NEW CENTURY BIBLE

General Editors

RONALD E. CLEMENTS
M.A., B.D., PH.D. (Old Testament)

MATTHEW BLACK
D.D., D.LITT., D.THEOL., F.B.A. (New Testament)

Ezra, Nehemiah
and Esther

NEW CENTURY BIBLE

Based on the Revised Standard Version

Ezra, Nehemiah and Esther

L. H. BROCKINGTON

*Sometime Senior Lecturer in Aramaic and Syriac,
University of Oxford*

OLIPHANTS

OLIPHANTS, Marshall, Morgan & Scott, a member of the Pentos group, 1 Bath Street, LONDON EC1V 9LB. © Thomas Nelson & Sons Ltd 1969; assigned to Marshall, Morgan & Scott 1971. First published 1969, reprinted 1977. ISBN 0 551 00777 X. The Bible references in this publication are from the Revised Standard Version of the Bible, copyrighted 1946 and 1952 by the Division of Christian Education, National Council of the Churches of Christ, and used by permission. All rights reserved. No part of this publication may be reproduced, stored in a retrieval system, or transmitted, in any form or by any means, electronic, mechanical, photocopying, recording, or otherwise, without the prior permission of the Copyright owner. Printed in Great Britain by Butler & Tanner Ltd, Frome and London. 772020L20.

CONTENTS

LISTS OF ABBREVIATIONS

TEXTUAL ABBREVIATIONS

A.A.S.O.R.	*Annual of the American Schools of Oriental Research*
A.J.S.L.	*American Journal of Semitic Languages and Literatures*
A.N.E.T.	*Ancient Near Eastern Texts relating to the Old Testament*, edited by J. B. Pritchard, 2nd ed., 1955
B.A.	*The Biblical Archaeologist*
B.A.S.O.R.	*Bulletin of the American Schools of Oriental Research*
B.Z.A.W.	*Beihefte zur Zeitschrift für die Alttestamentliche Wissenschaft*
Cowley, *Aram. Pap.*	A. E. Cowley, *Aramaic Papyri of the Fifth Century B.C.*, 1923
J.B.L.	*Journal of Biblical Literature*
J.Q.R.	*Jewish Quarterly Review*
J.T.S.	*Journal of Theological Studies*
Josephus, *Ant.*	Josephus, *Jewish Antiquities*
Josephus, *War*	Josephus, *The Jewish War*
Kraeling, *Brooklyn Pap.*	E. G. Kraeling, *The Brooklyn Museum Aramaic Papyri*, 1953
LXX	The Septuagint, i.e. the Greek translation of the Old Testament
Noth	M. Noth, *Die Israelitischen Personennamen*, 1928
Pfeiffer, *Intro.*	R. H. Pfeiffer, *Introduction to the Old Testament*, 2nd ed., 1952
R.B.	*Revue Biblique*
Syr.	The Peshitta, i.e. the Syriac translation of the Old Testament
V.T.	*Vetus Testamentum*

ABBREVIATIONS OF THE BOOKS OF THE BIBLE

OLD TESTAMENT (*O.T.*)

Gen.	Jg.	1 Chr.	Ps.	Lam.	Ob.	Hag.
Exod.	Ru.	2 Chr.	Prov.	Ezek.	Jon.	Zech.
Lev.	1 Sam.	Ezr.	Ec.	Dan.	Mic.	Mal.
Num.	2 Sam.	Neh.	Ca.	Hos.	Nah.	
Dt.	1 Kg.	Est.	Isa.	Jl	Hab.	
Jos.	2 Kg.	Job	Jer.	Am.	Zeph.	

APOCRYPHA (*Apoc.*)

1 Esd.	Tob.	Ad. Est.	Sir.	S 3 Ch.	Bel	1 Mac.
2 Esd.	Jdt.	Wis.	Bar.	Sus.	Man.	2 Mac.
			Ep. Jer.			

NEW TESTAMENT (*N.T.*)

Mt.	Ac.	Gal.	1 Th.	Tit.	1 Pet.	3 Jn
Mk	Rom.	Eph.	2 Th.	Phm.	2 Pet.	Jude
Lk.	1 C.	Phil.	1 Tim.	Heb.	1 Jn	Rev.
Jn	2 C.	Col.	2 Tim.	Jas	2 Jn	

BIBLIOGRAPHIES

GENERAL

(a) COMMENTARIES

L. W. Batten, *Ezra and Nehemiah* (International Critical Commentary), 1913.

H. Bückers, *Die Bücher Esdras, Nehemias, Tobias, Judith und Esther* (Herders Bibelkommentar), 1953.

T. Witton Davies, *Ezra, Nehemiah and Esther* (Century Bible), 1909.

J. de Fraine, *Esdras en Nehemias* (De Boeken van het Oude Testament), 1961.

K. Galling, *Die Bücher der Chronik, Esra, Nehemia* (Das Alte Testament Deutsch), 1954.

A. Gelin, *Esdras, Néhémie* (La Sainte Bible de Jérusalem), 1953.

J. M. Myers, *Ezra, Nehemiah* (Anchor Bible), 1965.

A. Noordtzij, *De Boeken Ezra en Nehemia*, 1951.

W. Rudolph, *Esra und Nehemiah samt 3 Esra* (Handbuch zum Alten Testament), 1949.

H. E. Ryle, *Ezra and Nehemiah* (Cambridge Bible), 1893.

H. Schneider, *Die Bücher Esra und Nehemia*, 1959.

M. Zer-Kabod, *Ezra and Nehemiah* (in Hebrew), 1948.

(b) GENERAL WORKS AND ARTICLES

H. L. Allrik, 'The lists of Zerubbabel (Neh. 7 and Ezra 2) and the Hebrew numerical notation', *B.A.S.O.R.*, 136 (1954), pp. 21–27.

J. Bright, *History of Israel*, 1962.

L. E. Browne, *Early Judaism*, 1920.

M. Burrows, 'Neh. 3:1–32 as a source for the Topography of Ancient Jerusalem', *A.A.S.O.R.*, XIV (1934), pp. 115–40.

—— 'The Topography of Neh. 12:31–43', *J.B.L.*, LIV (1935), pp. 29–39.

—— 'Nehemiah's Tour of Inspection', *B.A.S.O.R.*, 64 (December 1936), pp. 11–21.

H. Cazelles, 'La Mission d'Esdras', *V.T.*, IV (1954), pp. 113–40.

A. E. Cowley, *Aramaic Papyri of the Fifth Century B.C.*, 1923.

G. R. Driver, *Aramaic Documents of the Fifth Century B.C.*, 1954, 1957 (revised and abridged).

J. A. Emerton, 'Did Ezra go to Jerusalem in 428 B.C.?', *J.T.S.*, n.s., XVII (1966). pp. 1–19.

O. Eissfeldt, *The Old Testament: An Introduction* (English translation by P. R. Ackroyd), 1965.

K. Galling, 'The "Gola list" according to Ezra 2/Neh. 7', *J.B.L.*, LXX (1951), pp. 149–58.

G. B. Gray, *Hebrew Proper Names*, 1896.

M. Haran, 'The Gibeonites, the Nethinim and the sons of Solomon's servants'. *V.T.*, XI (1961), pp. 159–69.

E. G. Kraeling, *The Brooklyn Museum Aramaic Papyri*, 1953.

S. Mowinckel, *Statholderen Nehemiah*, 1916.

—— *Ezra den Skriftlærde*, 1916.

—— *Studien zu dem Buche Ezra-Nehemia*, I, II, 1964; III, 1965.

T. Nöldeke, 'Names', *Encyclopaedia Biblica*.

M. Noth, *Die Israelitischen Personennamen*, 1928.

R. H. Pfeiffer, *Introduction to the Old Testament*, 1952.

J. R. Porter, 'Son or grandson, Ezr. x. 6', *J.T.S.*, n.s., XVII (1966), pp. 54–67.

H. H. Rowley, 'The Chronological order of Ezra and Nehemiah' in *The Servant of the Lord and other essays*, 2nd ed., 1965, pp. 137–68.

—— 'Nehemiah's Mission and its Background' in *Men of God*, 1963, pp. 211–45.

—— 'Sanballat and the Samaritan Temple' in *Men of God*, 1963, pp. 246–76.

H. H. Schaeder, *Esra der Schreiber* (Beiträge zur Historischen Theologie, 5), 1930.

J. Simons, *Jerusalem in the Old Testament*, 1952.

C. C. Torrey, *Ezra Studies*, 1910.

—— *The Chronicler's History of Israel. Chronicles-Ezra-Nehemiah restored to its Original Form*, 1954.

R. de Vaux, 'Les Décrets de Cyrus et de Darius sur la reconstruction du Temple' *R.B.*, XLVI (1937), pp. 29–57.

A. C. Welch, *Post-Exilic Judaism*, 1935.

BIBLIOGRAPHY FOR ESTHER

(a) COMMENTARIES

H. Bardtke, *Der Prediger, Das Buch Esther* (Kommentar zum Alten Testament), 1963.

A. Barucq, *Judith, Esther* (La Sainte Bible de Jérusalem), 2nd ed., 1959.

M. Haller, *Esther* in M. Haller and K. Galling, *Die fünf Megilloth* (Handbuch zum Alten Testament), 1940.

G. A. F. Knight, *Esther, Song of Songs, Lamentations* (Torch Bible Commentaries), 1955.

L. B. Paton, *The Book of Esther* (International Critical Commentary), 1908.

H. Ringgren, 'Das Buch Esther' in H. Ringgren and A. Weiser, *Das Hohe Lied, Klagelieder, Das Buch Esther* (Das Alte Testament Deutsch), 2nd ed., 1962.

A. W. Streane, *The Book of Esther* (Cambridge Bible), 1907.

(b) GENERAL WORKS AND ARTICLES

F. Altheim and R. Stiehl, 'Esther, Judith, Daniel', *Die Aramäische Sprache unter den Achaimeniden*, Lief. II (1960), pp. 195ff.

D. Daube, 'The Last Chapter of Ezra', *J. Q. R.*, N.S. XXXVII (1946–47), pp. 139–47.

G. R. Driver, 'Problems and Solutions', *V.T.*, IV (1954), pp. 235ff.

H. S. Gehman, 'Notes on the Persian Words in the Book of Esther', *J.B.L.*, XLII (1924), pp. 321–28.

F. Justi, *Iranisches Namenbuch*, 1896.

INTRODUCTION TO
THE BOOKS OF

EZRA AND NEHEMIAH

INTRODUCTION TO EZRA AND NEHEMIAH

1. SUMMARY OF CONTENTS

EZRA

FIRST SECTION. CHAPTERS I–6 RETURN AND REBUILDING OF THE TEMPLE

(a) **1.1–11.** Return under Sheshbazzar the prince following the decree given by Cyrus *in his first year* (538 B.C.).

(b) **2.1–70.** A list described as of those who returned with Zerubbabel. (By its position the implication is that this is the same return as that under Sheshbazzar.)

(c) **3.1–13.** *In the seventh month* (of the year of return?) Joshua and Zerubbabel built an altar and began making sacrifices. *In the second month of the second year* they began preparation for building the Temple and finally laid the foundations. The people showed mixed feelings; some felt regret over the loss of the old Temple, others showed joy in the new one now to be built.

(d) **4.1–5.** Zerubbabel and Joshua rejected an offer of help in the building, and those who were thus rejected then offered serious hindrance *all the days of Cyrus* (538–529 B.C.) . . . *even until the reign of Darius* (522–485 B.C.).

(e) **4.6.** Then, *in the days of Ahasuerus* (=Xerxes, 485–465 B.C.) 'they' wrote an accusation against the Jews.

(f) **4.7.** following this there is a fragment that tells of a letter to *Artaxerxes* (465–425 B.C.) written by 'Bishlam and Mithredath and Tabeel'.

(g) **4.8–23.** Also *in the reign of Artaxerxes*, Rehum, Shimshai and their associates wrote to the king complaining of the likelihood of rebellion if the Jews continued to rebuild. The king answered that the building work should be stopped without delay. Rehum and Shimshai made the builders cease 'by force and power'.

(h) **4.24.** Then the work 'ceased *until the second year of the reign of Darius*' (520 B.C.).

(i) **5.1, 2.** It was *at this point* that Haggai and Zechariah encouraged Zerubbabel and Joshua who *began to rebuild*.

(j) **5.3–5.** *At the same time* Tattenai, governor of the province Beyond-the-River questioned them about their authority but took no further action against them until he had heard from Darius to whom he wrote.

(k) **5.6–17.** The letter that Tattenai and his associates wrote is then given at length and in it they reported their questioning of the Jews, which elicited from them the fact that Sheshbazzar had returned *in the first year of Cyrus* and had laid the foundation of the Temple and that '*from that time until now* it had been in building', and they asked the king for instructions.

(l) **6.1–12.** Darius had search made and found a copy of the decree of Cyrus at Ecbatana, the words of which he incorporated in his reply to Tattenai. The reply was to the effect that they were to let the Jews continue their building and to supply the cost and also materials for sacrifice.

(m) **6.13–15.** Tattenai acted on the letter and the Temple was finished on *the third day of Adar (the third month) in the sixth year of Darius* (516 B.C.).

(n) **6.16–18.** The completion was celebrated

(o) **6.19–22.** and the feast of Passover kept on *the fourteenth day of the first month*.

SECOND SECTION. CHAPTERS 7–10 EZRA'S RETURN AND THE MARRIAGE
REFORM

7.1–6. Ezra is introduced with a seemingly full genealogy

7.7–10. and there follows a summary statement of his return to Jerusalem *in the fifth month of the seventh year of Artaxerxes* (either Artaxerxes I, 465–425 B.C., or Artaxerxes II, 405–358 B.C.).

7.11–26. This section contains the letter of commission by Artaxerxes to the task of inquiring 'about Judah and Jerusalem according to the law of your God', and promising material help from the local treasurers.

7.27, 28. (From this point until 9.15, apart from 8.35f., the story of Ezra is told in the first person.) The chapter closes on a note of gratitude to God for his providence.

8.1–14. A list of the families who gathered to make the return with Ezra is given:

8.15–20. It was discovered that there were no Levites among them, so Ezra sent a mission to Casiphia and persuaded the leaders of the community there to send a number of Levites to join them.

8.21–30. Plans for departure were then made and the treasures which they carried were entrusted to twelve of the leading priests.

8.31–36. They left on *the twelfth day of the first month* and reached Jerusalem on *the first day of the fifth month* (7.9) where they handed the king's commission to the king's officers.

9.1–15. After these things a report was made to Ezra of the fact that many Israelites, priests, Levites and laymen, had married non-Israelites, whereupon Ezra made a long prayer of confession.

10.1–5. While Ezra was so engaged an assembly gathered round him and through their spokesman Shecaniah offered to make a covenant to divorce their foreign wives and called upon Ezra to undertake to see the task through according to the law.

10.6–9. The people were summoned to assemble and they gathered together on *the twentieth day of the ninth month;*

10.10–15. they were addressed by Ezra who invited them to make confession, to separate from the peoples of the land and to divorce foreign wives. With only four dissentients the people agreed and accepted the suggestion that a tribunal be held.

10.16–44. It began its work on *the first day of the tenth month* and had examined all the men concerned by *the first day of the first month.* The list of offenders is then given.

NEHEMIAH

FIRST SECTION. CHAPTERS **1–6** RETURN OF NEHEMIAH AND REBUILDING OF THE WALLS

1.1–3. In *the month Chislev, in the twentieth year,* Nehemiah's brother Hananiah reported a disaster to the walls of Jerusalem

1.4–11. at which Nehemiah made a prayer of confession to God.

2.1–8. When the opportunity came, Nehemiah told the king what was troubling him and received permission to go to Jerusalem. This was *Nisan in the twentieth year of Artaxerxes* (Artaxerxes I, 465–425 B.C.).

2.9, 10. His arrival gave great displeasure to Sanballat and Tobiah.

2.11–16. After three days he made an inspection, by night for secrecy, of the broken walls of the city.

2.17–20. Then he encouraged the people to build and in his confidence in God made light of the mockery of Sanballat, Tobiah and Geshem.

3.1–32. There follows a detailed description of the separate working parties and of the part of the wall on which they were each engaged. The description follows the line of the city wall travelling in an anti-clockwise direction.

4.1–5. Sanballat and Tobiah mocked Nehemiah's efforts, but he resorted to prayer,

4.6. and was able to record considerable progress.

4.7–9. Then Sanballat and Tobiah planned an armed attack and Nehemiah took defensive measures.

4.10–23. But the Jews began to feel the strain and complained of hardship, so Nehemiah redisposed the people and guard so that the work should proceed while guard was kept day and night.

5.1–5. Financial problems also arose within the Jewish community: they had been driven to the necessity of pledging themselves and their children and all they had for their food.

5.6–13. Nehemiah met this by arranging for loans to be made interest free and for pledges to be restored.

5.14-19. He himself as governor had refrained from drawing the allowances to which he was entitled.

6.1–9. Sanballat and Tobiah, with Geshem the Arab, now made personal attacks on Nehemiah: they tried to draw him away from the city and spread rumours that he was assuming the kingship. Nehemiah was rightly contemptuous of their efforts.

6.10–14. Then through false prophets they attempted to bring him into fault by trying to induce him to enter the Temple unlawfully, but he saw through their plan.

6.15–19. In spite of constant pressure from the enemy, and especially from Tobiah who was connected with highly placed Jews by marriage, the work was finished after fifty-two days, on *the twenty-fifth day of Elul* (444 B.C.).

SECOND SECTION. CHAPTER **7** SPARSE POPULATION OF JERUSALEM: A
LIST OF THE PEOPLE OF ISRAEL WHO HAD RETURNED

7.1–4. Nehemiah could now turn his attention to other problems, and he first tackled the problem of the sparse population of Jerusalem.

7.5. The first step towards this would be a census of the people, but Nehemiah found a convenient list to hand.

7.6–73. The list that follows is the same (with only minor deviations) as that given in Ezr. 2.2–70, purporting to be those who had returned with Zerubbabel.

THIRD SECTION. CHAPTERS **8–10** READING OF THE LAW BY EZRA: A
FAST AND A COVENANT

7.73b–8.8. The people assembled on *the first day of the seventh month* and summoned Ezra to bring the book of the law and then they held a solemn reading of it.

8.9–12. The people were persuaded by Ezra to change their sorrow at hearing the law into the joy of a festival.

8.13–18. The feast of booths was then celebrated.

9.1–37. On *the twenty-fourth day of the seventh month* the people held a solemn fast and Ezra publicly made a prayer of contrition.

9.38. The chapter ends with the decision to make a firm covenant.

10.1–27. This is followed by a list of the families (after two individuals, Nehemiah and Zedekiah, have been named) who 'subscribed' to the covenant

10.28–39. and then the terms of the covenant are given, namely, to observe the law, to adhere to the strictest marriage rules, to keep the sabbath and to pay tithes and Temple dues regularly.

FOURTH SECTION. CHAPTERS **11–13** SOCIAL AND RELIGIOUS REFORMS
CARRIED OUT BY NEHEMIAH, AND A NUMBER OF STATISTICAL LISTS

11.1, 2. The narrative here returns to the problem of the sparse population of the city and a decision was made to bring in one in ten to live in Jerusalem. Now follow sundry lists:

11.3–19(24). (a) of settlers in Jerusalem,

11.25–36. (b) of towns occupied by Jews of Judah and Benjamin,

12.1–9. (c) of priests and Levites who 'came up with Zerubbabel',

12.10, 11. (d) a genealogy of high priests from Joshua to Jaddua,

12.12–21. (e) of heads of priestly houses,

12.22–26. (f) of heads of Levitical houses.

12.27–43. Here the story takes up the dedication of the walls which was celebrated by a march along the wall by two processions going opposite ways and finishing up at the Temple.

12.44–47. Organization on behalf of the Levites.

13.1–3. Then in a series of rapid sketches Nehemiah's social and religious reforms and activities are outlined. First the law of racial purity was put into practice;

13.4–14. then the Temple room allotted to Tobiah was cleansed and arrangements made for regular payments of tithes to the Levites.

13.15–22. Measures were taken to prevent profanation of the sabbath;

13.23–27. and an oath was made not to continue the practice of mixed marriages;

13.28, 29. and finally Nehemiah expelled Sanballat's son-in-law, a son of Jehoiada, from his presence.

13.30, 31. The book ends with a summary statement of some of Nehemiah's good works and a call to God to remember him.

*

Thus, in twenty-three chapters, is written a record of the restoration of the Jewish community in Palestine after the exile, the rebuilding of Temple and city, the public recognition, by acclaim and by practice, of the authority of God's word as written in 'the book of the law of Moses which the LORD had given to Israel', and the safeguarding of the purity of the restored community. It is the only record we have of that restoration which makes any attempt to cover all the events from the time the exiles were given permission to return until they had settled down fully to their new life in the rebuilt city. For that reason, whatever judgment we may feel we ought to make on the author as a historian, we must naturally value his work highly and make the fullest possible use of it to construct our own idea of what happened in those eventful years.

Such rebuilding and restoration could not have proceeded without inspired leaders, and several such men find a place in the story: Zerubbabel the governor, Joshua the priest, Haggai and Zechariah the prophets, and Ezra and Nehemiah, priestly and lay leaders, respectively, of the post-exilic community at specific times during this period. But there were other leading figures; the Jewish community was not allowed to return home and re-establish itself on native soil without opposition from certain men and their followers who were already on Palestinian soil and resented the intrusion—as it would seem to them after nearly seventy years of undisputed occupation—of these returning exiles. These leaders too find their place in the narrative: Tattenai and Shethar-bozenai with their companions; Rehum the commander, and Shimshai the scribe; Sanballat the Horonite, Tobiah the Ammonite, the slave, and Geshem the Arabian.

No one knows for certain how long a period the narrative covers; at the very least it covers just over a century, from 538 to 432 B.C., and at most nearly a century and a half from 538 to 397 B.C., the terminus being determined by the date finally to be given to Ezra (see pp. 20, 29ff.).

In the present form of the story one of the characters, Nehemiah, is allowed to speak almost entirely for himself, since the author has included long sections of narrative in the first person and undoubtedly as written by Nehemiah. The story of another of the principal leaders, Ezra, is given partly in his own first-person narrative and partly in the author's rewriting of his story. This reproduction of first-person narrative, against the genuineness of which few have raised serious objections, is one of the valuable features of the story, enabling the reader to form his own judgment of the work and character of the two leaders concerned.

In this respect we may regret one of the characteristics of the approach to his material of the historian to whom we owe this record, namely, that events and the actors involved in them were more important to him than their correct sequence in time. It is a well-known fact, widely admitted, that the chapters in their present form, and probably also in the form in which they left their author's hands, have a letter to Artaxerxes, and the response it elicited, placed among events that happened in the time of Artaxerxes' predecessors. Recognition of this trait of the author inevitably prejudices the acceptance of other data in the books, more especially the relative chronological order of the two men whose names the books bear.

The reader who tries to reconstruct the order of events from this record will have to come to terms with this trait and accept the fact that the significance of events mattered more to him than the time at which they took place. The significance is that Jews who had been carried into exile, or, in a greater majority of cases, whose fathers or grandfathers had been carried into exile, had, within 150 years from the day when they were given permission by Cyrus to return to their own land (indeed were encouraged by him to do so), re-established themselves in the face of strong, if sometimes ill-informed opposition, as a Yahweh-worshipping community in a rebuilt Temple and city.

The author, who is to be identified with the chronicler who wrote 1 and 2 Chronicles, began his 'history of Israel' (apart from introductory genealogical tables) with David's capture of Jerusalem and his preparations for the building of the Temple by Solomon and ended it with the rebuilding of Temple and city and the renewed supremacy of the word of God.

2. THE AUTHOR-COMPILER AND SUBSEQUENT EDITING

The books of Ezra-Nehemiah continue the story told in 1 and 2 Chronicles and are to be attributed to the author-compiler known as the Chronicler. The last two verses of Chronicles are repeated in the first three verses of Ezra. The term 'author-compiler' is used here because it is clear that he not only wrote some of the narrative himself, but that he also borrowed much of the material from sources at his disposal, either transcribing it verbatim or editing it to suit his point of view. In all probability the Chronicler was responsible for assembling most, if not all, of the material now found in Ezra-Nehemiah (see 4, p. 24, for further comment on the Chronicler), but the question must be asked, how far the present *order* of the material was due to the Chronicler or to a subsequent editor?

A quick glance at the dates given in the two books (picked out in italic type in the summary given above) and at the order of some of the recorded events will show that, whoever was responsible for its final form, had no very great sense of chronological sequence or of the natural order of events. In chapter 4 of Ezra the mention of a letter to Xerxes (485-465) and the record of an incident in the reign of Artaxerxes (465-425) are placed between material belonging to the time of Cyrus (538-529) and material belonging to the time of Darius (522-485). Again, the record of the dedication of the repaired walls is separated from the record of their completion by the inclusion of nearly six chapters (Neh. 7.1-12.26) of mixed content, some of which concern Ezra and very little directly concern Nehemiah, while the recognition that something should be done about the sparse population of Jerusalem (Neh. 7.4) is followed by a list of those who 'came up with Zerubbabel' and is not taken up again for four chapters (11.1ff.). The account of the reading of the law, which is clearly Ezra's work, whatever view be taken of the relative dates of Ezra and Nehemiah (see pp. 20, 29ff.), is inserted right in the heart of the account of Nehemiah's activity and disrupts the narrative taken from Nehemiah's memoirs (see pp. 32ff.).

How much of this disordered arrangement can be attributed to the Chronicler and how much to a subsequent editing (assuming for the moment that such editing can be demonstrated)? We may begin to answer the question by reminding ourselves of the Chronicler's purpose and point of view (but see further, p. 13). Ezra-Nehemiah was written by him as part of a continuous history from David (or, by implication from the genealogical tables in 1 Chr. 1-9, from Adam; but the Chronicler's interest is not really roused until he comes to the point at which he can speak of David and of his plans for building a Temple) to the time of Ezra and Nehemiah. The effect of the dove-tailing of the records of the work of Ezra and Nehemiah is to allow the history to end with the reading of the law and the effecting of a number of reforms based on the law. Throughout the books of Chronicles-Ezra-Nehemiah the same interests can be seen coming into prominence as in 1 and 2

Chronicles: the tradition of the Davidic institution of Temple practices and the duties of its personnel (cf. Ezr. 3.10), particularly the Levites; the fondness for genealogies and lists of names, for he was an inveterate compiler; his dependence on earlier written material, not always reproduced slavishly, as is shown by his use of the books of Samuel and Kings in Chronicles. For Ezra–Nehemiah his most extensive source-material was the 'memoirs' of Nehemiah and of Ezra.

In view of the surprisingly unhistorical order and arrangement of some of the events in Ezra–Nehemiah, it is often felt that the Chronicler cannot be held responsible for it all, and that an editor, for reasons of his own, upset the Chronicler's original arrangement. It is argued that the material in these two books must at one time have existed in a more historical order of narrative. Now it does so happen that a document exists which has some of the material in a different order, although it also has additional material. That document is to be found in the book called I Esdras in the Apocrypha. The following table shows the difference in order at a glance:

I Esd. 1.1–58	=	2 Chr. 35.1–36.21
I Esd. 2.1–15	=	Ezr. 1
I Esd. 2.16–30	=	Ezr. 4.7–24
I Esd. 3.1–5.6	=	(additional material not in Ezra)
I Esd. 5.7–73	=	Ezr. 2.1–4.5
I Esd. 6.1–9.36	=	Ezr. 5–10
I Esd. 9.37–55	=	Neh. 7.73–8.13a.

It will be noticed that I Esdras is limited to the restoration of the Temple, chiefly the work of Zerubbabel (identified with one of the three guardsmen about whom the additional material is concerned), and to the work of Ezra. It is thought that, although the earliest form of I Esdras known to us is the Greek, it was originally written in a Semitic language, probably either Hebrew or Aramaic. Was that original (from which the Greek translation was made) identical with our Ezra–Nehemiah, from which the translator extracted what suited his purpose, altering the order as he thought necessary, and to which he added the story of the three guardsmen? Or was it an independent book with an order of narrative rather nearer the historical order and possibly nearer what the Chronicler originally gave for Ezra–Nehemiah?

In all probability the former of these alternatives is to be preferred, namely, that a Greek translator, in possession of a story about three guardsmen, of whom one could plausibly be identified with Zerubbabel, a story which he thought to have some importance, decided to incorporate that story into a translation of part of the book of Ezra–Nehemiah, and as he did so took the opportunity, as any translator might be tempted to do, to ease the chronological sequence of some of the material. The second alternative mentoned above demands the assumed existence of a Hebrew or Arimaic compilation of the Zerubbabel–Ezra material earlier thana that which we have in Ezra–Nehemiah, but of such a book there is so far no trace. All that we can really learn therefore from the different arrangement of material in 1 Esdras is that at least one writer or translator knew a different order from that found in the canonical Ezra–Nehemiah and also, apparently, had no interest whatever in the work of Nehemiah. If this man was the one who translated 1 Esdras into Greek, then a reminiscence of Dan. 2.37 and 2.22, 23 found in 1 Esd. 4.10a and 4.59, 60 suggests a date later than the book of Daniel.

The question remains: was the Chronicler himself better informed about the order of events than the present order of Ezra–Nehemiah would suggest? If there were evidence of substantial editing, apart from the compiling of the actual book, we might feel tempted to lay the blame for inaccuracy at the door of a later editor. But there is no such evidence. The only substantial piece of editorial work might conceivably be the insertion of the list of names in Neh. 10.1–27. That depends, however, on whether it be thought that the making of the covenant belonged to Ezra's work or to Nehemiah's; if to Ezra's then the list, which has Nehemiah's name in it, may be an editorial addition, but if to Nehemiah's then it could well belong to the original drafting of the book. Some of the lists of names are sometimes thought to have been added later than the Chronicler's time, but none can be shown to be necessarily later (see pp. 34ff.). The Chronicler himself must therefore apparently be credited with the unhistorical ordering of some of the material, and it probably has to be admitted that he conflated the work of Ezra and Nehemiah in spite of the fact that there is scarcely any reason why they should be thought to be contemporaries (see pp. 30ff.). If he could so confuse the dates of two such well-known leaders, we need not think it beyond him to introduce anachronisms elsewhere. There is therefore no need to posit a post-chronicler editor who substantially changed the order of what the Chronicler had written.

Those who do feel that the Chronicler's work showed a truer sense of historical sequence usually assume that he arranged the material in something like the following order (that of Rudolph):

Ezr. 1–8
Neh. 7.73*b*–8.18
Ezr. 9.1–10.44
Neh. 9.1–10.40
Neh. 1.1–7.73*a*
Neh. 11.1–13.31

There is, however, no close agreement about this proposed order and it still leaves the glaring anachronism of Ezr. 4.7–23 unless (with Browne) we suppose that the Chronicler placed this section immediately before Neh. 1.1. (There is also some uncertainty about the original intention and wording of Neh. 7.70–73*a*. These verses may be treated as an integral part of the introduction to the reading of the law. In this case they would belong to the Ezra story. But they may also be regarded as a slightly changed repetition of the words at the end of Ezr. 2.) Since no trace of the existence of an assumed original order of the Chronicler's story remains, it becomes a purely academic exercise to pursue it. It is much more important, though not always successful, to try to establish the true pattern of events behind the Chronicler's narrative.

3. THE COURSE OF EVENTS FROM THE EDICT OF CYRUS TO THE WORK OF NEHEMIAH AND EZRA: AN ATTEMPTED RECONSTRUCTION.

It may help here if we anticipate a little and state briefly from what sources the Chronicler drew his material. In the Temple (or state) archives he would probably find some record of the decree of Cyrus and a list of the Temple vessels that were returned. From the Aramaic document used by him (p. 26) he would learn that Sheshbazzar was a leading figure at the beginning of the return period, and from the prophecies of Haggai and Zechariah he would know something of the work of Zerubbabel and Joshua, and above all he could draw freely on the memoirs of Ezra and Nehemiah. It was from these sources, some official and some not, that he drew his material and welded it into a story, shaping it according to his own interests and convictions. Mention has already been made of his conviction that David instituted the whole system of Temple services and personnel and of his interest in the Levites and in statistical lists. To these may be added his firm conviction that the only element of the Jewish people that had any meaning and influence in post-exilic times was the group who had been in Babylon and who had returned or were still from time to time returning from exile. He apparently had no place for the people who had remained in Palestine and Judah throughout the exile beyond regarding them as a severe hindrance to progress in the days of restoration. It was therefore the remnant that had escaped from exile that was the effective nucleus of post-exilic Judaism (cf. Ezr. 3.8; 9.8, 14, 15). Another conviction he is thought to have held is that the Jewish people took immediate advantage of the decree of Cyrus and that their first task on their return was to set up an altar and recommence sacrificial worship, and then to proceed with the building of the Temple. This conviction would be strengthened by the references to the work of Sheshbazzar in his Aramaic source (Ezr. 5.16).

It must be admitted from the outset that any attempt to reconstruct the probable sequence of events from 538 B.C. onwards runs the risk of being as much of an exercise in creative reconstruction as we are prone to see in the Chronicler's own work. Sources for the period in question, i.e. the century and a half following the decree of Cyrus, are both rare and limited in scope. There is the Chronicler's story in Ezra–Nehemiah based on sources that are no longer extant, and to this we should add the Apocryphal book of I Esdras mentioned above, but, apart from the fact that it is probably as late as the second century B.C., the material in it, with the exception of the story of the three guardsmen, which is legendary, is virtually the same as that in Ezra–Nehemiah, although in a different order. The prophecies of Haggai and Zechariah, all dated within two and a half years, from the first day of the sixth month of the second year of Darius (Hag. 1.1) to the fourth day of the ninth month of the fourth year (Zech. 7.1), give a contemporary view of the situation in Jerusalem and of the mood of the people in the years 520–518 B.C., but, being mainly prophetic utterances, offer virtually no facts or events. Some inscriptional material exists which corroborates the decree of Cyrus (p. 48), and there are letters and other documents from Elephantine (Yeb, on the first cataract of the Nile) dating from 495 to 399 and containing certain details that might serve to fix some of the dates in the Ezra-Nehemiah period more clearly or otherwise throw some light on the social and religious background of the period. It will be obvious from this sketch that this period, though it ranks as one of the formative periods in Jewish history in that it saw the rise of Judaism, is one of the least-documented periods.

What, then, can be affirmed with any degree of certainty as the probable sequence of events and their dates from the decree of Cyrus to the work of Nehemiah and Ezra?

(i) *The decree of Cyrus*

Some time after Babylon fell into his power in 538 B.C., Cyrus issued a decree which sanctioned the return to Palestine of such Jews as wished to go back, encouraged the rebuilding of the Temple and offered grants in aid. The only evidence we have of this decree is the two copies of it (or excerpts from it, or paraphrases of part of it) in Ezr. 1.2–4 (in Hebrew) and 6.3–5 (in Aramaic). These two records of the decree do not agree in wording or in details, but this need occasion no surprise since the one (1.2–4) is recorded chiefly as evidence of the permission to return and rebuild the Temple, and the other (6.3–5) as evidence of the right to rebuild the Temple and of the existence of specific instructions about its size and about defraying its cost from the royal treasury. Both, doubtless, give only the minimal amount of wording to suit the purpose for which the decree is cited. We cannot be sure that either of them is in the language in which the decree was drafted (although in this respect the Aramaic version (6.3–5) would have greater claim to be so than the Hebrew, since Aramaic was used in the Persian empire as the *lingua franca*). On the other hand neither version of the decree is really out of keeping with what we know of Cyrus and of his treatment of subject peoples. On a cylinder found at Ur, Cyrus gives permission for the restoration of the gods, and therefore presumably, by implication, of the people of subject nations (*A.N.E.T.*, 315). The decree would almost certainly be made in the early months of his reign and it may therefore be dated 538 or 537 B.C.

(ii) *Sheshbazzar*

Whether the Jews took immediate advantage of the decree or not cannot be determined. The Chronicler clearly intended his readers to think they did. One of the first acts was the journey of a man named Sheshbazzar from Babylon to Jerusalem. He was appointed governor by Cyrus (Ezr. 5.14) and was commissioned by him to carry back the Temple vessels and whatever else was given by way of freewill offerings. His name is Babylonian and probably means 'Shamash protect the son', but we do not know whether the man himself was a Jew or a Babylonian. He is called the prince of Judah (Ezr. 1.8), but, beyond being the term used by Ezekiel, in anticipation, for the civil head of the post-exilic community, the term itself tells us nothing specific. The Hebrew word does not mean royal prince but is a word that could be applied to anyone who has been raised to authority over his fellows. It could be used of Sheshbazzar, whatever he was, whether Babylonian or Jew, whether of the royal line or not. In the Aramaic document (see p. 26) on the evidence of

the leading Jews, as reported by Tattenai and his associates, Sheshbazzar was also credited with laying the foundations of the Temple
(5.16).

This is where uncertainty begins, for if we did not possess Ezr. 1
and 5 we should be in no doubt that the Chronicler regarded
Zerubbabel as the chief figure in the 'return' period and in any
rebuilding work that was started. Ezra 2 lists those who 'came with
Zerubbabel' and is so placed as to be intended to serve as a list of
the first people who returned from exile, although Sheshbazzar is not
among them. Further, in chapter 3, apparently ignoring anything
that might have been done by Sheshbazzar, it is reported that
Zerubbabel and Joshua erected an altar and laid the foundations of
the Temple. Now one of the things that we learn from Haggai is
that in response to his preaching (and that of Zechariah) Zerubbabel
and Joshua were encouraged to make a start on rebuilding the
Temple, and that this happened in 520 B.C. This is also reported in
Ezr. 5.1, 2. (Hag. 2.18 can also be taken to mean that there had been
no previous foundation in post-exilic days.)

What, then, of Sheshbazzar? It used to be thought that he might
be identifiable with Zerubbabel, which is what the Chronicler
himself may have thought (but see below). This can be done if it be
assumed that a man could commonly have two names, a Jewish
name (Zerubbabel could equally well be either Jewish or Babylonian
in origin, see p. 53) and a Babylonian one. But nowhere does the
narrative bring the two names together or show explicit identification. Others, in spite of the Babylonian name, try to find a place for
Sheshbazzar among the more noble Jewish families, and, partly on
the basis of Greek transliterations of his name, Sabanassaro and
Sanabassaro, seek to identify him with Shenazzar, a son of
Jehoiachin and uncle of Zerubbabel (1 Chr. 3.18, 19). But this is
conjectural and not really necessary. There is no reason why Cyrus
should not have appointed a Babylonian as the first post-exilic
governor of Judah, especially if he were known to have Jewish
sympathies. And if Cyrus was indeed paying the cost of the Temple
out of his own treasury (Ezr. 6.4) he would want an officer of his
own in charge. Nor is there any reason why, in speaking to Persian
authorities (Ezr. 5), the Jews should not credit Sheshbazzar with what

he doubtless sanctioned, if not actually participating in, namely a beginning to the rebuilding of the Temple. If such was the case, and Sheshbazzar had been appointed to supervise return and restoration, the rebuilding may well have been started as early as 537 or 536 B.C. There is no further information about Sheshbazzar: he may have returned to Babylon at the end of a stated period of governorship, or he may have been recalled.

(iii) *Zerubbabel*

There are two possibilities about the date at which Zerubbabel began his work. The first is that he led a group of exiles home as soon as possible after the decree of Cyrus and that as leader of the Jews and a member of the royal house he played his part in laying the foundation of the Temple under Sheshbazzar's governorship. The foundations could properly be said to have been laid by Zerubbabel as principal Jewish participant, and also to have been laid by Sheshbazzar as responsible head of state. When Sheshbazzar gave up his office or was recalled, Zerubbabel became governor in his place. But 'adversaries' were successful in their opposition and work was brought to a standstill, or, alternatively, the returned exiles found so many other things that urgently needed to be done, that the Temple building had to be left in abeyance. Whichever it was, memory is short, and by 520 it might well appear as if nothing at all had happened, so a fresh start was made under the inspiration of the prophets Haggai and Zechariah.

The second possibility is that Zerubbabel did not return until 520, that this return surpassed that of 538/7 in importance and magnitude and that the work that was then begun (520) and finally brought to successful conclusion put Sheshbazzar's initial work almost into oblivion. If this was what happened, then the Chronicler, by identifying Zerubbabel and Sheshbazzar, projected Zerubbabel backwards into the events of 538 and the following years.

There is no urgent reason to dismiss the first of these possibilities, which would allow the Chronicler a little more credibility than would the second. Whatever may be thought about the real nature of the list in Ezr. 2, this reconstruction, coupled with the Chronicler's tacit identification of Zerubbabel and Sheshbazzar, enables the list for the moment to be taken at its face value, i.e. as a list of those who returned with Zerubbabel (and therefore implicitly with Sheshbazzar) at the earliest possible time after the decree permitting return (but see pp. 35-37).

(iv) *Opposition*

The attempt at rebuilding the Temple met with opposition. There is a report of one phase of opposition in Ezr. 4 and of another phase in chapter 5. As they now stand, the first of these refers to the earlier building effort under (Sheshbazzar and) Zerubbabel, and the second to the rebuilding inspired by Haggai and Zechariah. But the anachronistic nature of most of chapter 4 is patent and it becomes easy to assume that from beginning to end the chapter is wrongly put together and parts of it misplaced, in spite of editorial links in verses 5 and 24 which attempt to tidy it up. In all probability the work begun in 537 (or as soon thereafter as possible) lapsed more through insufficient labour, leadership, materials and money (but we cannot now discover how far Cyrus' monetary aid went), than through opposition even if the latter did show itself as early as 537. Doubtless there were many urgent things to be done which gradually crowded out the work on the Temple (cf. Hag. 1.2). Whether there was any at an earlier time (as is certainly implied in Ezr. 4.5) or not, there is no doubt that opposition did come in 520 or thereabouts. It is said to have come from the 'people of the land'. These people are to be identified partly with the northern Israelites (4.2) and partly with those Jews in Judah who would come to feel themselves unwanted because of the exclusionist policy of the returned exiles. Here, however, the Chronicler's view, namely, that only the returned exiles were the true Jews, must be regarded as an extreme one and not really tenable. There must have been many a true Jew among the people who had remained in Judah, or had been born there, during the exile. In any case they seem at first not to have been 'adversaries' but to have been ready to share in and help with the building, and only on their rejection did they become adversaries. Failing in their own efforts, assisted by hired counsellors (4.4, 5), they persuaded the governor of the province Beyond-the-River, Tattenai, to make inquiries with a view to getting official sanction to stop the work. When the king's answer came it was to the effect that the Jews should be encouraged to continue their building with all speed and diligence.

It is possible, on one interpretation of the prophecy in Hag. 2.10–14, that Haggai himself encouraged the Temple builders to refuse the proffered help of the people of the land. In this view what these people offered, namely their help in the rebuilding, was condemned by the prophet as unclean and therefore not acceptable.

After the opposition had been thus scotched, the work proceeded apace and the Temple was finished and dedicated in 516 B.C.

(v) *The years 516 to 457 or 444*

Between 516 and the middle of the fifth century B.C. lies a period for which we have no evidence of any significant event in Jewish history. There is nothing recorded by the Chronicler until the return of either Ezra or Nehemiah—whichever is to be deemed to have come first. This is not to overlook the incident recorded by the Chronicler in Ezr. 4.8–23 in the time of Artaxerxes, but that incident really belongs to the story of Nehemiah, since it must have been its results which provoked his return in 444. Nor is it intended to overlook the fact that the period was not barren from a literary point of view, although such literature as we have is difficult to date with certainty and much of it lies embedded in the collection of prophecies in the later parts of the Book of Isaiah, chapters 56–66. In any case, the literature does not record any significant incident. Not only is Jewish literature silent about this half-century or more, but neither is there any non-Israelite document which would enable us to fill in details of it.

(vi) *Nehemiah*

The reasons for preferring to put Nehemiah's work before that of Ezra will be set out in detail below (pp. 29ff.) and need not be mentioned here beyond the fact that the strongest argument is probably that of the different handling of the situation caused by the prevalence of mixed marriages, i.e. of an Israelite with a non-

Israelite. Ezra's handling of the problem was much more drastic than Nehemiah's and most naturally follows it at some interval of time.

Nehemiah's brother, Hanani, reported to him that 'the wall of Jerusalem is broken down, and its gates are destroyed by fire' (Neh. 1.3). There can be little doubt that the immediate cause of this state of the walls, which reads as if it was very recent at the time of the report, was the incident recorded in Ezr. 4.8–23 to the effect that Artaxerxes had given Rehum and Shimshai authority to make the men stop work, and so 'they went in haste to the Jews at Jerusalem and by force and power made them cease' (Ezr. 4.23). Nehemiah was cup-bearer to this same Artaxerxes (Artaxerxes I, 465–425) and evidently in sufficiently high favour to be able to influence the king's policy (it is known that Artaxerxes was susceptible to such influence) and secure permission to return to Judah and deal with the situation. He returned therefore in 444 B.C., the king's twentieth year, and was governor for twelve years (Neh. 2.1; 5.14). Whether he was resident in Jerusalem for the whole of that time is not known (see Neh. 5.14 and 13.6). During his governorship he rebuilt the walls of the city in the face of strong external opposition (Sanballat, Tobiah and Geshem) and embarrassing internal difficulties (Neh. 1–6); he established a covenant with the people to be more zealous in religious practices and instituted a number of social reforms, including an increase in the population of Jerusalem and an attempt to deal with the problem of mixed marriages.

(vii) Ezra

About thirty-five years after the last recorded date for Nehemiah (432), Ezra returned to Judah with a number of fellow Jews. His return took place in the seventh year of Artaxerxes (Ezr. 7.7), and if Nehemiah's priority is accepted this will be Artaxerxes II (405–358), thus giving 398/7 as the date of Ezra's return. His achievements were the reading of the law and its recognition by the people (Neh. 8) and a determined effort to root out the folly of mixed marriages (Ezr. 9, 10) sealed, so it may be argued (see below), by a fast day and a solemn covenant (Neh. 9.1, 38). It should be noted

that Ezra in his own memoirs nowhere gives an indication of the
year in which any event took place; the reference to the seventh
year of Artaxerxes is in narrative in the third person, presumably the
Chronicler's own writing-up of the introduction to Ezra's story.
On the other hand, several references to day and month are given
in the narrative and, since no year is specified for any one of them,
they could all be thought to have taken place within the same year.
The decision to travel was made in the first month (Ezr. 7.9), the
arrival in Jerusalem took place in the fifth, the law reading in the
seventh (Neh. 8.2), and later in the same month the feast of booths
was held (Neh. 8.13–18), and on the twenty-fourth day there was a
fast day (Neh. 9.1). On the twentieth day of the ninth month there
was an assembly to consider the marriage problem (Ezr. 10.9) and
the tribunal sat from the first day of the tenth month to the first
day of the first month (in the next year, Ezr. 10.16, 17).

We know comparatively little about the person, character, and
work of Ezra, and even that little is clouded with uncertainty. He
is described as a priest and scribe. As priest his duties would depend
on the place he occupied within his family, which was of the same
line, if the genealogy in Ezr. 7.1–5 is trustworthy (apart from some
faulty transmission, see note *ad loc.*), as the last high priest before
the exile, Seraiah, the line to which the Zadokite priests traced
their descent. But as a 'scribe' he may have been set free from the
duties of priesthood to be able to exercise his scribal work. We do
not, however, know for certain what was meant when Ezra was
described as a scribe: we have to remember also that we have an
edited record and that the editor may have meant by scribe something different from the original document. When the Chronicler
himself said that Ezra was a scribe, he was probably using the word
in its sense of 'student of scripture', but the Ezra memoirs on which
the Chronicler's account is based may have used it as an official
title. In general, it could mean secretary, such as Baruch was to
Jeremiah, and when Ezra is called 'scribe of the law of the God of
heaven' (Ezr. 7.12, 21; see note on 7.6) in the Artaxerxes document
it may be used as an official title for an office at court concerning
Jewish affairs. At all events he was concerned both with Jewish
affairs and with the law of Moses.

According to the terms of what is regarded as the document of commission from Artaxerxes, Ezra came to Judah' to make inquiries about Judah and Jerusalem according to the law of your God' (Ezr. 7.14). In the succeeding narrative there is nothing specific said about such an inquiry. Ezra arrived four months after he first planned his journey and after two months he read the law to an assembly of the people. In the same month they celebrated the feast of booths and immediately afterwards (at least as the narrative is now arranged) they held a fast-day and made a covenant (Neh. 8, 9). Two months later the leaders reported to Ezra about the deplorable situation in the matter of marriages with non-Israelites. An assembly was held and a commission of inquiry or tribunal was set up. The commission began its work at the beginning of the tenth month and finished it on the first day of the new year (Ezr. 9, 10). At this point one might well expect some mention—more indeed than the single verse at the end of chapter 10—of the way they acted upon the findings of the commission, or at very least of the holding of a solemn assembly of ratification. It so happens that, if we could disregard its present setting, the fast-day and covenant-making described in Neh. 9 would very nearly fit such an occasion. In its present position it is assumed that 'this month' in Neh. 9.1 was the seventh month, the month in which the events of Neh. 8 took place. But, if Neh. 9 is misplaced, 'this month' could conceivably refer to the month in which the commission finished its inquiry (Ezr. 10.17). This would leave just over three weeks, which might be thought a suitable, indeed a necessary, period, for the completion of everything involved in putting away the foreign wives. The statement in Neh. 9.2 that 'the Israelites separated themselves from all foreigners, and stood and confessed their sins' would certainly be appropriate to such an occasion. This is but another of the uncertainties that one meets as one probes into the Ezra record.

Two prayers are recorded as Ezra's: Ezr. 9.6–15 and Neh. 9.6–37. The first specifically concerns the marriage problem and is a fair sample of Jewish piety: it might well have come from Ezra himself, since it is embedded in an 'I' section and is closely tied to the actual circumstances. How far the words themselves were those used on that occasion is not possible to say. The occasion, however, would be memorable and one might expect the words used to be memorable too. The other prayer, that of confession in Neh. 9, stands in a different position. It is in effect a review of Israel's history showing the continuing proneness to sin. Although it suits the occasion well enough it is couched in general terms comparable with similar retrospects of Israel's history and could well have been reconstructed by an editor. It is in the third person part of the narrative. Its authorship must remain unknown.

Ezra is probably best known and remembered for the reading of the law. Ezra 7.14 speaks of 'the law of your God, which is in your hand', which, in the context, probably means the law that was at his disposal, i.e. to be the guiding principle of the inquiry that he was to make. Nehemiah 8.1 records that the people 'told Ezra the scribe to bring the book of the law of Moses which the Lord had given to Israel' and that he then read from it to the assembled people. In spite of some attempts to demonstrate that the book might have been Deuteronomy, it is generally felt, that, although Deuteronomy certainly long remained the favourite book of the law, by Ezra's time it would be the whole Pentateuch which was designated the book of the law of Moses. Deuteronomy, of course, would need no public introduction in Ezra's day, but the same could probably be said in some respects of the whole Pentateuch, since there is nothing in the narrative in Ezra-Nehemiah to suggest that Ezra brought something new with him. There is no reason why the Pentateuch should not already have been known in Palestine. What was probably wanted, and what Ezra did, was to hold a formal assembly at which the law was publicly read and accepted as authoritative. There is little doubt that this last is just what happened in Ezra's time. It is to be noted also that when the Samaritans finally separated from the Jews at about the middle of the fourth century they clung to the Pentateuch as their own sacred book. This they would scarcely have done if it had been a recent innovation. It had probably been known in Palestine for long enough to make public recognition of it under Ezra a timely necessity.

(viii) *Ezra as a legendary figure*

Whatever doubts have been entertained about Ezra as a historical figure (see p. 29), there is no doubt whatever that he became a legendary figure. In rabbinic tradition he was the most significant figure in post-exilic times. One text (*Seder 'Olam Rabbah*) fore-shortens the period of restoration so that Ezra appears as a contemporary of Zerubbabel and Joshua. One manuscript of the Targum of Malachi identifies Malachi with Ezra. In rabbinic tradition Ezra ranks as second to Moses in that he restored the law in its entirety after it had been forgotten in Palestine during the exile (cf. 2 Esd. 14.28-48 for one traditional form of the legend of the restoration of Scripture), and it is even claimed that he would have been qualified to have given it himself originally. He it was, according to tradition, who introduced a change in Hebrew writing, from the archaic script to the square characters. This change certainly took place after the exile, but it was probably not the work of one man, but rather the result of a gradual change which came at about the same time as Hebrew was steadily giving place to Aramaic as the popular language. The change in script was necessitated by a change in writing materials; potsherds (such as the letters found at Lachish were written on) gave place to leather and papyrus. Ezra was also honoured as the leader of the legendary company known as the 'men of the Great Synagogue'. This term was applied by the rabbis to a nebulous body, in actual fact the individual scholars, mostly unremembered by name, who were engaged in biblical transmission in the post-exilic period.

4. DATE OF COMPOSITION OF EZRA-NEHEMIAH

The earliest date for the writing of Ezra-Nehemiah, that is, for the work of the Chronicler, apart from any later editorial expansions, would be at a generation or two's remove from the completion of the work of whichever is shown to be later, Nehemiah or Ezra. If we assume Nehemiah's priority and put Ezra's return at 398/7 B.C., it gives 350 B.C. as the earliest possible date. This would allow just about enough time for the work of Nehemiah and Ezra to belong to the past and therefore to be subject to the possibility of chronological confusion such as memory is capable of and such as we have reason to think happened in these books. The latest date (assuming 1 and 2 Chronicles with Ezra–Nehemiah to be a literary unit) would be shortly before 180, say 200 B.C., because it is almost certain that ben Sira, writing at about 180, was dependent on 1 Chr. 23–29 for the ideas embedded in Sir. 47.8–10. There is no evidence, internal or external, that will allow us to define a date more closely and the writing may be placed at such time between these two limits as may reasonably fit all the known facts. There is inevitably much that has to be left to the imagination. For instance, if we were to date the Chronicler's work as late as 250 the question then arises, why did he not extend the history to bring it up-to-date with the rise of Alexander and the beginning of the Seleucid and Ptolemaic houses? One answer to this may be that for the Chronicler there was a clear beginning to Israel's history (at least such of that history as had meaning for the Chronicler) in the reign of David, to whom he ascribed the setting up of the full practice of worship and of its officers in the Temple, and there was probably an equally clear end-point or climax, namely the post-exilic restoration work culminating in the work of Nehemiah and Ezra, the promulgation of the law and the ensuring of the purity of the race by the handling of the problem of mixed marriages. The law had been restored and its supremacy established: history, for the Chronicler, could now be said to mark time and he would not be interested in subsequent events.

There is one thing within the book which, if it is part of the Chronicler's own work, would bring the date down to 330 B.C., namely, the extension of the list of high priests to Jaddua (Neh. 12.10, 11) who, according to Josephus (*Ant.* XI, vii, 2), was high priest at the time of Alexander. But this could well be editorial and therefore of no help in dating the original.

5. WRITTEN MATERIAL UPON WHICH THE
CHRONICLER COULD DRAW

(i) *An Aramaic document*

Part of the Book of Ezra is in Aramaic, namely, Ezr. 4.8–6.18 and 7.12–26. This Aramaic is very largely made up of official documents, as the following analysis will show:

4.8–16: Letter of Rehum and Shimshai to Artaxerxes.

4.17–22: The king's answer.

4.23: Rehum and Shimshai act upon it.

4.24: Stoppage of work.

5.1–3: Work starts on the Temple.

5.4, 5: Tattenai makes inquiry.

5.6–17: Tattenai's letter to Darius.

6.1, 2: Report of search and finding of decree.

6.3–12: Letter of Darius.

6.13–15: The Temple finished

6.16–18: and dedicated.

7.12–26: Letter of Artaxerxes giving Ezra his commission.

Thus, out of sixty-seven verses, only fifteen give narrative, the other fifty-two are records of letters. Presumably the Chronicler found much of this material, at very least the records of the letters, already written in Aramaic, and since he was writing for a community that could understand both Hebrew and Aramaic he not only retained the Aramaic but, since 4.24 must surely be his own comment, himself wrote connecting verses in Aramaic. A two-fold question arises: how much connecting narrative did the Chronicler add to his source material and how much of the Aramaic source, if any, did he fail to reproduce? These and any other questions that follow closely, such as whether 7.12–26 was part of the same source or was taken independently from elsewhere, can probably never be satisfactorily answered. Nor can we say how far the Aramaic source was trustworthy. Was it responsible for placing 4.8–23 in its unchronological position? If 7.12–26 does belong to the Aramaic source we may well hesitate before we give

full credibility to that source, for there is an element of the un-
believable about the letter which Artaxerxes wrote in support of
Ezra's mission. Is it really conceivable that a Persian king should
show so detailed an interest in Jewish affairs (see below for further
comment)? On the other hand, in regard to the position of 4.8–23,
it may be best to suppose that the Aramaic document had this
section in its more natural position after 6.18 and that the Chronicler,
with a greater concern for subject-matter than for sequence of
events, found it convenient to have a successful incident of opposition
to explain why the work was held up from 538/7 to 520 B.C.

Returning to 7.12–26, we cannot tell whether this was in the
source or not. Since it is now within narrative about Ezra in the
third person it need not be assumed that it was taken from Ezra's
memoirs and adapted. This leaves us free to think that it belonged to
the Aramaic document; in any case, being an official document,
7.12–26, if genuine, would as likely as not be written in Aramaic.
There is one small point that is sometimes thought to go against its
inclusion in the Aramaic document, and that is the spelling of the
name of Artaxerxes with a *sāmek* (7.12) instead of a *śin* (4.8, 23),
but this is not conclusive since the adjacent Hebrew has the same
spelling (7.11 and 4.7), possibly by attraction. That points to a
genuinely variable spelling.

(ii) *The Ezra memoirs, and date of Ezra's return*

Part of the Ezra story is told in the first person and part in the
third person, although it is not clear in some of the chapters now
embedded in the Book of Nehemiah (Neh. 9, 10) whether the
subject is properly Ezra or Nehemiah. The first-person narrative
is found in Ezr. 7.27–9.15 (but 8.35, 36 is third person) and the
third person in Ezr. 7.1–26; 10.1–44; Neh. 7.73*b*–8.18 and as much
of Neh. 9, 10 as might be agreed upon as belonging to Ezra's
story and not Nehemiah's. There are many difficulties about the
Ezra story. If the Chronicler found and used 'memoirs' of Ezra
that were complete in themselves, why did he not give the whole of
them rather than rewrite some of them in the third person? It is
obvious from 7.27f., which must have been preceded in the memoirs
by some account of Ezra's commission by the king, that they did

contain material that the Chronicler either rewrote or suppressed. The third-person narrative may have been based on the memoirs and rewritten to suit the Chronicler's convictions, or it may have been based on other Ezra material not known to us, or it could even be the Chronicler's own reconstruction of what he thought ought to have taken place. Again, why did the Chronicler separate the reading of the law from the rest of Ezra's work? Of this it might be said that once the Chronicler had convinced himself that Nehemiah and Ezra were contemporaries, he wanted *both* of them to share in this all-important event. The reading of the law, together with the reforms based on the law, is virtually the culminating point of the Chronicler's story (see p. 9).

Another question is why the fast-day and the covenant (Neh. 9, 10), which might seem to link up well with Ezra's marriage programme, was placed after the reading of the law and clearly intended to be shared by Nehemiah? About this we may say that there seems to be room for assuming that two fast-days were held and two covenants entered into, the one made under Nehemiah and looking forward to the reforms set out in chapter 13 and the other made under Ezra and rounding off the settlement of the mixed marriages problem. If this hypothesis could be proved, we could regard Neh. 9–10 as a telescoping of the two. As the narrative is at present arranged, the sequence of events raises the question why, after returning in the seventh year of Artaxerxes, Ezra waited until after Nehemiah's return in the twentieth year for the reading of the law. This question falls away if the two leaders are shown not to be contemporary and the documents to be in need of rearranging.

We have already touched indirectly on the next question, why does the report of the work of the marriage tribunal end so abruptly and with a corrupt text (Ezr. 10.44)? Even if we can restore a satisfactory form of that text, the ending still remains surprisingly inadequate for so important an issue. One solution, as hinted above, is to see in Neh. 9.1, 2 the record of a fast-day to solemnize the occasion, and in Neh. 9.38 a covenant to perpetuate the arrangement. The words used in Neh. 9.2 about separating themselves from all foreigners closely resemble those used in Ezr. 10.11, 'separate yourselves from the peoples of the land and from the foreign wives.' As they now stand, however, the fast-day and covenant refer to what took place after the reading of the law in Nehemiah's time. Something like such a covenant is indeed to be expected also in Nehemiah's work in order to prepare the way for his reforms.

More difficult than any of these, however, and much more fundamental, is the problem of the date of Ezra's return, and coupled with it the problem of his historicity.

To take the latter first: how seriously we consider it depends on how much importance is attached to (a) the silence of ben Sira about the existence of Ezra or the work he did although he knew about Nehemiah who 'raised ... the walls, ... set up the gates ... and rebuilt ... ruined houses' (Sir. 49.13), and (b) the unreal impression conveyed by the commission of Artaxerxes and by the sudden disappearance of Ezra from the scene. We have already noted the fact that if we dissociate Ezra from the Nehemiah story—and nowhere does Nehemiah mention Ezra or confer with him—then everything he did falls exactly within a year and a day (see p. 21). His plan to return was made on the first day of the first month in one year (Ezr. 7.9), and the end of the deliberations of the marriage tribunal was on the first day of the first month, presumably of the next year. As the material is at present arranged, he waited for thirteen years after his own arrival until Nehemiah's return and then he took his part in the law-reading. The narrative in itself does not say this; all it says is that the people assembled and that Ezra read the law on the first day of the seventh month. Only its present position demands a date thirteen years after Ezra's return. On the other hand, it may be said first that ben Sira, having a Sadducean outlook was undoubtedly prejudiced and we should not take his neglect of Ezra too seriously; and secondly, that what we can attribute positively to Ezra, namely the public recognition of the Pentateuch as Israel's scripture, is so important as not to be dismissed as fictional.

At what date did Ezra return? Some of what can be said about this has inevitably been anticipated above. In the absence of any serious textual uncertainty we ought to take Ezr. 7.7 at its face value, namely that Ezra went up in the seventh year of Artaxerxes. Any suggestion that the numeral should be deemed corrupt and twenty-seven (Rudolph) or thirty-seven (Bright and others) be read in its place is made in the interests of theory and should be resisted. If, then, we resist altering the text we must assume that the king meant is Artaxerxes II (405–358 B.C.) and that the year of Ezra's return was 398, nearly fifty years after Nehemiah. One very real advantage in dating Ezra later than Nehemiah is that their respective handlings of the mixed marriages problem fall into a more natural sequence. Instead of Nehemiah following Ezra's drastic divorce measures (Ezr. 10.3, 44) some years later with the less harsh method of a promise not to continue the practice, we now find that Nehemiah's measures had proved unworkable through a couple of generations and when Ezra faced the problem in his day, some thirty-four years later, he insisted on divorce for already existing marriages.

It may be said that the following are the main facts that stand in favour of regarding Nehemiah and Ezra as contemporaries: (a) the long-standing dove-tailing of the material taken from the memoirs makes their stories overlap; (b) both men returned during the reign of a king called Artaxerxes; (c) Nehemiah's name is found in Neh. 8.9 among those present at the law reading; (d) Ezra's name stands in Neh. 12.36 as a leading member of one of the processions at the dedication of the walls; (e) and one or two personal names recur as contemporaries of both men. Of these, (a) brings many problems in its train that cannot be solved; (b) is inconclusive, for the king is not more closely identified on either occasion; (c) the presence of Nehemiah's name in Neh. 8.9 involves a violation of grammatical usage, (d) the mention of Ezra in Neh. 12.36 virtually involves equating him with a leader of the singers (see verse 42) whereas a man of his standing would have been mentioned first if his name had stood originally; and (e) only one name, that of Meremoth son of Uriah is certainly identifiable as that of the same man (see p. 31).

Several things, apart from the mixed marriage incidents, fall into a natural perspective if Ezra is seen to follow Nehemiah.
(a) The high priest contemporary with Nehemiah was Eliashib, but with Ezra he was presumably Jehohanan (Neh. 3.1; Ezr. 10.6) According to Neh. 12.22f. Jehohanan was grandson of Eliashib

(see note on Ezr. 10.6). This is clearly not watertight as an
argument, but if it can be accepted as reasonable, then the later
date of Jehohanan is confirmed by the Elephantine Papyri, one
of the letters of which (Cowley, *Aram. Pap.*, No. 30) shows
that Jehohanan was high priest in 408 when the letter was
written.

(b) The identification of Hattush son of Shecaniah in Ezr. 8.2f.
(assuming a slight corruption of text, see note *ad loc.*) with
Hattush son (or grandson) of Shecaniah in 1 Chr. 3.22 would
not have much bearing on the date of Ezra unless we knew how
long each father lived before his son was born. The succession is
as follows: Jeconiah—Pedaiah (1 Chr. 3.19, or Shealtiel,
Ezr. 3.2)—Zerubbabel—Hananiah—Shecaniah—Hattush. If we
reckon that each son was born when his father was thirty years
old this would bring the birth of Hattush to about 470 B.C.,
making him a man of about seventy in 398, which would be
fitting for the head of a family. It must be conceded, however,
that such a method of reckoning could be made to fit a very
much earlier date.

(c) One or two proper names occur among Ezra's followers and
contemporaries as well as among those of Nehemiah, but there
is not one of the names that demands the assumption that the two
men were contemporaries and only one name that can be
identified with any certainty as that of the same man. This latter
is Meremoth the priest, son of Uriah, to whom Ezra handed over
the vessels and money on his return (Ezr. 8.33). In Neh. 3.4, 21
Meremoth son of Uriah, further designated as son of Hakkoz,
repaired two sections of the wall. If these refer to the same man,
although the longer designation in Neh. 3.4 might tell against
this, it can be represented that he was young and vigorous in
Nehemiah's day (witness a double stint of wall-repairing) and
old and trusted in Ezra's. Other names that occur in connection
with both men are either too common to be safely identified
or too little known, i.e. Hattush, Ezr. 8.2; Neh. 3.10; Hashabiah,
Ezr. 8.19; Neh. 3.17; Meshullam, Ezr. 8.16; Neh. 3.4, 30 (but
cf. Ezr. 10.15, 29; Neh. 3.6; 8.4; 10.7, 20; 12.25, 33—Meshullam
is obviously too common a name to distinguish any one individual

from another or to identify any two holders of the name); Malchijah, Ezr. 10.31; Neh. 3.11.

(d) The extent of Jerusalem's population, sparse in Nehemiah's day, is found, on the evidence of a large gathering in Ezr. 10.1, to be very much greater in Ezra's time, and this may be said to support a later date for Ezra, but it is almost purely subjective evidence.

(e) The mention of Protection (mg. Hebrew 'a wall') in Ezra's prayer (Ezr. 9.9) cannot, as the translation of RSV shows, be safely used as argument for date, because the word used is not a normal one for city wall and is doubtless used figuratively.

There are two problems that have to be faced by historians and scholars if the date of Ezra's return is found to be as late as 398. The first is that the Chronicler's date of writing must be assumed to be very late, for he clearly had no accurate knowledge of the temporal sequence of Nehemiah and Ezra; and the second is that if the Samaritan schism is put at about the middle of the fourth century, and if it be accepted that Ezra secured recognition of the completed Pentateuch in Palestine, half a century is a comparatively short time for the new (if it was new with Ezra) form of the law to establish itself not only among the Jews in Palestine but also among the Samaritans. But it may well be that the Pentateuch was known in Palestine long before Ezra's time and that what Ezra did was simply to ensure its final recognition.

(iii) *The Nehemiah memoirs*

We are on much more certain ground in discussing the memoirs of Nehemiah. The story of Nehemiah is told very largely in the first person and it is conceivable that the memoirs have been reproduced by the Chronicler almost, if not quite, in their entirety and that he did not add any narrative in the third person as he did in the story of Ezra, with the possible exception of such parts of chapters 9 and 10 as may be thought to belong to Nehemiah's story (see below). The first-person narrative runs from Neh. 1.1 to 7.5 and from 12.31 (to which verses 27–30 is introductory) to 13.31. While Ezra's style and interests are scarcely distinguishable from the Chronicler's, Nehemiah's style is very much his own, simple, straightforward and business-like, yet reflecting at the same time a genuine religious zeal. It is comparatively easy to pick out places where the Chronicler has introduced his own remarks, as, for example, in the preparation for the dedication of the wall in 12.27–30 where the Levites are brought into full prominence. Less clearly so is this true of 12.44–13.3, where the first person is not used but where the material is necessary introduction to the reforms of chapter 13.

We are accustomed to speak of Nehemiah's memoirs, but in fact they appear to be more in the nature of a *memorial* document to remind God and men of the work of Nehemiah, his piety, and his devotion to God and his people. This is clear from such a verse‍ as 5.19, 'Remember for my good, O my God, all that I have done for this people'; and the book closes with, 'Remember me, O my God, for good' (cf. also 6.9, 14; 13.14, 22: comparable words are frequently found on Aramaic votive tablets, see Lidzbarski, *Handbuch der nordsemitischen Epigraphik*, 1898, pp. 165–9). 'Like Hattushil and other ancient rulers of western Asia, Nehemiah reports his good deeds and justifies his actions before the deity, in the hope of receiving his reward' (Pfeiffer, *Introd.*, p. 838). If Nehemiah was a eunuch, as has been suggested, there would be no children to keep his memory alive, and that might have encouraged him to leave a 'memorial'. The Chronicler, however, did not transmit Nehemiah's memoirs just as he found them. He did not find a break at 7.5 (or 7.73a if we can, which is doubtful, attribute the list to Nehemiah), the story being resumed at 11.1 after three chapters of material which cannot be attributed to Nehemiah's memoirs. Why did the Chronicler insert chapters 8–10, and where ought they to be placed? The answer probably lies in his mistaken idea (or intention) that Ezra and Nehemiah were contemporaries. He put the chapters here so that Nehemiah would seem to have a full share in Ezra's work, and he added the words 'and Nehemiah who was the governor' in 8.9 in pursuit of this. The grammatical construction of the passage shows quite clearly that only one speaker, i.e. Ezra, is wanted. How much, then, of chapters 8–10 can be brought into Ezra's activity? The answer probably is that most of it could be said to fit Ezra's work, but that the latter half of chapter 10 better fits Nehemiah's background and work, first because it i based as much on Deuteronomy as on the laws in the rest of the Pentateuch (see the references in the commentary), and, second, because it looks forward in many respects to the actual details of reform carried out by Nehemiah. In the covenant (10.28–39) the people agree to keep the commandments, not to intermarry with the peoples of the land, not to buy from foreigners on the sabbath, to observe the fallow year and to remit debts every seventh year, to pay the one third of a shekel tax, to provide the wood-offering regularly and to contribute first-fruits and tithes. The reform, described in 13.10ff., was concerned with four of these, the bringing of tithes, sabbath trading by Jews and non-Jews, mixed marriages, and the wood-offering.

If the latter part of chapter 10 belongs to Nehemiah's story, at what point does the narrative switch from Ezra to Nehemiah? This has already been touched upon in dealing with the Ezra memoirs. As was suggested there, both leaders may have held a solemn ceremony with fasting and confession, followed by the making of a covenant, Ezra after his tribunal had done its work and Nehemiah before his reform. It is possible that the Chronicler has taken the first part of the Ezran account (Neh. 9.1–38a—although it will be noticed that the words 'and Ezra said' have been added in RSV from the Greek) and then completed it with the end of the Nehemian story of the fast and covenant (9.38b–10.39). The editing can be seen fairly clearly in 9.38b and 10.28, 29a, for it will be seen that the mention of priests and Levites in both 9.38 and 10.28 is typical of the Chronicler and the grammatical connection would be easier in the Hebrew text if it could be assumed that the infinitives 'to work . . . to observe and do' in 10.29 follow directly on the making of the covenant, 9.38a, and give its terms.

(iv) *Material from Temple or state archives*

Within the limits of the Nehemiah story there are several statistical lists that would scarcely have been appropriate in his memoirs, especially if he intended the 'memoirs' to be a memorial document. These, and other lists in the rest of Ezra-Nehemiah, were probably taken by the Chronicler from official archives.

(a) Ezra **1.9–11a**: This list of Temple vessels might well have been taken from the official archives. It is possible that it was written in the official language, i.e. Aramaic, since one of the words, that for bowl in verse 10, is in commoner use in that language than in Hebrew.

(b) Ezra **2** = Nehemiah **7**: This list (Ezr. 2.1–70; Neh. 7.6–73) is introduced in both places as that of the people who came up with Zerubbabel. In origin it is probably not such a list at all, and there are no strong internal reasons why it should be thought to be. It is much more likely to be a list of people who had already returned at some time before the list was made and had settled in their towns and villages, hence the inclusion of towns in part of the list (Ezr. 2.21–35; Neh. 7.25–38). The families mentioned in the list may have linked up, on their return, with other members of the family who had not been deported, since family solidarity was a strong feature of Israelite life, and we need not therefore feel that the list is limited strictly to people who had returned from exile. It may have been the record of a census taken in the early post-exilic period. On the other hand, it is not altogether an inappropriate list, for many of the families listed, if not indeed a majority of them, would in fact have returned from exile, and in the Chronicler's opinion it was these families who comprised the true Israel. The figures given in the two lists differ considerably at times and fail, in either list, to add up to the total given (see the commentary on Ezr. 2), but are so high in places as to appear quite unrealistic, whether as the number of those who actually returned or as the number of those who had settled in their towns and villages.

In some respects the list is welded better into its context in Neh. 7 than it is in Ezra 2. Although it is not the list one would have expected to find, namely a review of the population with a view to finding a tenth that could be called upon to live in Jerusalem, it does list the names of families living in Judah at some time in the post-exilic period and therefore was able to serve instead of a fresh census. This is not to say that it is the list that Nehemiah used for the occasion, but rather that it is the one the Chronicler thought suitable. At the end of Neh. 7 the list connects more easily with what follows than at the end of Ezr. 2, because it ends (both in Ezr. 2 and Neh. 7) with a reference to an assembly in the seventh month and runs straight on, in chapter 8, to the reading of the law in the seventh month. If this can be shown to be so, then, having used the list in Neh. 7, the Chronicler felt it to be an equally appropriate list to use for the first record of return from exile. The insertion in Ezr. 2 may not, however, be regarded necessarily as the work of the Chronicler. It will be seen later (see pp. 38, 187) that in all probability an editor (later than the Chronicler himself) inserted in 1 Chr. 9 a list which he found in Neh. 11. In the same way it is at least possible that it was not the Chronicler himself who put the list in Ezr. 2, but that an editor found the list in Neh. 7 and thought it an appropriate one to insert in Ezra. It is not by any means an integral part of the context in Ezra.

It is worth noting, in passing, that some of the family names in this list occur also in the list of Ezra's caravan, thus showing that family identity might remain even when part of the family was in Palestine and part still living in Babylon (see p. 44).

The differences in names in a few cases, but more frequently the differences in the numbers given for the families in the two lists, show how lists are liable to distortion in transmission. The total of the figures given in Neh. 7 comes to over 1,000 more than that in Ezra. To explain how the differences might have arisen, it has been suggested that there was a time when Hebrew documents used cyphers for the cardinal numbers as did the Aramaic documents found at Elephantine. On the papyri the cyphers represent 1, 10, and 20, and perhaps 100. Hebrew may have had more of these than the extant Aramaic papyri contain. They would be fairly easy to misread, especially when four or five single strokes were written together. But it cannot be proved that Hebrew did use such signs. Another possibility is that the numbers were abbbreviated by writing the initial letters only, but this would invite error because the same letter begins several numerals: the Hebrew letter šin, for instance, could then stand for 2, or 3, 6, or 7 or 8, 30 or 60, 70 or 80. it is true that some of the errors (or differences) could be thus explained, but not all of them, and in any case it would be a very uncertain way of representing numerals. The total, 42,360, also offers a problem: the total of the separate figures given in Ezr. 2 is 29,818, and in Nehemiah 31,089. The inclusion of the free women, it has been thought, might bring the total up to that given, but one would expect there to be more than 11,000 or 12,000 women to 30,000 men. We probably have to reckon with a confusion of numerals owing to several causes, and also to an accumulation of error over a number of copyings.

(c) Ezra **8.1–14**: This list of those who returned with Ezra seems capable of being taken at its face value. It is not alien to its context and, apart from the seemingly large number of the caravan about which we have no criteria to form a sound judgment, contains no serious improbabilities. On the other hand, it is of much historical significance in that it appears to be one of the earliest records of tracing back the priesthood to Aaron.

(d) Ezra **10.18–44**: The list of the men who married foreign women is also probably a genuine list. It is to be noted, however, that no Temple servants (nᵉṯînîm) are listed. There may be two reasons for this: either they may not have been regarded as full Israelites in view of their probable non-Israelite origin (see on Ezr. 2.43), or the numbers of their mixed marriages may have been so great as to deter the Chronicler from publishing them. It may also be noted that it is recorded only in the case of the family of the high priest Joshua that they pledged themselves to put away their foreign wives and made an appropriate guilt offering. The list has probably been given in an abbreviated form, and we are left to assume that the same procedure (verse 19) applied to them all in turn.

(e) Nehemiah **3.1–32**: This list of builders and the section of the wall on which they were engaged has no mention of Nehemiah in it, and indeed has nothing to suggest that he was the author. It may be, therefore, an official record which was copied by the compiler. There is little doubt that it is an ancient document, whether it was included in Nehemiah's own memoirs or added by the Chronicler, and is a valuable witness to the topography of Jerusalem in Nehemiah's time. (On Nehemiah 7, see above, pp. 35ff.)

(f) Nehemiah **10.1–27**: This is a list of 'those who set their seal' to the covenant. Apart from the first two names, Nehemiah and Zedekiah, which are those of individuals, the rest are family names, the first twenty-one priestly families, then seventeen levitical ones and finally forty-four lay families. Many of the names occur in other lists—those of the priests in 12.1–7 and 12–21, and those of the laymen in Ezr. 2.3–19. If the list be genuinely the list of names accompanying the covenant, and there is no obvious reason why it should not be, the name Nehemiah will be that of the governor and Zedekiah that of his second-in-command, although such a man is otherwise unknown in that capacity; there would presumably be no other reason for singling out two individuals. The rest of the names can be taken as representative of the family they name. If, on the other hand, it is an editorial list, the editor must have added the two individual names to attach it to the occasion. Against this it is said that no one would have invented an otherwise unknown man, Zedekiah, as second-in-command to Nehemiah. In any case, the list, in one form or another, was almost certainly taken from the official archives.

(g) Nehemiah **11.3–19**: This is a list of leading men of Judah and Benjamin and their families, together with certain priestly and levitical families, and families of gatekeepers, who lived in Jerusalem. It immediately follows the decision (by lot) to move a tenth of the population into Jerusalem. We would expect a list of those taken by lot, whether as individuals or as families, to move into Jerusalem, but this does not give the impression of being such a list. It seems to be a full list of all who lived in the city. The fact that it is also used in 1 Chr. 9.2–18 (with some differences) as a list of the first to settle in Jerusalem after the exile, and also the fact that it is followed (in Nehemiah, but not in 1 Chr. 9) by a list of towns, cast some further doubt on whether it was the actual list for the specific occasion. There appears to be no reason for doubting that it is a genuine document, made in Nehemiah's time, giving details of inhabitants of Jerusalem. Its inclusion here is therefore probably entirely due to the Chronicler, and there is evidence in the Chronicles form of the list to suggest that it was used in Nehemiah first and that an editor later than the Chronicler inserted it in 1 Chronicles.

(h) Nehemiah **11.25–36**: A list of towns in Palestine occupied by udahites and Benjaminites. This list, by its position after a list of families, invites comparison with Ezr. 2 (=Neh. 7), where there also occurs a list of place-names after a list of family names, but there the similarity ends. Like the previous list, this one is not obviously closely knit to its context, but it is probably a genuine list belonging in general to the Nehemiah–Ezra period and taken by the Chronicler from the official archives. It clearly reflects the gradual reoccupation of Jewish (or formerly Jewish) territory in post-exilic times.

(i) Nehemiah **12.1–9**: A list of priests and Levites who are described as those who came up with Zerubbabel. This, and the three lists that follow, break the apparent connection between the record of the settlement of Levites according to their divisions in 11.36 and the finding out of Levites for the wall dedication mentioned in 12.27. These lists do not therefore seem to enter into the Chronicler's scheme and must have been inserted here by a subsequent editor. But what was his purpose? He must have intended by the lists to give some further details about the nature of the population in Jerusalem and elsewhere. Or it may simply be a case of like attracting like: he knew of comparable lists to those already given and joined them on. It is difficult to see why this list is connected with the return of Zerubbabel. In Ezra 2.36–39 only four priestly families are named, but here twenty-two are named. It is conceivable that these twenty-two are subdivisions of the four named in Ezr. 2. In its present form it is virtually contemporary with the list of heads of father's houses (priestly) in the time of Joiakim, successor to Joshua (see on 12.12–21).

(j) Nehemiah **12.10, 11**: This is a table of the succession of high priests from Joshua, contemporary with Zerubbabel, to Jaddua, contemporary, according to Josephus, with Alexander the Great. Beyond the fact that this table supplies a thread of continuity for the post-exilic period from Joshua to Jaddua, with whom the editor was doubtless contemporary, it is difficult to see why it was inserted here.

(k) Nehemiah **12.12–21**: This is introduced as a list of the heads of the families listed in 12.1–7 who were contemporary with Joiakim. Since Joiakim was successor to Joshua, this list belongs to the next generation after that given in verses 1–7. It is not obvious why the list is given twice, i.e. in verses 1–7 and again in verses 12–21, nor why the families so changed by Nehemiah's time that the list of priestly families in Neh. 10.1–8 has only fifteen names in common with the two lists in chapter 12, nor what the relation of these lists of twenty-one (or -two) families each is to the list of twenty-four priestly families in 1 Chr. 24.7–18. (On family names, see p. 43 below.)

(l) Nehemiah **12.24–26**: This list of Levite heads of families rounds off the previous list. It is so short a list that little of historical value can be made of it; it serves at least as a counterpart to verses 8 and 9, where a short-list of Levite families is given.

6. HEBREW PROPER NAMES: THEIR FORMATION AND MEANING

In these two books, Ezra and Nehemiah, there occur 367 different personal proper names or names of families. In view of this it seems desirable to take some notice of these names and where possible to give a meaning to them in the commentary. Difficulties arise, however, because of unfamiliar verbal roots used in the names or because some names are capable of two meanings. Where two meanings are possible one would have to decide which of the two was more suitable as a proper name or which suited the bearer's circumstances better. It will be shown here, very briefly, how Hebrew proper names are formed, and thus on what basis they are translated in the commentary.

It may be assumed that most, if not all, Hebrew proper names were meaningful when first used, even though continued use deprived them of their significance. There is evidence within the Old Testament itself that meanings could be ignored or wrongly understood. When first used, a meaningful name might have some reference to the circumstances of the child's birth, or to his home or background, or to the hopes fulfilled in his birth, or the expectations raised by it, or the hopes placed in him by parents or well-meaning friends, or the gratitude of the parents to God. The majority of names are short, two-member sentences, but there are some that never seem to have been more than single words.

Single-word names may describe characteristics and may possibly have been given in later life and be more in the nature of nicknames, e.g.:

Ater	(Ezr. 2.16):	*Left-handed*
Bakbuk	(Ezr. 2.51):	*Flask*
Barzillai	(Ezr. 2.61):	*Man of iron (Iron-like)*
Bazlith	(Neh. 7.54):	*Onion*
Galal	(Neh. 11.17):	*Tortoise* (this could also mean *Dung*)
Hagab	(Ezr. 2.46):	*Locust* or *Grasshopper*
Hakkatan	(Ezr. 8.12):	*The little one ('Titch')*
Hakkoz	(Ezr. 2.61):	*The thorn*
Harumaph	(Neh. 3.10):	*Split-nose*
Hezir	(Neh. 10.20):	*Pig*
Parosh	(Ezr. 2.3):	*Flea*

Many that look at first sight like single-word names might in fact be abbreviations of two-member sentence names. The pronunciation of the shortened name sometimes differs widely from that of the full name (see pp. 42ff.).

The majority of Hebrew proper names were in origin short sentences which might be either verbal or nominal. They usually have two members, subject and predicate, and occasionally a preposition is included. Instances of prepositional names are:

Eliehoenai	(Ezr. 8.4):	*To Yahweh are my eyes* (cf. Ps. 25.15)
Michael	(Ezr. 8.8):	*Who is like God?*
Besodeiah	(Neh. 3.6):	*In the counsel/friendship/intimacy of Yahweh* (cf. Ps. 25.14)

Verbal sentence names may have a perfect tense:

Elnathan	(Ezr. 8.16):	*God has given*
Jozadak	(Ezr. 3.2):	*Yahweh has been righteous/acted rightly*

Or an imperfect tense, which is usually a wish or a hope for the future:

Eliakim	(Neh. 12.41):	*May God establish/set up*
Eliashib	(Ezr. 10.6):	*May God restore*
Joiakim	(Neh. 12.10):	*May Yahweh establish/set up*

Participial sentences are much less common—three only occur among the names in these books:

Mehetabel (Neh. 6.10):   *God is doing good/one who is doing good*

Meshezabel (Neh. 3.4):   *God is a deliverer/one who delivers*

Mahalalel (Neh. 11.4):   *God is one who illuminates/flashes light*

It will be noticed that all of the above verbal sentences have either God or Yahweh as their subject. It was natural that in a society so firmly based on religion as was Israelite society practically all the proper names should have a theophorous element. This seems to be particularly so of nominal sentence-names where the predicative element describes a characteristic of the God worshipped:

Eliezer   (Ezr. 8.16):   *God is help*
Uriah   (Ezr. 8.33):   *Yahweh is (my) light/fire*

The theophorous element is variable. It may stand either first or second and may be either *El*, God, or *Yah* (*iah*), *Yeho*, *Yo* (Eng. *Jo*) all short for Yahweh, or it might be a descriptive word like father, brother, lord, king. Examples are:

Jonathan   (Ezr. 8.6):   *Yahweh has given*
Benaiah   (Ezr. 10.25): *Yahweh has built*
Eleazar   (Ezr. 7.5):   *God has helped*
Zabdiel   (Neh. 11.14): *God has given: or Gift of God*
Abram   (Neh. 9.7):   *The father is high*
Adonikam   (Ezr. 2.13):   *The lord has risen up*
Ahitub   (Ezr. 7.2):   *The brother is good(ness)*
Malchijah (Ezr. 10.25): *Yahweh is (my) king*

One feature of some of these names remains uncertain, namely, the force of the 'i' sound in the middle. Grammatically it is capable of being taken in one of two ways, either as a first person singular pronominal suffix, e.g. Malchijah, 'Yahweh is my king', or as a connecting vowel between the two members of the sentence, so that Malchijah may mean simply 'Yahweh is king'.

As with proper names in all languages, there is a variety of shortened forms (of which the full form is not always discoverable):

Bunni	(Neh. 9.4):	for Benaiah, *Yahweh has built*
Giddel	(Ezr. 2.47):	for Giddeliah (perhaps, but the names does not occur in OT), *Yahweh has made great*
Zaccur	(Neh. 3.2):	for Zechariah, *Yahweh has remembered*

Some may have hypocoristic endings:

ai:	Ahzai	(Neh. 11.13):	for Ahaziah, *Yahweh has grasped*
	Zaccai	(Ezr. 2.9):	for Zechariah (?), *Yahweh has remembered*
i:	Zabdi	(Neh. 11.17):	for Zabdiel, *God has given*
on:	Shimeon	(Ezr. 10.31):	for Shemaiah, *Yahweh has heard*
oth:	Anathoth	(Neh. 10.19):	*Anath's man*
	Jeremoth	(Ezr. 10.26):	*Thick/Swollen*

Some names are capable of two meanings: Hattil may mean either 'Tall' or 'Garrulous', and since we know nothing more than the man's name (Ezr. 2.57; Neh. 7.59; and in any case it is probably a family name), we cannot tell which would fit. Hariph, Neh. 7.24 (see note on Ezr. 2.18), could mean 'Autumn' or 'Sharp/Keen'. Bakbukiah, Neh. 11.17 has a name that looks like a theophorous -iah coupled with Bakbuk, 'flask', but 'Flask of Yahweh' is too incongruous to be readily acceptable as a natural meaning. The ending -iah should perhaps here be taken as a longer hypocoristic ending.

There is some evidence that in post-exilic times the Jews began reviving some of the better-known pre-exilic names; hence we find Judah (Ezr. 10.23) and Benjamin (Ezr. 10.32) among others.

Family names

Many of the names used in Ezra-Nehemiah are not those of individuals as such, but of families, although this does not preclude the possibility that the family was named after one of its early or earliest fathers. Several such names are known to us only as family names, e.g. Parosh (Ezr. 2.3), Pahath-moab (Ezr. 2.6), Zattu (Ezr. 2.8), Adonikam (Ezr. 2.13), but they must originally have been personal names. The expectation is that family names would remain constant throughout the years and generations, and in general the several lists in these books tend to confirm this. On the other hand, there is evidence of some change and development. For instance, when families increased rapidly there would be a natural tendency to split into two or more new family groups. This seems to be the case with the family of Pahath-moab (Ezr. 2.6) which has two sub-families, Jeshua and Joab. There are many new family names among the laymen in the list in Neh. 10.14–27 as compared with that in Ezr. 2. The mention of three heads of houses in the Adonikam family and of two in the Bigvai family (Ezr. 8.13, 14) may also point to sub-families which might eventually separate as families in their own right. The several lists of priests' families (Neh. 10.1–8; 12.1–7, 12–21) are by no means constant in the names of families. This may be accounted for in one of several ways. Since there were twenty-four priestly families in the serving-list (1 Chr. 24.7–18), it may be that the lists in Nehemiah containing only twenty-one and twenty-two names may have suffered badly in transmission, but it is unlikely that *all* the differences could be thus accounted for. Another possibility is that the names of the priestly families changed more easily than those of the lay families and that the same families occur under new names. The third possibility is that there was a great deal of rivalry among the priestly families and that lists of the 'serving' families would be likely to change from generation to generation.

Occasionally a family name may be concealed in what appears to be the name of the father or grandfather. Usually the phrase 'of the sons of' introduces the family name, but in Neh. 11.17 'son of Asaph' appears to mean of the family of Asaph; cf. also Bebai in Ezr. 8.11 and Iddo in Neh. 12.4, 16.

Attention was drawn on p. 36 to the family solidarity implied in the fact that some of the family names of those who returned with Ezra are the same as those who are said to have returned with Zerubbabel.

Occasionally a family name denoted an occupation. Hallohesh, Neh. 3.12, means 'Whisperer', 'Magician', and the family may have been known for its skill as snake-charmers. Colhozeh, Neh. 3.15, meaning 'Every (one a) seer', implies that the family practised clairvoyance.

Lists of names which had no thread of meaning to hold them

together and lend them shape were particularly liable to corruption
or distortion. It would be easy for a scribe's eye to slip from one
name to another like-ending name, either forwards to omit a group
of names as in Ezra's genealogy in Ezr. 7 or backwards to repeat a
group of names. The lists may not have been faultless when the
Chronicler found them, and there is evidence that he or a subsequent editor or scribe glossed over corruptions of text by falling
back on imagination and supplying invented names. This is what
may have happened when we find pairs of like-sounding names
such as Gabbai Sallai, Neh. 11.8, Sallai Kallai, Neh. 12.20, Shashai
Sharai, Ezr. 10.40, and Milalai Gilalai, Neh. 12.36. With these we
may compare Muppim and Huppim in Gen. 46.21 and Huppim and
Shuppim in 1 Chr. 7.15. In Neh. 11.8 it is possible to demonstrate
that the two names stand where something else stood in the original
list.

7. THE TEXT AND EARLY VERSIONS

The book of Ezra is partly in Hebrew and partly in Aramaic. The
Aramaic parts are 4.8–6.18 and 7.12–26. The whole of Nehemiah is
in Hebrew. The text appears to have been well transmitted. However, lists of proper names were extremely liable to damage in
transmission, and this can be seen to have happened at many points
when comparison is made between Ezr. 2 and Neh. 7. Apart from
these, verses that are obviously corrupt can almost be counted on
the fingers of one hand; Ezr. 10.44; Neh. 4.12, 13, 23 may be
mentioned. Its worst feature, and this is a matter rather of composi-
tion than of text, is its non-chronological order leading to confusion
between Sheshbazzar and Zerubbabel, Nehemiah and Ezra.

The Aramaic sections help to date the books only in so far as they
appear to be later than the Elephantine documents, since the Aramaic
of Ezra can be shown to be later than that in the documents.

In Greek there are two forms of the book. The one, already
mentioned on p. 10, is called *Esdras a* (in LXX) and is 1 Esdras in
the Apocrypha. It is a Greek version of parts of the last two
chapters of 2 Chronicles, most of Ezra and those verses from
Nehemiah that report the reading of the law by Ezra, but in addition

it has two chapters of extra material in the form of a legendary story of three guardsmen in the court of Darius. The book is of value as an independent witness to a different order of narrative from that in the canonical book. Josephus evidently thought well of it and followed its version of events in preference to that in the Hebrew book. It would help if we could discover whether its Hebrew (or Aramaic) original was the canonical book or whether it translates an independent book. Further interest lies in its scope; it seems to be the story of the restoration under Zerubbabel and the work of Ezra, Nehemiah being left completely aside. This, admittedly, is an argument from silence, since it is conceivable that the translator also issued a translation of Nehemiah which has been completely lost.

The other form in Greek, called *Esdras b*, is the normal Septuagint translation and does not differ essentially from the Hebrew; it contains both Ezra and Nehemiah.

In view of the importance of the immediate post-exilic period, the period of restoration, in the development of Judaism, it is not surprising that we have three attempts to present a record of the events from the return to the work of Nehemiah and Ezra. The canonical Ezra-Nehemiah is one of these, the Septuagint version is a second, intended, of course, for the Greek-speaking Jews of the Diaspora, and the third, with an apparent emphasis on Ezra and neglect of Nehemiah, is the book known as 1 Esdras.

THE BOOK OF

EZRA

FIRST SECTION **1.1–6.22**   THE RETURN AND THE REBUILDING
OF THE TEMPLE

First Return under Sheshbazzar **1.1–2.70**

DECREE OF CYRUS **I.1–4**

Verses 1–3 as far as **let him go up** repeat the closing sentences of 2 Chronicles.

1. first year of Cyrus king of Persia: in 549 B.C. Cyrus, then king of Anshan and Persia, after revolting against Astyages king of the Medes, of whom he was a vassal, became king of the Medes and Persians. In 546 he defeated Croesus king of Lydia and in 538 Babylon fell to him without serious fighting. It was from this point that the Chronicler dated the reign of Cyrus, since only then did he become ruler over Palestine. The title king of Persia was retained after the conquest of Babylon and after the Persian empire was formed.

word of the Lord by . . . Jeremiah: the reference is probably to a seventy-year period of exile (Jer. 29.10; cf. 25.11ff.). The prophecy has to be interpreted very loosely because in fact only forty-eight or forty-nine years had elapsed from the fall of Jerusalem in 586 to the decree of Cyrus in 538. If we think rather of the restoration of the Temple, which was completed in 516, and which may well have been in the author's mind, we have the seventy years. There are two further possibilities, (a) that the number is reckoned from the deportation in 597 after Jehoiachin's surrender, and (b) that seventy is a round figure. Zechariah, prophesying in 520, could more easily speak of the seventy-year period (1.12; 7.5). Possibly the mention of Jeremiah is intended to cover any relevant prophecy of restoration, and if so, in view of the mention of building in the decree of Cyrus, we may also think of Isa. 44.28; 45.1, 13.

proclamation: there is no non-biblical evidence for this, but it is in keeping with the policy shown by Cyrus towards minorities, as seen on the cylinder found at Ur and written after the conquest of Babylon, allowing restoration of the gods, and therefore by implication of the peoples, of subject kingdoms (*A.N.E.T.*, p. 315).

in writing: the original decree might have been in the Babylonian language, in cuneiform script on a clay tablet, and deposited in the archives of the city in which Cyrus was resident at the time (see on 6.2). If it was written in Babylonian an Aramaic translation would have been made for Jewish purposes. But, since Aramaic was well understood at court, being for a long period the language of diplomacy, there is every possibility that it was written in Aramaic at the outset. Another form of the decree is given in Aramaic in 6.3–5. Close comparison of the two 'copies' with a view to establishing accuracy or authenticity is probably misapplied, since

neither reference set out in the first place to give an exact and verbatim record of
the decree, but simply to give the gist of it (see Introduction, p. 15). Moreover,
the version in chapter 1 came through different channels from that in chapter 6.
If either gives the original form, the balance of probability would be for the
Aramaic form.

2. The LORD: this recognition of Yahweh by Cyrus may well have been
genuine, since Cyrus, not being a strict monotheist, would be ready to increase his
pantheon to include the Jewish God. Otherwise we must ascribe it to Jewish zeal
in substituting Yahweh for whichever god Cyrus may have named, Marduk,
Nebo, or Bel.

3. who is in Jerusalem: this makes the Hebrew relative refer to God, but it
could refer back to 'the house'; the translation would then run: 'the house of the
LORD, the God of Israel—he is the God—which is in Jerusalem' (cf. verses 4, 5).
Whoever was responsible for the wording of this form of the decree, whether
Cyrus or a Jewish editor, was concerned with the fact that Yahweh was the (only)
God, not that he was merely the God in Jerusalem.

4. each survivor: lit. everyone who remains or, is left over; the Chronicler
clearly regarded the exiles as the remnant of the Jewish people (see on Neh. 1.2).
the men of his place: non-Israelite neighbours seem to be intended.
goods: the Hebrew word ($r^e k\hat{u}\check{s}$) sometimes means beast, and might here mean
pack-animals; **beasts** would then naturally be the domestic animals only.
freewill offerings: the picture is not clear. This seems to be over and above what
Cyrus expected the people to contribute. Possibly the latter was a minimum levy
to which people added what they wished (see on 6.4). The idea of voluntary giving
both in kind (1.4, 6; 3.5; 7.15f.; 8.28) and in service (2.68; 7.13) was important to
the Chronicler. We may also compare the coupling of compulsory measures with
voluntary in the matter of recruiting population for Jerusalem (Neh. 11.1, 2).

RETURN UNDER SHESHBAZZAR 1.5–11

5. and Benjamin: the Chronicler regularly associates Benjamin with Judah
(1 Chr. 6.65; 12.16; 2 Chr. 11.1, 3, 10, 12, 23; 15.2, 8, 9; 17.17; 25.5; 34.9;
Ezr. 1.5; 4.1; 10.9) and Judah and Benjamin inherit the name Israel (2 Chr. 10.17;
11.3, 23). Originally only Judah separated from the northern tribes (1 Kg. 12.20),
but Benjamin, the southernmost 'northern' tribe, gradually became attached to
Judah.

6. all who were about them: are the people who are called 'the men of his
place' in verse 4.
vessels of silver: of what immediate use would *vessels* of silver be? 1 Esd. 2.9 has
'with everything, with silver'; the Hebrew text underlying this would involve only
slight change (*bakkol bakkesep* for *bik̲lê k̲esep*); if we accept this reading the silver
and gold come into the same category.

7. vessels: tradition about the Temple vessels was uncertain and confused:
2 Kg. 24.13 says that Nebuchadrezzar carried off the vessels of gold and cut them

in pieces, but 2 Chr. 36.7 knows nothing of the cutting up. Jeremiah 27.16; 28.6 show that the vessels still existed to be restored when the time came. If they were destroyed the reference here might be to bronze vessels, but the Chronicler clearly thought that the silver and gold vessels remained.

8. Mithredath: a Persian official. The name, which means 'given by Mithras', occurs again in 4.7 as that of a Persian official of a later date and not to be identified with this one.

Sheshbazzar: a Babylonian name probably meaning 'Shamash protect the son', but another suggestion is 'Sin protect the son'. The uncertainty is due to the several Greek transliterations of the name, Sabanassaro, Sasabalassaro, and Sanabassaro.

the prince: a title used by Ezekiel for the Davidic king as the civil head of the post-exilic community (Ezek. 34.24), but in other parts of O.T. for any man raised to authority. Nothing is known of Sheshbazzar except what is told us in Ezra. In 5.14 it is said that Cyrus appointed him governor. He may have been a Babylonian charged with the supervision of Judah in the early days of return and if so confusion by later Jewish historians with Zerubbabel, who also held authority in the early days of return, would be possible (see on 2.1 and Introduction, pp. 15–18).

9–11. In these verses RSV, by following the Greek text of 1 Esd. 2.13f., provides an English text in which the total agrees with the figures given for the individual items. This is not so in the Hebrew, which runs: 'This was their number: thirty basins of gold, a thousand basins of silver, twenty-nine vessels of various kinds [this word is translated 'censers' in RSV and LXX], thirty bowls of gold, four hundred and ten various silver bowls and a thousand other vessels; all the vessels of gold and silver were five thousand four hundred.' The list given in the other Greek version (Esdras b) agrees with the Hebrew except for one item, namely six various silver bowls instead of 410. 1 Esdras is a secondary text (in all probability) and should be followed with caution in spite of the numerical accuracy. The Hebrew text is certainly corrupt, but whether the figures themselves are wrong or whether some items are missing is hard to say. The total of well over 5,000 is unduly large. There could be at least two sources of error. First, if the Hebrew list is itself a translation—and the non-Hebrew word '$^a\bar{g}art^el\hat{e}$ 'basins', translated 'wine-coolers' in the Greek, suggests that it is—and if signs were used for the numerals, then the translator or copyist might have misrepresented them. Secondly, the list may have been copied and recopied and each time been subject to error (see further, Introduction, pp. 35–37).

A NUMERICAL RECORD OF THOSE WHO RETURNED **2.1–70**

Introduction 2.1, 2a

This describes the people covered by the list as belonging to the province, i.e. Judah, cf. 5.8, the territory of which Sheshbazzar was made governor, and then later Zerubbabel and later still Nehemiah.

1. each to his own town: this may give a clue to the nature of this document, for it implies that the people had already settled where they belonged and had not immediately returned from Babylon. It is not a list of individuals, with the exception of those in verse 2, but partly of families (lay, verses 3–20; priestly, verses 36–39; and levitical, verses 40ff.) and partly of towns and their inhabitants (verses 21–35). This difference in character between parts of the list suggests that it may have been compiled and was not a single document made at one time for one occasion. In the latter case one would have expected uniformity of character. The same document is found, with some variations probably due to copying, in Neh. 7.7–69. It is possible that, although it is not the document originally intended for the place it now occupies in Nehemiah, it was used in Nehemiah first and borrowed for use in Ezra. Whether this is so or not, the reference to a gathering in the seventh month at the end of the list fits more easily into place before the reading of the law recorded in Neh. 8 than it does in Ezra. This, however, would commit us to assuming that the Chronicler edited Nehemiah first and then turned to Ezra, which is not convincing, or that he found Nehemiah already edited and the list included by that editor, but of this there is no direct evidence. If he himself inserted the list in both places he seems to have made a better job of working it into Nehemiah than into Ezra. It is conceivable that it was inserted in Ezra by an editor later than the Chronicler (Introduction, p. 36).

In Ezra the Chronicler or editor seems to have used it with the intention of producing evidence of an immediate and generous response to Cyrus' permission to return. It is more of a 'settlement' list than a 'return' one, but it must not be overlooked that, although they are described as 'people of the province' and are said to have returned each to his own town, very many (if not all) of them must have returned from exile at some time. In the record of those who joined Ezra's caravan (8.1–14), some of the same family names occur. At least some families still recognized their kinship even when some of their number were in Judah and some remained in exile (see also Introduction, p. 44).

The eleven names in verse 2 must be intended to be those of the leaders of the community at the time of return. Zerubbabel and Jeshua (i.e. Joshua—the form of the name by which he is better known and which will be used in this commentary except when quoting, as it has been already, in the Introduction) were leaders in 520 (Hag. 1.1), but there is no certain evidence at what time they became such or at what time they returned. It is tempting to think that a new return took place in the beginning of the reign of Darius giving Haggai and Zechariah a chance to infuse new heart into the people. Zerubbabel and Joshua may have returned in 537 with Sheshbazzar, or, less probably, they may have been leaders of a fresh return in 520. The rest are not otherwise known as leaders unless we identify Nehemiah as the man of that name who returned in 444 B.C., and treat it here as an anachronism. Nehemiah 7.7 gives twelve names, adding Nahamani, and so does 1 Esd. 5.8, adding Resaiah. Mordecai and Bilshan are Babylonian names in form and reflect the practice by Jews of assuming Babylonian names as is attested by names on business documents found at Nippur and dated in the fifth century B.C.

2. Zerubbabel: in Ezr. 3.2 he is said to be the son of Shealtiel and therefore presumably grandson of Jeconiah the king (cf. 1 Chr. 3.17), but 1 Chr. 3.19 makes him son of another of Jeconiah's sons, Pedaiah. Perhaps this is to be explained by the assumption that the elder son Shealtiel died without a son and that his brother married his widow according to law and the first son was counted as Shealtiel's. The mention of Zerubbabel as among those who first returned and the subsequent statements that it was he who began the restoration work at this early time (3.2, 11; 4.2) seem to conflict with 5.16 which explicitly ascribes this work to Sheshbazzar, and, indeed, with 1.8 which speaks of Sheshbazzar as prince of Judah and charged with the return of the vessels. Why is Sheshbazzar not mentioned in chapter 2? Attempts are made either to identify Sheshbazzar and Zerubbabel, as the Chronicler himself must have done when he left chapter 2 without mention of Sheshbazzar, but this stretches ingenuity; or to show that references to Zerubbabel before 520 are anachronistic. The former overlooks the fact that Zerubbabel himself with his companions is the ultimate source for the statement that Sheshbazzar laid the foundations (5.2, 11ff.). The latter only increases the burden of historical error laid on the Chronicler.

Zerubbabel was clearly Jewish by birth and of the line of David, but it is not certain whether the name is Hebrew with the meaning 'born in Babylon' (shortened from $z^e r\hat{u}'b\bar{a}bel$) or Babylonian (zer-babel, 'seed of Babel') also meaning 'born in Babylon'. It would simplify the problem if, accepting the historicity of Sheshbazzar, we could assume that he had sole responsibility and authority for the initial attempts at restoration (in 537). Then we should be free to picture Zerubbabel and Joshua as leading a fresh company back from exile, and under the stimulus of the prophets Haggai and Zechariah giving fresh impetus to the work in 520. But we ought not, without more certain evidence, to credit the Chronicler with too much distortion of fact. If Sheshbazzar was a Babylonian charged with official responsibility for the restoration there is no reason why he should not be credited with laying the foundations, and at the same time Zerubbabel as leader (probably unofficial at that time) of the Jewish community could also be spoken of as building the altar (3.2) and laying the foundations of the Temple (3.12).

Jeshua: i.e. Joshua, 'Yahweh has saved', was son of Jozadak (=Jehozadak), 'Yahweh is right/has acted rightly' (5.2), whose descent from Levi is traced in 1 Chr. 6.1–14. Jehozadak was carried into exile (1 Chr. 6.15) and his father Seraiah was the last officiating priest in the pre-exilic Temple (2 Kg. 25.18). Joshua's name seems also to be used as the family name of his successors (see verse 36 and 10.18).

Nehemiah: 'Yahweh has comforted', apart from the governor of that name and a Nehemiah who ruled half Beth-zur (Neh. 3.16) this (=Neh. 7.7) is the only other mention of the name. There is no compelling reason why there should not have been a man named Nehemiah among Zerubbabel's companions, but it is tempting to regard this as an anachronistic inclusion of Nehemiah the governor among the first leaders.

Seraiah: 'Yahweh has become master', is a fairly widely used name both for laymen, priests, and Levites and, apart from well-known men like David's secretary (2 Sam. 8.17), the last high priest before the exile (2 Kg. 25.18) and Ezra's father (Ezr. 7.1), bearers of the name cannot be closely identified.

Reelaiah: a name of uncertain meaning, is used only here; Neh. 7.7 has Raamiah ('Yahweh has thundered'?).

Mordecai: 'Marduk's man'; occurs only here and Neh. 7.7 apart from the well-known Mordecai in Esther.

Bilshan: of uncertain meaning and occurs only here and Neh. 7.7.

Mispar: only here, Nehemiah has Mispereth. As pronounced it would mean 'Number': if pronounced *m^esappēr* it could mean 'Story-teller', 'Narrator'; but it may be a corrupt form of a Persian name Aspadat (cf. Aspatha, Est. 9.7).

Bigvai: of Persian origin, meaning 'Happy': three uses of this name are known: (a) this one (=Neh. 7.7); (b) a family name Ezr. 2.14, 8.14, Neh. 10.16; and (c) on the Elephantine papyri (Cowley, *Aram. Pap.*, Nos. 30, 31, 32).

Rehum: 'Has been shown compassion'; the name occurs five times: (a) here (Nehemiah has Nehum); (b) Neh. 12.3 a priestly family name; (c) Neh. 3.17, a Levite; (d) Neh. 10.25, a family name; and (e) Ezr. 4.8, a Persian official.

Baanah: this may be a contracted form of a name compounded with Baal, but its meaning is unknown. In post-exilic times it occurs only here (=Neh. 7.7) and as a family name in Neh. 10.27 .In pre-exilic times there were (a) a Benjaminite named Baanah, the murderer of Ishbosheth (2 Sam. 4.2); and (b) the father of one of David's heroes (2 Sam. 23.29).

Names of lay families **2.2b–20**

3. The family names in verses 3–19 are closely echoed by those listed in Neh. 10.14–19; see note on Neh. 10.14.

Parosh: 'Flea'; apart from its use as a family name, here and 8.3; 10.25; Neh. 3.25; 7.8, it occurs only in Neh. 10.14 as among those who sealed, but there is every reason to think that the names in Neh. 10.1–27 are all family names. If that is so, this is one of the names that occurs only as a family name.

4. Shephatiah: 'Yahweh has judged'; this is a fairly common name and some nine different men of the name can be distinguished.

5. Arah: 'Traveller' or 'Wild-ox'; the name occurs also in Neh. 6.18; 7.10, and 1 Chr. 7.39, where it is the name of an Asherite.

Seven hundred and seventy-five: Nehemiah has 'six hundred and fifty-two'. This and other errors or differences in the figures may be due to the use of abbreviations or signs for the numerals (see Introduction, p. 36). It so happens that in the order in which the numbers comprising this figure occur in the Hebrew text, this particular case could be due to mistaking initial letters, but this is not true of every difference in figures.

6. Pahath-moab: meaning unknown; occurs only as a family name 2.6; 8.4; 10.30; Neh. 3.11; 7.11; 10.14.

Jeshua and Joab: appear to be the family names of two sub-divisions of the very large family of Pahath-moab. Joshua (2.2) is a widely used name, but **Joab,**

'Yahweh is father', occurs only as (a) the son of David's sister, (b) a descendant of Judah (1 Chr. 4.14), and (c) as a family name here, Neh. 7.11 and Ezr. 8.9.

two thousand eight hundred and twelve: Nehemiah has 'two thousand eight hundred and eighteen'.

7. **Elam:** of unknown meaning; in addition to being a family name, as here, it occurs at least three times as the name of an individual, 1 Chr. 8.24; 26.3, Neh. 12.42, and also as a place-name in 2.31=Neh. 7.34.

8. **Zattu:** of unknown meaning; occurs only as a family name; Ezr. 8.5 (supplied from 1 Esd.); 10.27; Neh. 7.13; 10.14.

nine hundred and forty-five: Nehemiah has 'eight hundred and forty-five'.

9. **Zaccai:** meaning either 'Pure' or, as a short form of Zechariah, 'Yahweh has remembered'; it occurs only here and Neh. 7.14 (unless Zabbai be deemed an error for Zaccai in Neh. 3.20).

10. **Bani:** probably a short form of a name compounded with *banah*, e.g. Benaiah, 'Yahweh has built'; it is a fairly common name, but is liable to confusion with the name Binnui which Neh. 7.15 has, and also with *b'nê*, 'sons of'. The names Bani, Binnui, and Bunni (Neh. 9.4) mainly belong to the post-exilic period.

six-hundred and forty-two: Nehemiah has 'six hundred and forty-eight'.

11. **Bebai:** 'Pupil/apple of the eye' (or it may be a contracted form of a name otherwise unknown); it occurs only as a family name, 8.11 (possibly an individual), 10.28; Neh. 7.16; 10.15.

six hundred and twenty-three: Nehemiah has 'six hundred and twenty eight'.

12. **Azgad:** 'Gad is strong'; it occurs only as a family name in 8.12; Neh. 7.17; 10.15. Gad in this name probably originally referred to the god of fortune, cf. Isa. 65.11.

one thousand two hundred and twenty-two: Nehemiah has 'two thousand three hundred and twenty-two'.

13. **Adonikam:** 'The lord has risen up'; occurs only as a family name 8.13; Neh. 7.18. In Neh. 10.16 it appears to be given as Adonijah.

six hundred and sixty-six: Nehemiah has 'six hundred and sixty seven'.

14. **Bigvai:** see on verse 2.

two thousand and fifty-six: Nehemiah has 'two thousand and sixty-seven'. This difference may be a copyist's error in repeating the last two figures of the previous number.

15. **Adin:** 'Rapture'; occurs only as a family name, 8.6; Neh. 7.20; 10.16.

four hundred and fifty-four: Nehemiah has 'six hundred and fifty-five'.

16. **Ater:** 'Left-handed'; (a) the name of a lay family, Neh. 7.21; 10.17, and (b) the name of a levitical family of gatekeepers, 2.42; Neh. 7.45.

Hezekiah: 'Yahweh has strengthened'; a branch of the Ater family (cf. the division of the family of Pahath-moab, verse 6), Neh. 7.21; 10.17. As the name of an individual it occurs only in pre-exilic times.

17. Bezai: Probably a short form of a name like Bezalel, 'In the shadow of God'; it occurs as a family name only, Neh. 7.23 and 10.18.

three hundred and twenty-three: Nehemiah has 'three hundred and twenty-four'.

18. Jorah: 'Autumn rain'; it occurs only here, Nehemiah has Hariph. Was the change an accidental one due to association of meaning? *Ḥōrep* means the autumn season. Hariph could mean 'sharp', 'keen', or it could mean 'autumn'. The latter is not a natural meaning for a proper name, so that if the former be regarded as the meaning it may indicate that Hariph was the original name and that a scribe, mistaking the meaning, absent-mindedly wrote Jorah, its near-synonym.

19. Hashum: 'Broad-nosed'; is the name of an individual in Neh. 8.4, otherwise it occurs only as a family name, here, 10.33; Neh. 7.22; 10.18.

two hundred and twenty-three: Nehemiah has 'three hundred and twenty-eight'.

20. Gibbar: 'Strong man'; occurs only here. Nehemiah 7.25 has Gibeon which does not occur as a personal or family name but only as a place-name. Gibeon is in Benjaminite territory. If Nehemiah has the original reading, then the list of places begins with this verse.

Laymen enumerated according to towns 2.21–35

21. sons of: Nehemiah has 'men of' as in 22, 23 etc., which is obviously right. 'Sons of' has probably crept in during copying—similarly in verses 24, 25, 26, 29–35.

Bethlehem: in Judah.

22. Netophah: in Judah. The list in Nehemiah links Bethlehem and Netophah with a total of one hundred and eighty-eight; the total for both in Ezra is one hundred and seventy-nine.

23. Anathoth: in Benjamin, Jos. 21.18.

24. Azmaveth: also called Beth-azmaveth (as in Neh. 7.28), lies in Benjaminite territory, near Geba (Neh. 12.29). Its original pronunciation may have been 'Azmoth', i.e. incorporating the name of the god *Mot*, a prominent figure in Ugaritic (Canaanite) mythology.

25. Kiriatharim: in Neh. 7.29 he more familiar name Kiriath-jearim is used. It is a town of the Gibeonites (Jos. 9.17) assigned to Judah in Jos. 15.60 and lying near the Benjaminite border (Jos. 15.9), but in Jos. 18.28 assigned to Benjamin.

Chephirah: also Gibeonite and assigned to Benjamin (Jos. 9.17; 18.26).

Beeroth: Gibeonite, assigned to Benjamin (Jos. 9.17; 18.25).

26. Ramah: 5 miles N. of Jerusalem in Benjaminite territory.

Geba: in Benjaminite territory (Jos. 21.17).

27. Michmas: in Benjamin, north of Geba and Jerusalem.

28. Bethel: in Ephraim on the border of Benjamin.

Ai: near Bethel.

two hundred and twenty-three: Nehemiah has 'one hundred and twenty-three'.

29. Nebo: Neh. 7.33 calls it 'the other Nebo'. Perhaps it is another form of Nob (1 Sam. 21.1; Neh. 11.32) which was occupied by Benjaminites (Neh. 11.32). It is to be distinguished from Nebo in Moab (Num. 32.3). Confusion might well arise with the family name Nebo (Ezr. 10.43), or with the personal name Nebai (Neh. 10.19).

30. Magbish: not in Nehemiah and nothing is known of it. Again, there may be confusion between Magbish and the personal name Magpiash (Neh. 10.20).

31. the other Elam: nothing is known of an Elam in Palestine. It is perhaps designated 'the other' to distinguish the name of the town from that of the family in verse 7. It is strange that both family and town should be credited with one thousand two hundred and fifty-four men.

32. Harim: a place not known; in verse 39 it is the name of a family of priests. Here again confusion may have arisen between personal name and place-name.

33. Lod: i.e. Lydda (modern Ludd) 11 miles SE. from Jaffa; a Benjaminite town.
Hadid: a Benjaminite town, only here and Neh. 7.37; 11.34.
Ono: a Benjaminite town, only here, Neh. 6.2; 7.37; 11.35, and 1 Chr. 8.12.
seven hundred and twenty-five: Nehemiah has 'seven hundred and twenty-one'.

34. Jericho: a Benjaminite town (Jos. 18.21).

35. Senaah: here, Neh. 3.3 (where it has the definite article, Hassenaah) and Neh. 7.38. The number given here, **three thousand six hundred and thirty** (for which Nehemiah has 'three thousand nine hundred and thirty'), is very large for an otherwise unknown place, and it has been thought that the name may have the same force as the participial form $s^e n\hat{u}$'$\bar{a}h$ would have, i.e. 'hated', and be a derogatory term for the lower classes of the people (? in Jerusalem). Its occurrence in Neh. 3.3 tells against taking it as a place-name. This, and the instances given above of possible confusion between place and person (verses 29, 30, 32), raise the question whether these four really are place-names.

Of the twenty-one towns listed here, two are placed in Judahite territory and fourteen can be connected with Benjaminites or Benjaminite territory. What is the reason, first, for listing towns at all, and secondly that so many belong to Benjamin? No certain answer can be given. It may be that the men were reckoned by towns because they could not be connected with any known family, but in verses 59, 60 others are listed who could not prove their fathers' houses. It may also be that it is meant to be derogatory to Benjamin inasmuch as it suggests that so many living in Benjaminite towns had no family connections. That only two towns are in Judah may be the result of Edomite encroachment on Judah during the exile. The list of towns in Neh. 11.25-36 is a comparable list.

Names of priestly families **2.36–39**

With this short list is to be compared the list in Neh. 12.1–7 of priests 'who came up with Zerubbabel'. Two of these five names occur again there, but for the other families listed in Neh. 12 we must probably assume that the main families could be subdivided (cf. the Jedaiah-Jeshua sub-branch in verse 36).

36. Jedaiah: 'Yahweh has known/cared for'; this may be an old name for a priestly family, but all instances of the occurrence of the name are post-exilic and all are priests (1 Chr. 9.10; 24.7; Neh. 7.39; 11.10; 12.6, 7, 19, 21; Zech. 6.10, 14). **Jeshua:** i.e. the branch of the Jedaiah line that was called Jeshua. It is a widely used name, mostly of priests or Levites (see verses 2, 40). 10.18 shows that the family came to be named after Joshua son of Jozadak.

37. Immer: 'Lamb'; the personal name Immer appears to be used only of the priestly family so named (1 Chr. 9.12; 24.14; Jer. 20.1; Ezr. 10.20; Neh. 3.29; 7.40; 11.13). In verse 59 it is a place-name.

38. Pashhur: meaning unknown, perhaps of Egyptian origin; always a priestly name, sometimes a family name as here, and sometimes that of an individual, as in Jer. 20.1.

39. Harim: 'Dedicated'; occurs probably only as the name of families, both lay (Ezr. 10.31) and priestly (as here); but see Neh. 3.11, 10.5. In verse 32 it is a place-name.

Names of Levite families **2.40–42**

For a comparable list, see Neh. 12.8, 9.

40. Jeshua: see on verses 2, 36.

Kadmiel: 'God is the first/ancient one'; appears to be mainly, if not entirely, limited to the designation of a levitical family (see on 3.9).

Hodaviah: 'Give praise/thanks to Yahweh'; the name of a Benjaminite in 1 Chr. 9.7 and of a Manassite in 1 Chr. 5.24, of a descendant of Zerubbabel in 1 Chr. 3.24, and here (=Neh. 7.43) of a levitical family. It may be assumed that this verse mentions two families, those of Joshua and Kadmiel, branches of the line of Hodaviah. The number of Levites is small compared with that of priests, but the same is true of the caravan that assembled to return with Ezra (8.15, 18, 19). Some scholars, after slight change of text and pronunciation (*ûbinnûy weʰôdawyāh*), make four family names, Jeshua, Binnui, Kadmiel, and Hodaviah (cf. Neh. 12.8, where Jeshua, Binnui, Kadmiel, and Judah (? standing for Hodaviah) occur among other Levite names).

41. Asaph: 'He (Yahweh) has removed (reproach?)'; is well known as the name of one of David's chief musicians (1 Chr. 6.39). Other men bearing the name appear to be mentioned in Neh. 2.8; 11.17; 12.35, but in the last two of these Asaph is probably the family name.

one hundred and twenty-eight: Nehemiah has 'one hundred and forty-eight'.

42. Shallum: 'Reward' or 'Complete'; a widely used name for laymen, priests, and Levites, some sixteen different men may be distinguished. It was, for some reason, an alternative name for Jehoahaz, king of Israel (Jer. 22.11, 1 Chr. 3.15). One of the two was probably given him on his accession.

Ater: see verse 16.

Talmon: 'Light/brightness'; used only of the family of gatekeepers (1 Chr. 9.17; Neh. 7.45; 11.19; 12.25).

Akkub: 'Protector'(?); is also the family name of Temple servants, verse 45, the name of a descendant of David (1 Chr. 3.24), and of a Levite (Neh. 8.7).

Hatita: 'Furrowed'; the name occurs only here and Neh. 7.45.

Shobai: possibly a short form of Shebaniah (Neh. 9.4), but meaning unknown; it occurs only here and Neh. 7.45.

Note: Three of these six names are listed as those of gatekeepers also in 1 Chr. 9.17, namely, Shallum, Akkub, Talmon.

one hundred and thirty-nine: Nehemiah has 'one hundred and thirty-eight'.

Temple servants 2.43–54

43. temple servants: the Hebrew word so translated is *nᵉṯînîm*, a word used only by the Chronicler and, apart from 1 Chr. 9.2, only in Ezra and Nehemiah. In 1 Chr. 9.2 the people are divided into Israelites (lay), priests, Levites, Temple servants. In Ezr. 2.58; Neh. 7.60; 11.3 they are coupled with the 'servants of Solomon'; and in Ezr. 8.20 it is recorded that they were appointed by David and his officials to serve the Levites. (Other references to them are: Ezr. 2.70; 7.7; 8.17, 20; Neh. 3.26, 31; 7.46, 73; 10.28; 11.3, 21.) The name is reminiscent of the term *nᵉṯûnîm*, 'given', used to describe the Levites in Num. 3.9; 8.16, 19. They were given to the Lord and to Aaron to do the odd jobs in the Tabernacle. The association with the servants of Solomon raises the possibility that they were foreigners, and this in turn invites comparison with the 'Gibeonites' whom Joshua appointed to draw water and cut wood (Jos. 9.23–27; cf. 2 Sam. 21.2).

Of the thirty-five families listed in verses 43–54, two occur only in the Ezran form of this list, namely:

46. Hagab: 'Grasshopper/locust'.

50. Asnah: possibly Egyptian in origin.

Twenty-one occur only here and in the list in Neh. 7, namely:

43. Hasupha: 'Swift/speedy'.

Tabbaoth: 'Signet-ring'.

44. Keros: of unknown meaning.

Siaha: of unknown meaning.

Padon: 'Ransom'.

45. Lebanah: 'White'.

Hagabah: 'Grasshopper/locust'.

46. Shamlai (Shalmai): 'Garment/cloak'.

47. Gahar: an Arabic name meaning 'Reticent'.

48. Gazzam: 'Bird of prey'.

49. Besai: possibly a short form of Besodiah, Neh. 3.6, 'In the counsel/ friendship/intimacy of Yahweh'.

51. Bakbuk: 'Flask'.

Hakupha: 'Humpbacked'.

Harhur: 'Raven'(?).

52. Bazluth: 'Onion'.

Mehida: meaning unknown.

Harsha: 'Magic spell'.

53. Barkos: possibly a Babylonian name but of unknown meaning.

Temah: meaning unknown.

54. Neziah: 'True' or 'Sprinkled'.

Hatipha: 'Robbed'.

The other names, listed below, occur also outside this list:

43. Ziha: perhaps of Egyptian origin, meaning unknown; occurs otherwise only in Neh. 11.21 as an overseer of Temple servants.

45. Akkub: see verse 42. It is not in the Nehemiah list.

46. Hanan: probably a short form of Hananiah, 'Yahweh has been gracious'; a Levite name (Neh. 8.7; 10.10; 13.13), and the name of other Israelites (1 Chr. 11.43; Jer. 35.4, etc.).

47. Giddel: 'He (Yahweh) has made great'; also the name of one of the families of Solomon's servants, verse 56=Neh. 7.58.

Reaiah: 'Yahweh has seen'; occurs otherwise as the name of a Judahite in 1 Chr. 4.2 and a Reubenite in 1 Chr. 5.5.

48. Rezin: 'Spring/source'; otherwise only the king of Syria (Aram) (2 Kg. 15.37).

Nekoda: 'Freckled'; in 2.60=Neh. 7.62 it is the name of a family without genealogy. It does not occur elsewhere.

49. Uzza: 'Strength'; apart from this family name, the name is that of (a) a Benjaminite in 1 Chr. 8.7, (b) the ill-fated driver of the Ark in 2 Sam. 6.3, and (c) the owner of a burial garden in 2 Kg. 21.18.

Paseah: 'Limping/cripple'; only here and (a) a Judahite in 1 Chr. 4.12, (b) the father, or family name, of a wall-builder in Neh. 3.6.

50. Meunim: an Arabian (or Bedouin) tribe (possibly Nabataeans) mentioned in Jg. 10.12 (RSV, Maonites); 2 Chr. 20.1; 26.7. The last reference is to king Uzziah's overmastering of the Meunites, so they may have been prisoners of war.

Nephisim: a Bedouin tribe whose place of origin is unknown; they are mentioned in Gen. 25.15 (RSV, Naphish) as descended from Ishmael. See also 1 Chr. 1.31; 5.18–22 (RSV, Naphish in each case).

These are both plural in form and designate tribes; they may originally have been prisoners of war who never lost their tribal identity but were nevertheless held in the slave system of Temple worship.

53. Sisera: a non-Israelite name of unknown meaning; it occurs otherwise only of the Canaanite defeated by Barak and Deborah, Jg. 4.2ff.

Note: It has been seen that some of the names of the Temple servants, in addition to the Meunites and Nephisites, are non-Israelite names, e.g. Rezin, Sisera, a fact which supports the view that the Temple servants may have been non-Israelite in origin, the survivors of prisoners of war.

Solomon's servants 2.55–57

55. Solomon's servants: mentioned only here and Neh. 7.60; 11.3. Possibly they were descendants of prisoners of war taken by Solomon and eventually (or perhaps immediately after capture) dedicated to the Temple service. There is evidence that Sennacherib gave forty-one people to the god Zababa as slaves. 1 Kg. 9.20, 21 shows that captives and other non-Israelites were taken up into the slave system. In the Temple they may have had similar duties to those of the Temple servants. If Neh. 10.28 is intended to be an exhaustive list it may well be that Solomon's servants are meant to be included there in the term 'temple servants'. Of the ten names given here, eight occur only here and in Neh. 7.57–59; namely:

55. Sotai: meaning unknown.

Hassophereth: Nehemiah has Sophereth, for meaning see below.

Peruda: Nehemiah has Perida; 'Grain/pebble' or 'Only one'.

56. Jaalah: 'Mountain goat'.

Darkon: 'Hard'.

57. Hattil: either 'Tall' or 'Garrulous'.

Pochereth-hazzebaim: see below.

Ami: Nehemiah has Amon; either 'Master-workman' or 'Confident'.

Note: Two of these names are feminine in form and may denote an office or an occupation, thus **Hassophereth** may mean the office of scribe or the holder of that office, and **Pochereth-hazzebaim** Gazelle-binder. Of the other two names, see on verse 47 for **Giddel** and on verse 4 for **Shephatiah**.

Total of temple servants and Solomon's servants 2.58

The total given, **three hundred and ninety-two**, is small for a list of forty-five families, giving an average of less than nine in a family, and one is bound to wonder if these Temple slaves were unable to develop a 'family' system as the Israelites did and whether the names here are not family names but the names of the actual father.

Those who could not prove their descent 2.59–63

59. who came up: this is the same form as the verb in verse 1 and we would expect the following places to be places of exile. They may well be so, but first it should be noted that nowhere else do we get notice of places in Babylon from which exiles returned, except in the case of the Levites for whom Ezra specifically sent to Casiphia (8.17), and second, none of the places are known and they are not mentioned outside this list (here and Neh. 7.61). The first two places begin with *tel*, a word which is used in Hebrew to mean a mound of ruins (Jos. 8.28), but apart from these places the only other places beginning with Tel in the O.T. are Tel-abib, which we know to be in Babylon (Ezek. 3.15), and Tel-assar (2 Kg.19.12), which was probably in Mesopotamia. It is tempting to think that these places were not in Babylon, but nevertheless were places outside Judah from which Jews took the opportunity to return to their own country. The 'sons of Barzillai' may have come from a place east of Jordan. If Tobiah (verse 60) were, by chance, to be connected (as an ancestor) with Tobiah the Ammonite (Neh. 2.10) his family may have lived east of Jordan.

60. Delaiah: 'Yahweh has drawn'; apart from this one, there was a Delaiah who was descended from Zerubbabel (1 Chr. 3.24) and one who was the father of Shemaiah (Neh. 6.10). From the Elephantine papyri we know that one of Sanballat's sons was so named.

Tobiah: 'Yahweh is goodness/my good'; occurs elsewhere (a) as the name of a Levite in 2 Chr. 17.8 (RSV, Tobijah), (b) of a returned exile in Zech. 6.10, 14 (RSV, Tobijah, and who probably does not belong to this family), and (c) the Ammonite in Neh. 2.10.

Nekoda: see verse 48.

six hundred and fifty-two: Nehemiah has 'six hundred and forty-two'.

61. Habaiah: 'Yahweh has hidden'; occurs only here and Neh. 7.63 (Hobaiah). **Hakkoz:** 'The thorn bush'; also Neh. 3.4, 21; 7.63; 1 Chr. 24.10. In each case it is almost certainly the family name of the same line of priests. If Meremoth the priest, son of Uriah in 8.33, can be identified with the Meremoth son of Uriah son of Hakkoz in Neh. 3.4, then it may be assumed that they did make good their claim to the right of priesthood.

Barzillai: 'Man of iron'; see 2 Sam. 17.27; 19.31ff. Evidently an Israelite priest had married into this family and adopted their family name. Did he thereafter lose or surrender the record or title of his priesthood which he now sought to re-establish?

63. governor: the word used, *tiršātā*', is the Persian title for a local or provincial governor. Zerubbabel was probably so designated and Nehemiah certainly was (Neh. 8.9; 10.1). Either Zerubbabel or Sheshbazzar must be the governor intended by the editor here, but if Sheshbazzar were a non-Israelite he would scarcely determine a priestly matter. The identity of the governor depends on the date of origin of the list.

priest . . . Urim and Thummim: this could be one way of speaking of the high priest and may mean no more than the advent of a new high priest. It could imply, however, that at that time they were conscious that the full worship and practice of the Temple could not be re-established until the Temple was built and the ancient ritual of Urim and Thummim restored. (This, of course, depends very largely upon what date the list may be ascribed to.) It may hint at a desire to recover some of the lost ceremonies of the priesthood. The Greek text of 1 Sam. 14.41 has become the key passage for any attempt to discover the nature of Urim and Thummim, and points to their use to distinguish one party from another and to reach an answer by an eliminating process. The meaning of the two words is uncertain. Urim begins with the first letter of the Hebrew alphabet and Thummim with its last, which may or may not carry any significance. Whatever hopes may have been entertained, the fact was that the Urim and Thummim were not restored to the post-exilic Temple and the community mourned their loss, together with that of the Ark, the Shekinah, the holy fire, the spirit of prophecy, and the oil of anointing.

A summary of totals 2.64–67

64. forty-two thousand three hundred and sixty: it is impossible to see where this total comes from. The sum of the figures already given in the chapter is twenty-nine thousand eight hundred and eighteen (or, if we take the figures in Neh. 7, thirty-one thousand and eighty-nine). No total was given for the priests in verses 61–63, but these would not make up the difference. It has been suggested that the total included the free women but not the children. This is possible, but one would have expected a much greater proportion of women to men than this would allow. The corruption of the figures must be deeper seated than the present differences between those in Ezr. 2 and Neh. 7 (see Introduction, p. 36).

65. menservants and maidservants: properly, slaves.

male and female singers: distinguished from the Temple singers (verse 41) and regarded as comparable with the slaves. 2 Sam. 19.35 hints at the existence in pre-exilic times of professional singers; but was the immediate post-exilic community large enough or rich enough for such extras? 2 Chr. 35.25 shows that professional mourners existed (cf. Ec. 2.7, 8).

two hundred: Nehemiah has 'two hundred and forty-five' (but this may have come in from the next verse by anticipation, see note on Neh. 7.67f.).

Freewill offerings 2.68–69

68. With the exception of the first six (English) words, this verse is not in Neh. 7. If Neh. 7 was the earlier use of the list, then this verse was added here to adapt the list to the circumstances of the first return.

on its site: apart from being a natural thing to do, this would ensure continuity of worship and tradition.

69. darics: taking the Hebrew word *dark^emônîm* to represent the Persian gold coin, the daric; but it is equally possible that it is the Hebrew form of the Greek drachma. The Chronicler's use of the list is probably late enough to make the use of the Greek word quite natural.

minas: mina, on the other hand, is of Babylonian origin and was apparently the familiar unit for silver coins (Ezek. 45.12, if LXX be followed, makes it equivalent to fifty shekels).

Settlement **2.70**

70. lived in Jerusalem and its vicinity: this addition from 1 Esd. 5.46 may be
justified in that it makes tolerable sense of the verse, but it may be questioned
whether in fact all the priests and Levites settled in or very near Jerusalem (there
were over four thousand priests) and all the lower ranks of Temple personnel in
their towns. The text of Neh. 7.72 is slightly different and somewhat easier than
the Ezran form, but both are awkward statements and it may be that they are both
expansions of a much shorter verse which simply said, 'and all Israel dwelt (or,
settled) in their towns'.

RESTORATION OF TEMPLE (WITH INTERPOLATIONS RELATING TO
LATER TIMES) **3.1–6.22**

THE ALTAR BUILT **3.1–7**

1. seventh month: this is to be understood as the seventh month of the year of
return (verse 8). According to verse 6 it was the first day of the month. The
seventh month was Tishri, of which month the first was the day of trumpets
(Num. 29.1; cf. Lev. 23.24f.), the tenth the day of atonement and the fifteenth the
first day of the feast of booths. A reference to a gathering on the first day of the
seventh month occurs also in Neh. 7.73. Are both dates right and is it coincidence
that they are identical? Or was one borrowed unthinkingly from the other? There
is little doubt that the seventh month would be an appropriate time for the reading
of the law (Neh. 8), since it was enjoined in Dt. 31.10f. that at the end of every
seven years the law should be read during the feast of booths. Moreover, there is
nothing in the context in Ezra, apart from the keeping of the feast of booths in
verse 4, that makes the seventh month more appropriate than any other month.
There has been no previous mention of day or month. There are other reasons
for doubt about the historicity of the chapter. According to Haggai the activities of Zerubbabel and Joshua took place in the second year of Darius, i.e.
520 B.C., and, while there is no reason why they should not have been active also
in 537, there is the clear statement that Sheshbazzar 'laid the foundations of the
house of God' (see on 2.2). We may say tentatively that when the list was used
here the Chronicler or editor retained the date reference that was meant for its
present position in Nehemiah.

in the towns: Neh. 7.73 has 'in their towns', which is to be preferred.

2. Jeshua the son of Jozadak: see 2.2.

Zerubbabel the son of Shealtiel: see 2.2. Shealtiel may be a Hebrew form of an
Accadian name *šalti-ilu* of uncertain meaning, but so written and pronounced in
Hebrew as to suggest the meaning 'I have asked God'.

his kinsmen: probably men of his own race, i.e. fellow-Jews. The Hebrew word,
which commonly means brother, is used frequently in Deuteronomy in this sense.

altar: the Chronicler's interest is uppermost here; the worship of God is given
first place. It is not inconceivable that there had been an altar of some sort during

the exile (cf. Jer. 41.5), and if so the people who returned may not have regarded it as duly authorized.

3. in its place: in an effort to secure the utmost continuity; cf. 2.68.

fear was upon them: this seems to be an anticipation of the opposition that would eventually be offered them. The Hebrew (*be'ēmāh*) may be an abbreviation for 'fear came upon them' (*bā' 'ēmāh*).

4. feast of booths: this is a jump from the first day of the month to the fifteenth. The feast was a vintage festival interpreted in Jewish practice as a celebration of the wandering in the wilderness (Lev. 23.33ff.; Dt. 16.13–15). The celebration of it at this time seems to contradict what is said in Neh. 8.17 about it not having been celebrated since the time of Joshua. This may be further evidence for thinking that much of chapter 3 is the Chronicler's own reconstruction of events.

by number: referring to Num. 29.12–38, or at least to the tradition underlying that chapter, where the numbers of animals for the feast are given.

5. freewill offering: the Chronicler is at pains to emphasize the freewill gifts and service; cf. 1.4.

7. to the sea, to Joppa: as translated, **the sea** would only refer to the Mediterranean, but they would be there from the start of their journey. The Hebrew could be translated 'to the sea of Joppa', which would then mean the anchorage at Joppa; cf. 2 Chr. 2.16.

grant: 'permission' would probably catch the meaning better than **grant**. The rule of Cyrus did not include Phoenicia and what Cyrus probably did was to permit the Jews to bargain with the Phoenicians for the building material.

THE PART PLAYED BY THE LEVITES **3.8–9**

8. second year . . . second month: it could be argued that the second month, when the harvest had been completed, would be a suitable time to begin building operations, but if the Chronicler is reconstructing an ideal course of events the source of the date may well be the time when Solomon is said to have begun his Temple, namely the second month of his fourth year (1 Kg. 6.1; 2 Chr. 3.2). The Chronicler's intention, clearly, is to follow up the building of the altar with the rebuilding of the Temple as soon as possible. His evidence for an early start on the Temple is probably to be found in the Aramaic source (5.16), and the Chronicler may have taken Sheshbazzar to be another name for Zerubbabel. There is no urgent reason to doubt that Sheshbazzar, the Babylonian governor of the province, fulfilled the instructions of Cyrus and procured a beginning of the building of the Temple. The Jews evidently failed to maintain the work. Uncertainty creeps in when we seek to fill in events between that beginning, presumably soon after return in 537, and the fresh start made under the leadership of Zerubbabel and Joshua in 520 at the instigation of Haggai and Zechariah.

twenty years old: this was the responsible age according to 1 Chr. 23.27 and 2 Chr. 31.17. In Num. 8.24 it is given as twenty-five and in Num. 4.3, 23, 30 and 1 Chr. 23.3 as thirty.

oversight: the work itself, presumably, being done by the laymen.

9. Jeshua: see on 2.40, where Jeshua is the family name of a group of Levites. It is possible that it is so used here.

Kadmiel: in 2.40 and elsewhere this is a family name, and may be so here too. In 2.40 Jeshua and Kadmiel appear to be two branches of a family of Hodaviah; it may be that Hodaviah is concealed here in the name Judah (meaning uncertain). It is not clear otherwise why sons of Judah (the tribal name here) are among the Levites, although Judah does appear as a Levite name in 10.23.

the workmen: if *all* the Levites were in a supervising capacity as verse 8 suggests, then this will not here refer to the laymen doing the work, but the unnamed Levites: it must here bear the meaning 'those responsible for the work'. In Est. 3.9; 9.3 the phrase clearly means officials of some sort. cf. Neh. 2.16.

Henadad: Possibly an Aramaic name meaning 'Favour of Hadad'; the name occurs only here and Neh. 3.18, 24; 10.9 and is probably a family name in each case. In this verse, therefore, three families of Levites are mentioned, Joshua, Kadmiel, and Henadad.

CELEBRATION AT FOUNDING OF TEMPLE 3.10–13

The celebration is reminiscent of that described by the Chronicler for the dedication of Solomon's Temple (2 Chr. 5.13f.). For the trumpet-blowing, see Num. 10.10.

11. The psalm quotation is to be found in Ps. 107.1; 118.1, 29; 136.1, and is also referred to in 2 Chr. 5.13; 7.3; 20.21. The first phrase could bear the meaning 'for that (i.e. giving thanks to the LORD) is a good thing to do'.

steadfast love: the quality of remaining true to all that his election of Israel as his own people demanded of him; cf. Neh. 1.5.

shouted: the verb is that used for raising a shout of acclamation; cf. the use of the noun in Ps. 47.5.

12. foundation: evidently little or nothing was left of the former Temple.

who had seen: fifty years had passed since its destruction and many would now be old men; cf. Hag. 2.3.

OFFER OF HELP REJECTED 4.1–3

On the face of it this chapter seeks to explain why the work was soon broken off and not resumed until 520. The Chronicler drew on Aramaic documents for his material and seems, either deliberately or unwittingly, to have confused dates.

1. Judah and Benjamin: see 1.5.

adversaries: this is how they are described long after the event. They were clearly not adversaries when they seriously asked to be allowed to help to build. The reference to their deportation (verse 2) in the days of Esarhaddon (681–669 B.C.) (although this is the only evidence for a second deportation to northern Israel, there is no need to doubt it), makes it clear that people living in the province of Samaria are meant. The Judean Jews came to regard them with suspicion and ultimately with hostility, seeing them as a mixed people, partly Israelite, partly foreign, as is clear from 2 Kg. 17, which offers an account of how a mixed race and an eclectic religion came into being. The Chronicler's view of them as adversaries reflects this attitude.

On the other hand, there is plenty of reason for thinking that the Samaritans held to a religion that was very much the same as that of their Judean neighbours: they came later to share a common literary tradition which became the sacred book of both parties, the law of Moses. Since they worshipped the same God in the same way their offer to help to build may be taken as genuine; during the exile there had been some attempt by northerners to continue to worship on the Jerusalem site (Jer. 41.5), and now they have an opportunity to offer help to restore that worship. They may not necessarily have been resident in Samaria. Samaritans, like the Edomites, may have made inroads into Judea during the exile. There may have been some tension within the Samaritan community itself, some being in favour of restoring a Yahweh-worshipping community centred on a rebuilt Jerusalem and some for setting up a separate place of worship, as they ultimately did on Mount Gerizim. The Chronicler has probably simplified the picture by reducing the people to two interested parties, the one being returned Jews who were eager to rebuild Jerusalem and at the same time to foster purity of race and worship, the other being the 'adversaries', among whom he clearly included not only the Samaritans but by implication all people in Judea who were not returned exiles.

A further problem raised by this offer is that of the date at which it was made. The Chronicler's intention was to date the request in 536 or thereabouts, i.e. soon after the first attempt to lay the foundations and to rebuild. The result of the rejection of the offer is given in verses 4 and 24: the Jews were prevented from continuing the work until the reign of Darius. If this can be shown to be so, then a completely fresh start in 520 would be necessary. It is widely recognized, however, that the document which immediately follows, and is intended to enlarge this incident, properly belongs to a very much later time (the reign of Artaxerxes) and has nothing to do with the offer to help to build the Temple, but rather with the rebuilding of the city itself. This leaves open the possibility that verses 1–3 could refer to an offer made when Zerubbabel and Joshua began their work (or restarted it) in 520 B.C. Verse 24 must then be regarded as part of the Chronicler's reconstruction.

2. we have been sacrificing to him: this raises the question as to where they made the sacrifices, to which the answer would probably be, on an improvised altar in Jerusalem. The only other answer would involve an illicit sanctuary elsewhere. Another reading is, 'we have not been sacrificing', which would less readily alienate the Jews from Babylon who had had no chance of offering sacrifice. In this latter case the sacrifices mentioned in Jer. 41.5 would be deemed exceptional.

3. nothing to do with us: a rejection made on religious grounds: a strong sense of purity of race and religion possessed the Jews who had returned from exile. See also Introduction, p. 18.

as Cyrus . . . commanded: cf. 1.2–4.

WORK ON THE TEMPLE HINDERED **4.4–5**

4. people of the land: a term of wide and flexible meaning. Normally it would mean the common people of the land, i.e. over against the governing class. It would, in a sense, carry political implications in that they are the people who are accorded political status and rights in their 'land'. This meaning is clear in 2 Chr. 23.21, but in Ezr. 9.1, 2 it will be seen to be used in distinction from the people of Israel and to comprise the other inhabitants of Canaan. Here it must mean the same people as are intended by the adversaries in verse 1, mainly the Samaritans, but doubtless any others who did not have the purity of the returned exiles.

people of Judah: the pure Jews; those who had returned and settled in Judea.

5. counsellors: some think these are to be identified with the seven referred to in 7.14f. (cf. Est. 1.14); others think they were pro-Samaritan officers in the Persian administration with whom an arrangement had been made. Another possibility is that by counsellors the Chronicler means the people mentioned by name in verses 7 and 8, at least one of whose names is non-Jewish.

all the days of Cyrus . . . even until Darius: Cyrus, 538–529 B.C.; Darius, 522–485 B.C.

AN ACCUSATION AGAINST THE JEWS IN THE REIGN OF XERXES **4.6**

6. The verse stands by itself. In its present position the people who wrote must be the adversaries mentioned in the preceding verses. Ahasuerus is the Hebrew form of Xerxes (485–465 B.C.) and the letter would be written shortly after 485. What the letter was about, some thirty years after the Temple was finished, and what result it had is not known. Were the Samaritans jealous of the rate of progress made by the Jews?

A LETTER TO ARTAXERXES **4.7**

7. Artaxerxes ruled from 465 to 425 B.C. and this verse records that some men, of whom we know nothing beyond their names, wrote to him. We do not know what was in the letter, which cannot be equated with that mentioned in verses 9ff., because the personal names are completely different. Was this a further letter of accusation like the one written earlier to Xerxes (verse 6) or was it a letter written on behalf of the Jews?

Bishlam: this, if a proper name, occurs only here. With slight vowel change (*bišᵉlôm*) it could be taken as a noun with preposition meaning 'in agreement with' (cf. LXX), or, possibly, 'with the approval of '. If this is right the letter was written by Tabeel in agreement with Mithredath (or with his approval). Another possibility is that it is an abbreviation made up of the first and the last three letters of *bidᵉḇar yᵉrûšālaim*, 'in the matter of Jerusalem'. We are not told enough to enable us to understand it fully.

Mithredath: see 1.8. Presumably he is a Persian official with whose approval (or collaboration) Tabeel and his associates wrote to the king.

Tabeel: 'God is good'; an Aramaic or Hebrew name. The only other instance of its use in the O.T. is Isa. 7.6.

written in Aramaic: this would be no difficulty; Aramaic was for long the language of the court, and in any case Est. 1.22 shows that the king was expected to write to the provinces in their own language. The footnote to RSV (Heb. adds 'in Aramaic', indicating that 4.8–6.18 is in Aramaic. Another interpretation is 'The letter was written in the Aramaic script and set forth in the Aramaic language') shows the difficulty of the text. The repeated word 'in Aramaic' is probably best understood as a scribe's indication that what follows is in Aramaic. The Aramaic text runs from 4.8 to 6.18.

LETTER TO ARTAXERXES AND HIS REPLY **4.8–23**

These verses refer to an incident relating to the rebuilding of the walls of Jerusalem in the time of Artaxerxes I (465–425 B.C.). It was presumably placed here, probably by the Chronicler himself, because it provided an example of the kind of hindrance to building work which the Jews suffered and which could account for a stoppage of work between 537 and 520.

It will be seen that there are virtually three introductions or prefaces to the letter: (a) a statement that the letter was written (verse 8); (b) a full list and description of the persons who sent the letter (verses 9f.); and (c) a statement that the document is a copy (or abstract, or contains the text) of the letter. How much of this would appear on the document, and where? Aramaic letters when folded with the writing inside often had a note written on the part of the reverse that was exposed after folding to say from whom it came and what was its theme. The gist of either verse 8 or of verses 9 and 10 may have been written outside the letter Verse 11a must be taken to be the editor's pledge that he is giving an accurate copy.

8. Rehum: see 2.2.

commander: evidently ranking higher than scribe; possibly more like a high commissioner. It is not clear whether he was Persian or Samaritan.

Shimshai: 'Sun', but it may be a shortened form of a name comprising Yahweh or El (God); the name occurs only in this chapter; he may have been a Persian official.

scribe: in the O.T. in general the Hebrew word, of which the Aramaic cognate stands here, is used to describe a high-ranking officer of state, for instance Seraiah in 2 Sam. 8.17 (where RSV has secretary). See further on Ezr. 7.6.

9. judges: this translation, the only one possible in the context, presupposes some vowel changes in the Aramaic word (*dayyānayyā'* instead of *dînāyē'*).

governors: a Persian loan word, *apara-saraka*.

Erech: a city in Babylon (*Warka*).

Babylonians: here means men of the city of Babylon.

Susa: a city in Elam which lay east of Babylon: Elam's chief cities were Ecbatana (Achmetha) and Susa; cf. 6.2.

that is: this rendering, necessary in the context, involves reading *dî hû'* instead of *dᵉhāwē'*.

10. Osnappar: to be identified with Ashurbanipal (669–626 B.C.). Verse 2 mentioned a deportation by his predecessor Esarhaddon: are we to understand a succession of deportations, under Sargon II (722–705 B.C.) (2 Kg. 17.24) and under each of his successors? The colonists are not necessarily in ignorance of the other deportations, but mention the name of one of the better-known kings.

cities: this is the reading of LXX. The Aramaic has 'city'.

and in the rest of: this could also be construed as nominative, i.e. 'and the rest of ' ='and the remaining people in . . .'.

province Beyond the River: this probably included practically the whole of Syria between the Euphrates and the Mediterranean, but these colonists doubtless thought in terms of Samaria only, which may have been one of the administrative centres of the province, and diplomatically spoke of the whole province. The place of residence of the satrap is not known; Damascus seems most likely. Was Jerusalem without a governor at this time? The command to hinder the work should at least have been communicated to him.

12. from you to us: implies a recent caravan, which is not improbable, as the stories of Nehemiah and Ezra show.

finishing the walls and repairing the foundations: an unlikely order of operation which would be slightly eased if we translate the second phrase 'examining the foundations', which is a possible meaning of the verb.

13. revenue: the word occurs only here in the O.T. and is a loan-word from Zend. It could also mean either 'suddenly', as does the Accadian cognate (*apitti*), or 'in the end' (cf. the Pahlavi *afdom*), thus offering two other possible translations, either 'they will at once be injurious to the kings' or 'they will in the end be injurious to the kings'.

tribute, custom or toll: the use elsewhere of the Aramaic words thus translated suggests closer definition as 'a general levy [? assessed by produce], poll-tax, and land-tax'.

14. eat the salt of the palace: i.e. in the pay of the court. Elsewhere in the O.T. it implies the closest friendship and intimacy (2 Chr. 13.5; cf. Lev. 2.13; Num. 18.19).

15. records: these would be Babylonian records; it must be assumed that they would be readily accessible to the Persian king.

18. plainly read: this implies either careful reading with a pause between each word to make it distinct, or with a Persian translation after every sentence or two. The Aramaic verb can mean either 'separate' or 'expound'.

20. ruled over the whole province Beyond the River: this is an exaggeration; the greatest extent of Israelite rule was in the days of David and Solomon, but even their territories did not cover all that was included in the province Beyond the River (see verse 10). The **mighty kings** may refer, grandiosely, to some of those who rebelled.

21. until a decree is made by me: at first sight this may seem meaningless since verse 21a implies the making of a decree that can only be a royal decree, and it was accepted that royal decrees were not to be revoked (Dan. 6.8, 12, 15; Est. 1.19; 8.8). It may therefore be intended here either to imply an added safeguard against the possibility that a pro-Jewish party might cause the king to change his mind, or to prepare for the fact that the king did sanction Nehemiah's return to build.

23. by force and power: this may mean that they not only prevented further work, but actually dismantled what had been done. If this incident is rightly understood as taking place shortly before Nehemiah heard of the plight of Jerusalem, then we may infer that they did substantial material damage.

STOPPAGE OF WORK ON THE HOUSE OF GOD 4.24

Here the narrative harks back to verse 5 since the stoppage was to the work on the Temple and not on the city and its walls as in verses 8-23. With this statement about work ceasing until the time of Darius the way is now prepared for the work of Zerubbabel and Joshua reported in chapter 5.

HAGGAI AND ZECHARIAH ENCOURAGE WORK ON THE TEMPLE 5.1-2

1. Haggai and Zechariah: the prophecies of both are dated and all fall between the first day of the sixth month of the second year of Darius, and the fourth day of the ninth month of his fourth year. They were concerned with the necessity of rebuilding the Temple and with the part to be played by Zerubbabel and Joshua in that rebuilding. Haggai='Festal' and Zechariah='Yahweh has remembered'.

son of Iddo: according to Zech. 1.1 he was a grandson of Iddo. There are other places where 'son of' must be deemed to stand for 'grandson of'. Iddo might, however, be the family name; see Neh. 12.4, 16. The meaning is not certain, it might be a shortened form of a name meaning 'Yahweh has bedecked (himself/his servant)'.

2. Zerubbabel: see 2.2.

Jeshua: see 2.2.

began to rebuild: if there had been any previous attempt to rebuild since the return the lapse of time would have rendered it negligible.

TATTENAI MAKES ENQUIRY 5.3-5

3. Tattenai: the name occurs only in this chapter and the next. It is probably a Babylonian name, cf. the name Nabu-tattanu-uṣur='Nabu protect him you gave'. He is described as governor, but presumably over the province Beyond the River, a much larger territory than that over which Sheshbazzar had been governor (verse 14). On contract tablets a man named Ushtani is mentioned as satrap of the combined Beyond the River and Babylonian satrapy. It is not possible either to identify Tattenai and Ushtani or to deny their identity. If they are not to be identified, then Tattenai may have been answerable to Ushtani. Tattenai in any

case was highly placed in Persian affairs. But why should the governor and his colleagues be concerned at this point? Were they put up to it by 'the adversaries' of Judah and Benjamin (4.1)? Was this their first attempt to hinder the work or a renewed attack? Doubtless the trouble-makers approached Tattenai when they could get nothing out of the Jews themselves. It is very unlikely that Tattenai would have any grounds for the action he took unless complaint had been made.

Shethar-bozenai: occurs only in Ezr. 5.3, 6 and 6.6, 13 and is perhaps a Persian name meaning 'One who sets the kingdom free', but it might be an altered form of the name *šaṯbarzan* used at Elephantine (Cowley, *Aram. Pap.*, No. 5, line 16); cf. the name Shethar, Est. 1.14.

their associates: these are designated 'governors' in 6.6; they may have been the principal officers in each of the administrative districts into which the province would be divided. Cf. the mention of **treasurers** in 7.21.

structure: another possible meaning is 'furnishings', a meaning it seems to have on three papyri from Elephantine. In one case it clearly refers to the contents of the temple there (Cowley, *Aram. Pap.*, Nos. 26, 27, 30).

4. they: this reading from LXX and Syr. is clearly right; the 'we' has crept into the Hebrew text from verse 10.

TATTENAI WRITES TO DARIUS **5.6–17**

6. the governors: (*'ᵃpars'ḵāyē'*) a different word from that used in verse 3 (*peḥāh*). It is probably a modified form of the word *'ᵃparsaṯḵāyē'* in 4.9, also translated governors. It is not known what authority these governors exercised.

8. the province of Judah: see 2.1.

the great God: cf. Dan. 2.45. Such an ascription need not seem strange from the pen of a non-Israelite; it would be a proper term of respect to apply to the currently worshipped God of the territory, and there is no need, as some do, to translate 'the great house of God'.

huge stones: lit. stones of rolling; so large as to need rollers for handling.

timber: cf. 1 Kg. 6.15f. for the timber in Solomon's Temple.

9. those elders: there has been no previous mention of these, and it may well be that 1 Esd. 6.8 is right in reading 'built by the Jewish elders' instead of 'built' in verse 8.

structure: see verse 3.

10. names: a list may have been drawn up to accompany the letter. If so, it was either not included in the Aramaic document used by the Chronicler, or was dropped by him. The suggestion has been made that such a list was the basis for the list in Ezr. 2=Neh. 7.

11. great king: Solomon is meant.

12. This is a typically Jewish approach to history: the initiative is in the hands of the God of heaven and earth and Nebuchadrezzar is but a tool in his hands. For the destruction of the Temple and the deportation, see 2 Kg. 25.8–12.

the Chaldean: a Babylonian could be so called because an Aramaean people named Chaldeans had infiltrated into Babylon from the eleventh century onwards and become the dominant element.

13. decree: see 1.2ff.; 6.2ff.

14. cf. 1.7, 8.

governor: see verse 3. The word (*pehāh*) seems to have been in use for both a Persian satrap and a provincial governor. Both Tattenai and Sheshbazzar are so described.

16. laid the foundation: cf. 3.3, where it is recorded that Zerubbabel built an altar, and 3.8–10, where it is recorded that the foundations were laid by Zerubbabel in the time of Cyrus (cf. also 5.2). It is obvious that the Chronicler and the source he was using had different views. They could be reconciled if it could be shown that Sheshbazzar laid the foundations in his official capacity as governor and that Zerubbabel assisted in an unofficial capacity as leader of the Jewish community.

from that time until now: not knowing of any stoppage of the work such as is recorded in 4.5, 24. Another possible view is that the elders were unwilling to admit to the Persian authorities that the decree of Cyrus had become void by default, and that a fresh start had become necessary.

17. send us his pleasure: i.e. either ratifying or rescinding the decree, if found.

SEARCH RESULTS IN DISCOVERY OF DECREE OF CYRUS **6.1–5**

1. archives . . . documents: the two Aramaic words thus translated mean literally 'books' (or 'documents') and 'treasures' *in that order*. The order of the words is peculiar; one would have expected 'the treasure-house where books (or documents) were stored'.

2. The Chronicler here does not reproduce the king's letter to Tattenai verbatim, but gives in his own words (or those of the Aramaic document which he used) the gist of the first part.

Ecbatana (Aramaic: 'Achmetha'): Cyrus used to live in different parts of his empire, according to Xenophon, either Babylon, or Susa, or Ecbatana the capital of Elam. Susa was the winter residence; cf. (4.9); Neh. 1.1; Est. 1.2.

A record: this may mean that the document was a copy of the original. It is unlikely that the actual document would be moved from place to place as the court moved. The same word is used on one of the Elephantine papyri for the record made by the bearer of a verbal message (Cowley, *Aram. Pap.*, No. 32).

3. Concerning the house of God at Jerusalem: this probably stands first to form a heading and to give on its first line the subject of the decree. Whether this record or that in 1.2ff. comes nearest to the actual decree will possibly never be known. It is sometimes maintained that this one cannot be original because Cyrus would not have troubled about measurements. On the other hand, if he was providing the cost from his treasury he would naturally be concerned. The greater detail here, showing closer knowledge of the Temple building, may be due to the fact that the king would almost certainly have Jewish advisers with him as the decree was drafted. The copy in chapter 1 was written in a context that was more concerned with the return from Babylon, but here the return has already taken place and building is uppermost in mind. May it not be that the relevant parts of the decree, or simply the gist of those parts, is given in each case? However that may be, it is possible that the record made in Ecbatana was a memorandum giving only the main points of the decree.

burnt offerings are brought: this translation involves a slight change in the pronunciation of the Aramaic (*'eśśôhî* for *'uśśôhî*) and gives a better sense in the context than the other possible translation 'and let its foundations be maintained', which involves making a participle do the work of a finite tense. (For the meaning 'maintain', see Kraeling, *Brooklyn Pap.*, Nos. 5, line 11; 9, line 17.)

height . . . sixty . . . breadth . . . sixty: Solomon's Temple was sixty by twenty by thirty (1 Kg. 6.2). The text may have become disordered here, for it is not to be expected that the length would remain unspecified. The original may have run something like this: 'Its height shall be thirty cubits, its length sixty cubits and its breadth twenty cubits.'

4. The method of construction mentioned here is similar to that for the wall of the inner court of Solomon's Temple (1 Kg. 6.36). The timber was doubtless in such lengths as to bind the stone courses.

great stones: stones so large that they had to be handled on rollers.

the cost: there is no good reason to doubt that Cyrus did intend to bear the cost. He may have felt some gratitude towards the Jews in view of the welcome given him in Babylon by some of their leaders, if we may understand the passages about Cyrus in Isa. 40ff. in this way. That Cyrus should bear the cost need not be thought to contradict 1.4 where the 'men of his place' are to assist, for this assistance being in addition to freewill offerings, may have been some form of taxation, and the term 'royal treasury' may have been wide enough to include provincial revenues. Verse 8 of this chapter would then be providing for the same thing more explicitly. The more serious objection to this provision for the cost is that Tattenai appears to know nothing at all of it, but by his time it may have fallen into abeyance.

5. vessels: cf. 1.7; 5.14.

INSTRUCTIONS TO TATTENAI **6.6–12**

6. See 5.6.

7. governor of the Jews: Zerubbabel is meant. The term governor could clearly be used for the head of any administrative district; cf. 5.3, 14. Tattenai and his colleagues had only mentioned the elders, 5.9.

8. cost . . . royal revenue: whereas Cyrus is said to have promised the money from the royal treasury (verse 4), Darius offers it from the revenue of the particular province in which the building was situated. It is possible that 'royal treasury' and 'royal revenue' stand for the same thing, that part of the local taxes which was due to the king.

without delay: evidently there had been some delay. Another possible meaning is 'so that there be no delay (i.e. stoppage in the building)'.

9–10. Such gifts in kind would perhaps readily be made in return for prayers and sacrifices offered on behalf of the king and his sons. On the Cyrus cylinder we read, 'May all the gods whom I have resettled in their sacred cities ask daily Bel and Nebo for a long life for me' (*A.N.E.T.*, p. 316b). Isaiah 60.16 seems to hint that foreign kings and princes might be exploited by the revived Jewish community. For the animals mentioned here, see Lev. 1.3, 10; Num. 28.

11. impaled: probably after being put to death; see Dt. 21.22f.; cf. also Gen. 40.22; 41.13; Est. 5.14; 9.14.

dunghill: this would be to no one's advantage. The word (*nᵉwālû*) could be connected with an Arabic root (*wly*), one of whose meanings is 'the right of succession to property', and then be translated 'confiscate' or 'forfeit', which is how the Greek version understood it (cf. Josephus, *Ant.*, xi, iv, 6). Confiscation of property is spoken of in 7.26.

12. caused his name to dwell: this is the phrase found in Deuteronomy (12.11; 14.23; 16.2, 6, 11; 26.2) and kindred writings (Jer. 7.12; Neh. 1.9). A similar phrase, 'to put his name there', occurs also in Deuteronomic writings. It may be understood as meaning that Yahweh was *personally* present in the Temple in so intimate a way as would be impossible elsewhere on earth. The use of the 'name' conception enables a language unaccustomed to philosophical expression, as Hebrew was, to represent God as being wholly present in the sanctuary and yet at the same time wholly transcendent, as we should say.

THE WORK CONTINUES AND IS FINISHED 6.13–15

14b. The Jews feel that all possible aid, divine and human, has been granted them for the completion of the work. God's command is implied in the prophesying of Haggai and Zechariah and in such prophecies as Isa. 44.26–28; 54.11f.; Jer. 31.38–40; 33.7; Ezek. 40.5–43.12.

Artaxerxes: possibly an editorial addition (perhaps by the Chronicler himself) due either to the present position of 4.8–23, or because the editor was familiar with the Ezra-Nehemiah stories and coupled them in his mind with the Zerubbabel period to make a historical unit.

15. third day of . . . Adar: 1 Esd. 7.5 gives the twenty-third day of Adar, and so also does Josephus (*Ant.*, xi, iv, 7). This latter date may be due to a desire to have what may be regarded as a liturgically apt date. Adar is the twelfth month, and if the dedication festival was an eight-day festival then the new year could be celebrated immediately afterwards.

DEDICATION CEREMONY 6.16–18

16. people of Israel: lit. 'sons of Israel'. In 2.2 the term 'men of the people of Israel' and in 7.7 the term 'sons of Israel' are used to signify lay Israelites, but in 3.1 and 6.21 'sons of Israel' is applied to all the people, lay and cleric alike. It is possible to take this verse, therefore, in two ways: (a) the people of Israel are defined as priests, Levites (to include singers and gate-keepers), and the rest of the people who

had returned from exile, i.e. the laymen; (b) each phrase may designate a group
of the people—the laymen, the priests, the Levites, and the rest of those who
returned (singers, gatekeepers, and Temple servants). The first is to be preferred,
but in any case the Chronicler seems to limit true Israelites to those who had
returned, as in verse 21. In this latter verse he envisages the possibility of extension
of the true Israel.

17. Contrast the abundance in Solomon's time (1 Kg. 8.5, 63).

twelve he-goats: this is an interesting blending of the traditional and ideal with
the actual. It was traditional to offer twelve to represent the tribes of Israel,
although the Chronicler recognized only two tribes, Judah and Benjamin.

sin-offering: cf. Exod. 29.36 for sin-offering at the dedication of Aaron and his
sons; Ezek. 43.22–26 for sin-offering for the altar; and 2 Chr. 29.24 for sin-offering
for the dedication of the restored Temple under Hezekiah, which is the immediate
parallel to the present occasion.

18. divisions . . . courses: according to the Chronicler (1 Chr. 23–26) these
were fixed by David.

written in the book of Moses: there is no specific mention of divisions, etc., in
the Pentateuch, but they are perhaps implied by the duties assigned to priests and
Levites in Num. 3.5–10; 4.15; 8.1–26; 10.8.

With this festival the rebuilding of the Temple was complete. The narrative now
changes back from Aramaic to Hebrew.

CELEBRATION OF PASSOVER **6.19–22**

19. fourteenth day of the first month: i.e. of Nisan: the date is confirmed
by Exod. 12.2, 6; Num. 9.3.

returned exiles: these constitute the true Israel in the Chronicler's view (cf.
verse 16 and 8.35).

20. clean: the law laid down that if a man was unclean at the proper time he
could celebrate Passover a month later (Num. 9.10f.).

21. The Chronicler seems to widen his horizon at this point and recognizes that
some of the Jews who had remained in Palestine could be regarded as 'clean' and
could share in the Passover.

pollutions: this must mean the heathen worship of the non-Israelite people who
had taken advantage of the exile to enter Judah. Some Jews had fraternized
(Ezr. 9.1; 10.11; Neh. 9.2; 10.29f.), and this statement may mean that they had
been willing to dissociate themselves from such pollution as fraternizing involved,
but it will also include such as had never fraternized. It might even include the
possibility of proselytes being made from the surrounding peoples who had
encroached on Judah during the exile. If there were such they would have to be
circumcised before they could eat the Passover; cf. Exod. 12.44, 48.

22. feast of unleavened bread: this was celebrated as part of the Passover
festival; see Exod. 12.15–20; Lev. 23.6–8; Num. 28.17. See 2 Chr. 30.21 for the
celebration of the feast in Hezekiah's time.

king of Assyria: the king of Persia, Darius, is meant. It looks like a slip of the pen owing to familiarity in biblical literature with the phrase 'king of Assyria' which occurs some ninety times (although 'king of Babylon' is more frequent with 127 times). In Neh. 9.32 'kings of Assyria' is used to include Assyrian, Babylonian, and Persian kings.

SECOND SECTION 7.1–10.44 EZRA'S RETURN AND THE MARRIAGE REFORM

EZRA'S RETURN 7.1–8.36

INTRODUCING EZRA 7.1–6

1. **Artaxerxes:** the Chronicler's intention is clearly to identify this king with Artaxerxes I (465–425 B.C.; see Introduction, pp. 29ff.). (Artaxerxes II reigned from 405–358 B.C.)

Ezra the son of Seraiah . . .: the name Ezra is probably a shortened form of Azariah, 'Yahweh has helped'. On **Seraiah** see 2.2. Two purposes may be served by this longer (but by accident incomplete; see below) genealogy. The first is to ensure that Ezra is known to belong to the true priestly line that runs from Aaron (see 8.1ff.); the second is to strengthen the importance of his person and work (cf. Neh. 11.4 for a 'longer' genealogy). In naming Seraiah the intention clearly is to connect Ezra with the priest who was last in office before the exile (2 Kg. 25.18–21), although according to 1 Chr. 6.15 it was Jehozadak son of Seraiah who went into exile. The connection with Seraiah would ensure proper succession. It is impossible, however, that Ezra could be the son of a priest who was active at the time the exile began. The list has suffered some shortening in transmission; comparison with the similar genealogy in 1 Chr. 6.1ff. shows that in the Ezran form six names have been omitted, perhaps due to the repetition among the names of three that stand in a row, Zadok, Ahitub, and Amariah. Between the second Azariah (verse 3) and Meraioth the table in 1 Chronicles has the following: Johanan, Azariah, Ahimaaz, Zadok, Ahitub, and Amariah. Moreover, here Ezra stands where Jehozadak stands in 1 Chronicles as son of Seraiah. If Seraiah could be shown to be in fact the name of Ezra's father, we may assume an omission here too, owing to the scribe's eye having jumped over several names from the mention of the Seraiah who was father of Ezra to the Seraiah who was father of Jehozadak. The first few names of the table might then have run: 'Ezra the son of Seraiah, son of "x", son of "x", . . . son of Jehozadak, son of Seraiah, etc.'

How much trust can be placed in this record? Is the Chronicler using a list already to hand, but compiled for another purpose (1 Chr. 6.1ff.), to enhance the prestige of Ezra by associating him with the last high priest before the exile? Was the list already in the source he used for the Ezra material? The uncertainty is increased when it is realized that the list in 1 Chr. 6.1ff. is probably as much an artificial one as this one which is based on it. The list in 1 Chr. 6 seems to have been intended to secure recognition of the Zadokite line of priests by incorporating it in the line from Aaron (and Levi). Some of the names may be no more than links in a manufactured chain.

Azariah: 'Yahweh has helped'; occurs also in verse 3. It is a very common name, at least twenty-two men bearing it may be distinguished; cf. Neh. 3.23.

Hilkiah: 'Yahweh is (my) portion'; another quite common name, chiefly of priests.

2. Shallum: see 2.42.

Zadok: probably a short form of Zedekiah, or the like, meaning 'Yahweh has been righteous/right'; of the six or seven men so named the best known is the priest of David's time, called son of Ahitub in 2 Sam. 8.17 (but the text there is uncertain and the name Ahitub should belong to Abiathar's designation and the text run: 'Zadok and Abiathar son of Ahimelech son of Ahitub'; see 1 Sam. 22.20).

Ahitub: 'Brother is goodness'; a recurring name in lists of priests (1 Chr. 6.1ff.; 9.11; Neh. 11.11), but otherwise occurs only as that of the grandson of Eli (1 Sam. 14.3) father of Ahimelech (1 Sam. 22.9).

3. Amariah: 'Yahweh has promised', is a fairly common name; there are at least eight men of this name in the O.T.

Meraioth: apparently a name with a hypocoristic ending *oth*, and perhaps meaning 'Rebel'. Apart from an instance in Neh. 12.15, where it may be an error for Meremoth, it occurs only in forms of this genealogical table; cf. Neh. 11.10f.

4. Zerahiah: 'Yahweh has shone forth/risen'; apart from its occurrence in forms of this table, it occurs only as the name of the father of a head of a family (8.4).

Uzzi: probably a short form of Uzziah, 'Yahweh is (my) strength', 10.21; it is the name of five or six different men.

Bukki: this may perhaps be a short form of Bakbuk, 2.51, meaning 'Flask'; apart from this table (here and 1 Chr.) it occurs only as the name of a Danite in Num. 34.22.

5. Abishua: '(my) Father is deliverance'; outside this table only the name of a Benjaminite (1 Chr. 8.4).

Phinehas: an Egyptian word meaning 'Negro'; there are two: (a) grandson of Aaron, as here; (b) son of Eli (1 Sam. 1.3).

Eleazar: 'God has helped'; six different men are so named.

Aaron: possibly of Egyptian origin, but of uncertain meaning. It occurs only as the name of the brother of Moses.

6. scribe: in verse 21 he is also described as a priest, which is patent in the genealogy just given. As far as the narrative in Ezra-Nehemiah goes, the latter is secondary; it is as scribe that he is most spoken of. What is meant by scribe? There are in the main two biblical uses of the word, the one developing from the other at a more or less late date. First, it appears as the title or description of a high-ranking officer of state (2 Sam. 8.17; 20.25; 1 Kg. 4.3, etc. (RSV 'secretary')), and in this usage it corresponds to the Aramaic word *sāpᵉrā'*, which occurs on the Elephantine papyri (Cowley, *Aram. Pap.*, No. 17, lines 1, 6). A military officer whose task was that of a modern marshal was called 'scribe' (Jer. 52.25; Jg. 5.14). It could also be used in a way closely corresponding to the English 'clerk', as in 1 Chr. 24.6, which speaks of Shemaiah recording the organization of the priests in David's time. Baruch was 'scribe' to Jeremiah, that is, he acted as his amanuensis, or secretary, or clerk (in Jer. 36.26 RSV has secretary and in 36.32 scribe). Shimshai in Ezr. 4.8, 9, 17, 23 is secretary to Tabeel.

A second use in biblical literature which probably came later is to designate a student of Scripture, i.e. scribe in the now traditional sense; cf. Jer. 8.8. Since it is clear that Ezra was one who had much to do with the law, its study and dissemination, the title scribe in this sense is not out of place for him.

It is possible that in the books of Ezra-Nehemiah both uses of the term are found and both applied to Ezra, the one in the document used by the Chronicler (the Ezra memoirs) and the other by the Chronicler himself. It has been argued that when Artaxerxes gave Ezra a letter and in it called Ezra 'the scribe of the law of the God of heaven' (7.12), he was giving him an official title as minister or secretary for Jewish affairs. There is something to be said for this view, for there can be little doubt that Ezra was invested with authority when he travelled back to Judah, even if he had not already held an office in Babylon. When the Chronicler took up the title it was at a time when students or scholars of the law had evidently greatly increased in numbers and importance and it is natural that he should associate Ezra with them as an early leader. That may be why this verse, which is in an editorial passage, has simply 'scribe', while verse 11 has 'priest, scribe', and the next verse (12) has the longer title. It is to be noted that even if we date Ezra's return at 457, let alone a very much later date, the presence of a Jew so well versed and so highly placed in Babylon suggests that the Jewish community there, despite such returns as had already taken place, was by no means negligible in numerical strength and in administrative and intellectual capacity.

all that he asked: we are not told what this was.

the hand of the LORD . . . upon him: a phrase used by Ezra himself in his memoirs (7.28, 8.18, 22, 31) and by Nehemiah in his (2.8, 18), sometimes with the adjective 'good' added; it is used also by the Chronicler here, in verse 9 and in 2 Chr. 30.12. It shows a lively sense of dependence upon God. For 'the hand of the LORD against' with the opposite meaning, see Dt. 2.15 and Ru. 1.13.

SUMMARY STATEMENT OF RETURN 7.7–10

7. seventh year of Artaxerxes: either 458/7, the seventh year of Artaxerxes I (465–425 B.C.), or 397, the seventh year of Artaxerxes II (405–358 B.C.). The Chronicler presumably found the date in the Ezra memoirs and referred to it here but did not mention it again later. Any other date for Ezra's return would involve textual change. Some scholars have assumed that a 'twenty' or a 'thirty' has dropped out before the seven, but there is no evidence of such a slip.

people of Israel: cf. chapter 2 for the different sections of the people. The details of the caravan are given in 8.1–20 and taken from Ezra's own account.

8–9. We learn from 8.31 that it took eleven days to assemble, so that the journey itself took just over three and a half months. Although only about 500 miles as the crow flies, it would probably be a journey of nearly twice that distance by the caravan route avoiding the desert.

began to: this translation involves a different pronunciation of the Hebrew consonants (reading *yissaḏ* for *yᵉsūḏ*); the traditional reading means 'foundation'.

10. A summary of Ezra's credentials, either as being the reason for God's protection (verse 9) or more probably as being the right man for this mission.

LETTER OF COMMISSION FROM ARTAXERXES **7.11–26**

11. letter: i.e. of sanction and authority to Ezra for his mission to Jerusalem. The letter is in Aramaic (see on 4.7).

learned in: lit. 'scribe of', i.e. repeating the word scribe; see verse 6.

12. king of kings: cf. Ezek. 26.7; Dan. 2.37.

the priest, the scribe: the first gives Ezra's position among his own people; the second may give his official title; see verse 6.

of the God of heaven: Jewish universalism (of thought, more than of practice) could tolerate this non-Jewish description of God, for it would be readily understood by the Persians; cf. 1.2.

13. freely offers: the Chronicler laid much store by this; cf. 2.68; 2 Chr. 17.16; Neh. 11.2. See on 1.4.

14. seven counsellors: cf. Est. 1.14. Some think it is these (i.e. those in office at the time) who were hired by the people of the land (4.4f.).

inquiries . . . according to the law: did Ezra have an authorized, and therefore authoritative, copy of the law, and was he commissioned by the king, acting under advice from his Judean advisers, to make sure that religious matters were regulated in Judah according to it? In verses 25–26 Ezra is given the necessary power to enforce the law. There is insufficient evidence to answer these questions, but it is very probable that the whole Pentateuch was already known in Judah but had not really taken the place in people's minds that Deuteronomy had come to occupy. What had happened that prompted Ezra's journey and the king's commission? No event is known that could serve as a reason for the king to introduce new measures, under Ezra, for discipline in Judah. An incident mentioned by Josephus (*Ant.*, XI, vii, 1) about the brutality of a certain Bagoses, following the murder of the high priest Johanan by his brother, cannot be confirmed, and cannot in itself be claimed as likely to raise serious problems. On the other hand, Ezra's mission may have seemed opportune to the Persian authorities and might even have been inspired by them. Shortly before 400 B.C., during the early years of the reign of Artaxerxes II, the Persians lost their control of Egypt. They might well be expected, in consequence, to do all they could to strengthen their authority in what territory remained to them by the Mediterranean. It has been suggested (H. Cazelles, *Vetus Testamentum*, IV, pp. 113–40) that this fully accounts for the details of the king's commission. Ezra's mission would result in a closer-knit community.

in your hand: taken literally this means either 'which you carry with you' or 'with which you are entrusted', but taken metaphorically, as it probably should be, it means 'which is at your disposal', 'which is part of your duty'; we may compare the same phrase used of the wisdom of God which was at Ezra's disposal (verse 25). There is nothing in this narrative to demand that this means that Ezra had a copy of the law with him which he had either edited or helped to edit. Moreover, (a) it is unlikely that the king would authorize Ezra to act on an entirely new law, and (b) much, if not all, of what is contained in the Pentateuch may well have been known in Palestine before Ezra's return. When the law was read by Ezra (Neh. 8) it was not on Ezra's initiative but at the people's request, and there is no hint that what he read was entirely new to them; all that need be implied is that it had not been acted on.

15. freely offered: in 6.10 reference is made to prayers offered on behalf of the king and the silver and gold freely contributed by the king would cover the cost of these and the sacrifices involved. Mention of freewill offerings for the first Tabernacle is found in Exod. 25.2. See also 1.4.

16. silver and gold which you shall find: this must mean the silver and gold which was freely offered throughout the province of Babylon by Jews and non-Jews (8.25) who followed the example of the court.

17. This purchase of sacrificial victims may be to supply part of the regular daily sacrifices; in that case it would amount to a subsidy, but it may be for special sacrifices to accompany prayers for the king (6.10).

18. the rest of the silver: it is not clear how much, or little, of the money contributed would be spent on sacrificial victims and materials, but this statement is indicative of the unlimited generosity that was felt to be fitting to the occasion.

19. vessels: these must be new vessels dedicated by the Persian authorities, for it is unlikely that at this time there were any left in Babylon of those that had been brought over by Nebuchadrezzar. This may be a further example of a generosity called forth by the occasion; the account may be modelled on that of Sheshbazzar's return (1.7-11).

20. out of the king's treasury: see 6.8.

21. all the treasurers: i.e. of each administrative district; see note on 5.3.

22. Apart from the **silver**, the things mentioned here were probably required for sacrificial purposes, **wheat** as one of the staple products (Exod. 23.19), **wine** for drink offerings (Hos. 9.4) and probably to accompany the sacrificial meals, **oil** as an ingredient in offerings (Exod. 29.2) or as an independent offering (Lev. 14.10ff.), and **salt** as a cleansing or preserving ingredient in sacrifices (Lev. 2.13). A talent of silver was equivalent to two thousand five hundred shekels: according to 2 Kg. 23.33 a hundred talents of silver was part of the tribute imposed by Pharaoh Neco on Judah, and in 2 Chr. 25.6 Amaziah hired 100,000 mercenaries from Israel for a hundred talents. A measure (*cor*) of wheat was probably an ass's load. The estimated capacity of a *bath*, based on the size of broken jars (found at Lachish and Beit Mirsim) marked as '*bath*', i.e. capacity one *bath*, is five gallons.

23. his wrath: recognized as one of the most powerful of forces: the word (in its Hebrew form *keṣep*) is used almost exclusively of divine anger. 2 Kg. 3.27 records great wrath (Yahweh's or Chemosh's?) against Israel after the sacrifice of Mesha's eldest son. However, there is no pronoun to qualify it in the Aramaic text here, and it could be taken in the sense of 'trouble'; i.e. 'lest trouble come upon'.

24. The exemption of the Temple personnel from tax may well be because the Temple was under subsidy from the state by reason of the contributions made by the king and the court and it would be pointless to tax its servants. Similar exemption was given by Artaxerxes III (Josephus, *Ant.*, XII, iii, 3).

other servants: it is not clear what part these servants played: a noun from the same root (*pᵉlaḥ*) occurs in verse 19 to mean the 'service' for which the vessels were intended.

25. in your hand: see on verse 14.

all the people in . . . Beyond the River: this must surely be limited to the Jewish people, as is implied in verse 14 where Ezra's enquiry is to be in Judah and Jerusalem. It may be intended to include Jews settled outside Judah in other parts of the province Beyond the River.

26. banishment: lit. uprooting.

27. From this point the narrative reverts to Hebrew, and also Ezra's own memoirs in the first person begin to be used and continue as far as 9.15. The abrupt transition to a cry of thanksgiving may be due to the way in which the source material was awkwardly joined on to the Chronicler's own introductory account.

28. his steadfast love: there is no pronoun in the Hebrew text, which could, and probably should, be translated: 'he has made the king and his counsellors well-disposed towards me', lit. 'to show me steadfast love'; cf. 9.9.

hand of the LORD: see 7.6.

leading men from Israel: the order of words in the Hebrew sentence suggests a slightly different emphasis, namely, 'I gathered from Israel leading men to go up with me.' It is noteworthy that the term Israel could here be used of those who still remained in Babylon, and they were clearly not a negligible group. The leading men were either those who were capable of taking a leading part (cf. 5.10), or were heads of families (cf. 8.1).

LIST OF HEADS OF FAMILIES, PRIESTLY AND LAY, WHO WENT WITH EZRA **8.1–14**
The family name is given first ('this is the genealogy'), and then the name or names of the leader(s) from that family. It is not clear why the family of Adonikam (verse 13) is credited with three leaders and Bigvai (verse 14) with two. The list, though much shorter, has close connections with that in chapter 2. The first three families, two priestly and one Davidic, have no counterpart in chapter 2, but the rest all occur in the first part of that chapter; five of them from Bani to Bigvai

occur in the same order as in 2.10–14. The reference to the two priestly houses of Phinehas-Gershom and Ithamar-Daniel is of some importance. Phinehas was the son of Aaron's third son Eleazar (Exod. 6.23–25) and Ithamar was Aaron's fourth son (Exod. 6.23). This list, if it is to be attributed to the Ezra memoirs, is one of the earliest records we have of the tracing back of the priesthood to Aaron. The table in 7.1–5 traces Ezra's descent to Aaron, but that table is almost certainly editorial and may well be later than Ezra's memoirs. The Aaronite ancestry of the priesthood is given formal expression in the Priestly writings; cf. Num. 3.1–4. It is of course possible that this priestly record is as early as, or even earlier than, Ezra's memoirs, but the interval of time will not be a long one and in either case, whichever can be shown to be the earlier record, the probability is that the Aaronite ancestry of the priesthood originated among the Jews in Babylon. The references to priestly families in 2.36–39 and 10.18–22 make no mention of descent from Aaron. Noteworthy also is the existence of two lines of priestly descent, both from Aaron, one through Phinehas and Eleazar, and the other through Ithamar. It has been suggested that the rival claims of two lines of priests are represented here, both claiming descent from Aaron, the Zadokites through Phinehas son of Eleazar (cf. 1 Chr. 6.1ff. where Zadok is in that line) and another line, possibly that of Abiathar, through Ithamar. 1 Chr. 24.6 implies that if Zadok belonged to the Eleazar line (1 Chr. 6.1ff.; Ezr. 7.1–5) then Abiathar-Ahimelech belonged to the Ithamar line. This is doubtless tied up with the record in 2 Sam. 8.17 and 1 Chr. 18.16 that Zadok son of Ahitub and Abiathar son of Ahimelech (1 Sam. 22.9, 20 show this to be the right order) were priests in David's time. There were therefore two legitimate lines of priests. 1 Chr. 24.3–6 shows a numerically smaller group of non-Zadokite priests associated with the names of Ithamar, Ahimelech, and Abiathar sharing office with the Zadokites, who are there also linked with Phinehas through Eleazar.

Apart from the two priestly families and the Davidic one, there are, if two additions to the present Hebrew text be admitted (as in RSV, verses 5, 10), twelve families, possibly based on the tribal number, although with no present tribal significance. In chapter 2 laymen stand first in the list, here priests. Is this because Zerubbabel was a layman whilst Ezra was a priest? Or were the priests a more important part of the community in Ezra's time? It is not clear why a total is given for each group of laymen but not for the priestly and Davidic groups (verse 2).

2. Phinehas: see 7.5.

Gershom: 'Bell'; this is the only post-exilic occurrence of the name. The Levitical family of Gershom is sometimes associated with Moses (Exod. 2.22) and sometimes with Levi (1 Chr. 6.16). Moses, however, is always associated with Levites.

Ithamar: occurs only as the name of the youngest son of Aaron, Exod. 6.23 etc., meaning uncertain, possibly 'Land of Palms'.

Daniel: 'God has judged'; occurs again as a priestly family name in Neh. 10.6, otherwise the name is used only of (a) a son of David, 1 Chr. 3.1, and (b) the hero of the book of Daniel (cf. Ezek. 14.14, 20; 28.3).

David: 'Beloved': occurs only as the name of the king.

Hattush: meaning not known; according to 1 Chr. 3.22 Hattush was in the line of descent from David and is a grandson of Shecaniah (or, son of Shecaniah—if we regard 'sons of Shecaniah' as a scribal addition, as is suggested by the total of six at the end of the verse). Another Hattush, son of Hashabneiah, is found in Neh. 3.10, and a third, a family name, in Neh. 10.4; 12.2.

3. **of the sons of Shecaniah:** this, as it stands, seems to designate a sub-family of Hattush, but it would be better to regard 'of the sons of' as a copyist's error for 'son of' (reading *ben* for *mibb'nê*). This would link up with 1 Chr. 3.22 mentioned above. Shecaniah means 'Yahweh has taken up his dwelling'.

Parosh: see 2.3.

Zechariah: see 5.1; this name is of too frequent occurrence, at least twenty-eight men, for any but the best-known bearers of the name to be identified.

registered: i.e. included in the genealogy.

4. **Pahath-moab:** see 2.6.

Eliehoenai: 'To Yahweh are my eyes'; a name borne by several people (but none clearly identifiable).

Zerahiah: see 7.4.

5. **Zattu:** see 2.8. The name here is a necessary addition to complete the sense of the verse (cf. 1 Esd. 8.32).

Shecaniah: this is another fairly common name, see verse 3.

Jahaziel: 'May God see'; five men of this name can be distinguished, but are not otherwise known (1 Chr. 12.4; 16.6; 23.19; 2 Chr. 20.14).

6. **Adin:** see 2.15.

Ebed: probably a shortened form of Obadiah, 'Servant of Yahweh'; occurs otherwise only in Jg. 9.26, the father of Gaal.

Jonathan: 'Yahweh has given'; the name of at least sixteen different men in the O.T.

7. **Elam:** see 2.7.

Jeshaiah: 'Yahweh has saved/delivered'; this is virtually the same name as that of the prophet Isaiah, but has been transmitted differently. Apart from the prophet, the other six bearers of the name are not identifiable, each being mentioned once only.

Athaliah: 'Yahweh is exalted'; as a man's name it belongs to three people, this one, one in 1 Chr. 8.26, and a third (Athlai), Ezr. 10.28. It is also a feminine proper name (2 Kg. 8.26).

8. **Shephatiah:** see 2.4.

Zebadiah: 'Yahweh has given'; nine different people are so named and there are ten who bear the father's name **Michael,** 'Who is like God?'

9. **Joab:** 'Yahweh is father'; in 2.6 Joab is a sub-branch of the family of Pahath-moab; here it is listed as a separate independent family. There is other evidence that families might change their names or status in Israel (see Introduction, p. 44).

Obadiah: 'Servant of Yahweh'; the name of ten different men.

Jehiel: 'May God live'; the name of eleven men.

10. Bani: see 2.10. The name here is a necessary addition to complete the sense of the verse (cf. 1 Esd. 8.36).

Shelomith: 'Reward'; a frequent Levite name in 1 Chronicles.

Josiphia: 'May Yahweh add', occurs only here; but cf. 10.42 (Joseph).

11. Bebai: see 2.11.

Zechariah: see verse 3.

Bebai: normally a family name, as at the beginning of the verse and in 2.11. This is the only instance of it as a personal name, but it may here be a repetition of the family name, i.e. 'Zechariah of the family of Bebai'.

12. Azgad: see 2.12.

Johanan: 'Yahweh has been gracious'; the name of at least thirteen individuals. See also Ezr. 10.6 (Jehohanan); Neh. 12.22.

Hakkatan: 'the little one', occurs only here.

13. Adonikam: see 2.13.

those who came later: it is difficult to see in what way members of Adonikam's family can be called 'those who came later'—any younger members of the family could perhaps be so called. It may suggest that members of this family were late in arriving to join the caravan. It is more probable that it should be translated 'the last' and mean that these were all that remained of Adonikam's family to transfer from Babylon to Judah.

Eliphelet: 'God is escape'; it is the name of five individuals, but this and 10.33 are the only two in post-exilic literature.

Jeuel: another reading is Jeiel; cf. 10.43. It may mean 'Yahweh has stored up' or 'Yahweh has healed (a wound)'; there are eight or nine men so named.

Shemaiah: 'Yahweh has heard'; it is a very common name, some twenty-eight different men being distinguishable.

Note: It is not known why three individuals of the family of Adonikam are named as heads of families; it may indicate that the family was composed of three sub-families (see Introduction, p. 44).

14. Bigvai: see 2.2, 14.

Uthai: this could be a shortened form of either Athaliah (verse 7), or Athaiah (Neh. 11.4), 'Yahweh has shown himself pre-eminent'. Apart from this instance the name occurs only as the name of a Judahite (1 Chr. 9.4).

Zaccur: probably a shortened form of Zechariah (5.1); it is the name of at least seven other men; cf. Neh. 3.2; 10.12; 12.35; 13.13. Again it is to be noted that more than one member of the family of Bigvai are mentioned as of Adonikam.

STEPS TAKEN TO GET LEVITES TO JOIN THE CARAVAN **8.15–20**

15. the river that runs to Ahava: presumably this is one of the canals near Babylon.

three days: this seems to have been a common and doubtless conventional after-journey rest period; cf. verse 32 and Neh. 2.11; also Jos. 3.2; Jg. 19.4; cf. 2 Chr. 20.25f.

none of the sons of Levi: why should Levites be specially missed? The answer is not clear, but we may think that Levites were perhaps not very numerous in Babylon because at the time of the deportation they were not in Jerusalem but remained scattered about the land near the shrines which had been closed during Josiah's reform. They were reorganized after the exile and Ezra himself may have had a share in that operation, hence his desire to have Levites in his company. It is clear from Neh. 8.7f.; 9.4 that they played an important part in the ceremony of the reading of the law.

16. sent for: if this is the right way to translate the Hebrew, one wonders where he sent to for them to come to him; but the Hebrew may mean no more than 'sent' (with the object introduced by a preposition), and the men will then be taken from those already assembled with him. Two of the names occur in the list just given, Shemaiah and Zechariah. It is strange to find three of the eleven named Elnathan with another named Nathan. If all eleven names are original (see below) one is bound to wonder why the choice stopped at eleven rather than going on to the ideal and tribal twelve. Another peculiarity, however, is that as the list now stands there appear to be two groups, nine being called leading men ('heads') and two men of insight. Why such a distinction was made is not easy to understand unless we assume faulty transmission of text. The last two names, Joiarib and Elnathan, are repetitions of the fifth (Jarib being a short form of Joiarib) and sixth names, and are not found in 1 Esd. 8.43. This may indicate that the original text had only nine names and they were described both as leading men and also as men of insight.

Eliezer: 'God is help'; an Eliezer is listed among Levites in 10.23 as having taken a foreign wife, but the two are not to be identified for this man is unlikely to have been a Levite and almost equally unlikely to have been one of those culpable in the matter of a foreign wife. It is a fairly common name; cf. 10.18, 31.

Ariel: 'Herald'(?); only here as a personal name.

Shemaiah: see verse 13.

Elnathan: 'God has given'; in post-exilic times only used of the three men mentioned here; otherwise only (a) grandfather of Jehoiachin (2 Kg. 24.8), and (b) son of Achbor (Jer. 26.22).

Jarib: probably a short form of Joiarib, 'May Yahweh plead'; elsewhere only (a) a son of Simeon (1 Chr. 4.24), and (b) a priest (Ezr. 10.18).

Nathan: probably a short form of either Elnathan (above) or Nethanel (Ezr. 10 22), both meaning 'God has given', or of Jonathan (Ezr. 8.6), 'Yahweh has given'. It is borne by nine individuals.

Zechariah: see verses 3, 11 and 5.1.

Meshullam: 'Rewarded' or 'Fulfilled'; the name of at least twenty different men in the O.T.

Joiarib: 'May Yahweh plead'; it occurs as the name of a priestly family in Neh. 11.10 and elsewhere, and as the name of a Judahite in Neh. 11.5.

men of insight: the verb of which this translates the participle is much used in the writings of the Chronicler and occurs in the following ways: (a) 'to understand', (i) God understands the thoughts of men, 1 Chr. 28.9, (ii) men understand what they are taught, Neh. 8.12; (b) 'to come to understand' (i) in the sense of 'discover', Neh. 13.7, and (ii) of 'review', Ezr. 8.15; (c) 'to be clever' (i) in general, 1 Chr. 27.32; 2 Chr. 11.23, (ii) at hearing, Neh. 8.2, and (iii) at music, 1 Chr. 25.7; 2 Chr. 34.12; (d) 'to instruct', 'teach', 1 Chr. 15.22; 25.8 (participle meaning teacher); 2 Chr. 26.5; with Levites as subject, 2 Chr. 35.3; Neh. 8.7, 9.

17. **Iddo:** either 'Strength' or a hypocoristic form of '*Adôn*, 'Master'; this is the only occurrence of it. Zechariah's grandfather Iddo (5.1) is spelt differently in Hebrew. He is 'head' of the Levite and Temple-servant community at Casiphia. To attempt to describe this community in more detail would be a purely imaginative effort.

Casiphia: may perhaps be identified with Ktesiphon on the Tigris. Here it is called **the place**; does this mean a sanctuary of some sort? Deuteronomy speaks of 'the place which the LORD your God will choose' (12.5), and Jeremiah of 'this place' (7.3, 6, 7). The narrative here gives the impression that it was a place where the Levites were established (and possibly segregated) and this would be more likely at a sanctuary or synagogue than at any other place.

and his brethren: this reading (*w^eehāw*) is necessary for sense, but the Hebrew has 'his brother' (*'āhîw*). As the translation stands Iddo is one of the Nethinim—Temple servants—and yet appears to be in authority over the whole community, Levites and Temple servants. This seems unlikely, especially if it be proved that the Temple servants were descended from former prisoners of war (see on 2.43). One way of reducing this difficulty has been to insert an 'and' before Temple servants, thus making **his brethren** capable of being applied to the Levites. Another way, perhaps preferable, is to take the word translated Temple servants as a passive participle of the verb 'to give' (which in form it very nearly is) and take it to mean 'set' in the sense of 'appointed' or 'settled'. This gives the meaning 'telling them what to say to Iddo and his brothers who were settled (or appointed) in the place Casiphia'. This may be thought to be partly confirmed by the way it was understood by the translator in 1 Esd. 8.45f., the relevant part of which runs: 'Iddo who was the leading man at the place of the treasury, and ordered them to tell Iddo and his brethren and the treasurers at that place. . . .'

temple servants: see 2.43.

18. **good hand of our God:** see 7.6; as used here it could be a recognition of the nobility of the spirit of the men who left their homes and positions at short notice.

Mahli: meaning unknown; it seems to be used here as a clan or family name going back to Mahli son of Merari son of Levi (Exod. 6.16, 19). Another tradition is that Mahli was son of Mushi son of Merari (1 Chr. 6.47).

Sherebiah: 'Yahweh has sent burning heat'(?). The name occurs only in Ezr. 8.18, 24; Neh. 8.7; 9.4, 5; 10.12; 12.8, 24. In each instance it belongs to Levites, and at least twice it is a family name (Neh. 10.12; 12.8). Whether the man named here can be identified with the one in Neh. 8.7; 9.4, 5 depends on the dates assigned to Nehemiah and Ezra.

19. Hashabiah: 'Yahweh has taken account of'; at least seven different men bear this name, mostly Levites; see on Neh. 3.10.

Jeshaiah: see verse 7.

Merari: meaning either 'Bitter' or 'Strong'. Merari son of Levi is the only instance of the name.

20. and his officials: if there is genuinely ancient tradition behind this statement, then it may refer to David's generals, who would assist him in handling his prisoners of war. If, on the other hand, it belongs to the Chronicler's acceptance of the late tradition that David established an elaborate Temple procedure, it will refer to David's administrators. The figure of 220 Temple servants seems very high when compared with the figure of 392 given in 2.58 for both Temple servants and servants of Solomon together. We do not know why there were so many with Ezra.

PRAYER FOR A SAFE JOURNEY **8.21–23**

21. fast: cf. 2 Chr. 20.3; Neh. 1.4.

humble ourselves: cf. Dan. 10.12.

22. wrath: see 7.23. The attitude expressed in this verse is typical of the Chronicler's outlook—even in battle the most important thing was the cry to God and the blowing of trumpets by the priests (2 Chr. 13.14, 15).

ARRANGEMENTS FOR THE CARE OF THE MONEY AND TREASURES **8.24–30**

24. According to tradition the priests alone were to handle sacred objects and the Levites were to carry them (Num. 3.8, 31; 4.5ff., 15). Since the two names mentioned here are those of two of the Levites mentioned in verses 18f., it is natural to identify them. In view of this one would expect this verse to have mentioned twelve priests for oversight and an equal number of Levites for carrying. **Sherebiah, Hashabiah,** and their ten kinsmen are the twelve Levites. The twelve priests remain unnamed; possibly through faulty transmission of the Hebrew text. The supposition that a clause has been lost is supported by the fact that in 1 Esd. 8.54 there is a conjunction before Sherebiah. Twelve is the traditional tribal number.

25. offering: the word (*tᵉrûmāh*) is used in Exod. 30.13, 14, 15 of the half-shekel for sanctuary maintenance, and this was virtually the purpose of the silver and gold given by the king (7.15). Another passage that may have influenced its use here is Exod. 25.2, where the people made a *tᵉrûmāh* willingly (see on 7.15) for the building of the sanctuary.

26. talents: see 7.22.

27. darics: see 2.69.

fine bright bronze: this kind of bronze may be that known as orichalc, a bright yellow alloy of copper highly prized in ancient times. The word translated 'fine bright' occurs only here in the O.T. In the Targum of 2 Chr. 4.16 in its Aramaic form it renders the Hebrew for 'burnished bronze'.

28. holy: the gifts, being dedicated to God, were evidently already deemed holy and therefore their bearers were holy.

29. weigh them: a second check, see verses 25–26.

ARRIVAL AT JERUSALEM AND HANDING OVER OF GIFTS **8.31–34**

31. twelfth day: they began assembling on the first day (7.9).
hand of our God: see 7.6.
enemy and . . . ambushes: these are but the natural hazards to expect on a caravan journey of close on 1,000 miles; much of it was through desert country.

32. three days: see verse 15.

33. Meremoth . . . son of Uriah: a Meremoth son of Uriah is mentioned at Neh. 3.4, 21, and since he built two sections of the wall it may be surmised that he was a man of energy and possibly young: here Meremoth is a treasurer and would now be old if Ezra came later than Nehemiah. They could be identified as the same person whether we date Ezra before or after Nehemiah, but the identification is easier if Ezra be assumed to follow Nehemiah. The name Meremoth, the meaning of which is unknown, occurs without a father's name attached in Neh. 10.5; 12.3 and Ezr. 10.36. These are unlikely to be the same person as the one mentioned here; indeed it is a family name in Neh. 10.5; 12.3, and may imply that the name was not altogether an uncommon one.
Uriah: 'Yahweh is (my) light/fire'; the name of (a) the Hittite husband of Bathsheba (2 Sam. 11.3); (b) a priest in the time of Ahaz (Isa. 8.2); (c) father of Meremoth; and (d) a priest (Neh. 8.4), who may or may not be the same person as (c).
Eleazar the son of Phinehas: assuming that Uriah is the name of an individual and not of a family, it may be supposed that Phinehas is also a personal name, which is not unlikely, although otherwise the name occurs only of (a) the grandson of Aaron (Exod. 6.25) and (b) the son of Eli (1 Sam. 1.3). **Son of Phinehas** could mean a member of the family of Phinehas, although the more usual expression is 'of the sons of'; cf. 8.2. For the name Eleazar, see 7.5.
Jozabad: 'Yahweh has given'; is a frequently occurring name among priests and Levites, see 10.22, 23; Neh. 11.16.
Jeshua: see 2.2.
No-adiah: meaning either 'Yahweh has revealed himself' or 'Yahweh has kept his appointment'; the latter is preferable in that it connects with the word 'meeting' in the phrase 'tent of meeting': it occurs only here as a man's name (cf. Neh. 6.14).
Binnui: 'Yahweh has built'(?). This is a fairly common Levite name; see on 2.10, 40.

34. recorded: Ezra may have been responsible to the Persian authorities and had to render account; but the phrase may be editorial, as are verses 35f., and may imply that the Chronicler knew of an official record.

THE PEOPLE SACRIFICE AND THE KING'S COMMISSION IS HANDED TO THE AUTHORITIES
8.35–36

These two verses are written in the third person and may be regarded as editorial and not as a part of Ezra's memoirs.

35. twelve bulls: see on verse 24 and 6.17.

ninety-six rams: allowing eight for each tribe.

seventy-seven lambs: is this a scribal error for seventy-two? 1 Esd. 8.66 has seventy-two. The figure seventy-seven may be due to misunderstanding of an abbreviated numeral by a thoughtless scribe, or if it is correct we may assume that some private personal offerings were also included in the total.

sin offering: goats as well as bulls were permitted for sin-offerings (Lev. 9.2, 3; Ezek. 43.21, 22). It would be intended to purge of any impurities and uncleanness contracted on the journey.

burnt offering: we may compare the fact that Noah sacrificed burnt-offerings after leaving the ark (Gen. 8.20).

36. satraps . . . governors: both words are here used loosely for officers in general; the terms of the commission concerned only officers of the province Beyond the River (treasurers in 7.21), a province that was only a part of the larger satrapy of Babylonia; cf. 5.3.

aided the people: see 7.21–24.

THE PROBLEM OF MIXED MARRIAGES 9.1–10.44

A COMPLAINT LAID **9.1–5**

1. After these things had been done: as it stands this can only naturally refer to (a) checking the money and gifts and (b) making the burnt-offering. Since the enquiry rose out of a complaint, it cannot be claimed that the marriage problem was one of the chief things for which Ezra returned, and would not be very likely to be the very first thing he undertook. There must therefore, in all probability, be something else to which **these things** refers. Moreover, a date in the ninth month is given in 10.9, which leaves four and a half months (see 7.9) during which no activity is recorded in this part of the narrative. It has been suggested above that 8.35f. may be editorial and that the editor may then have passed over a portion of the Ezra memoirs and omitted that part of the narrative to which **these things** might refer. What should stand between the end of chapter 8 and the beginning of chapter 9 is probably the narrative that now stands in Neh. 8 together with some of the material that is in Neh. 9–10, i.e. the story of the reading of the law and of the fast-day that followed.

officials: i.e. leading Jews, doubtless heads of fathers' houses. To which group did they belong? Those who had remained in Judah throughout the exile, or those who had returned? Probably the latter, for it is they in whom the Chronicler's interest is centred and it was returned exiles who were accused of committing the offence (9.4; 10.6).

separated themselves: see 6.21.

Canaanites. . . : Nehemiah, speaking of the same problem of mixed marriages, as it showed itself in his day, mentions Ammonites, Moabites, and Ashdodites (13.23). Did Ezra himself mention these eight or did the Chronicler expand what Ezra had written by drawing upon similar lists of pre-Israelite inhabitants of Canaan; cf. Exod. 3.8, 17, where six are listed: Canaanites, Hittites, Amorites, Perizzites, Hivites, and Jebusites? (Cf. also Gen. 15.19–21; Exod. 33.2; Dt. 7.1.) **Egyptians** are not a normal member of such lists but were equally distasteful to the Jews. It is thought that **Amorites**, which often means no more than Canaanites, is here an error for Edomites, who might well be expected to have a place in such a list in post-exilic times. It is implied that the surrounding peoples had taken advantage of the exile to encroach on Judean territory; cf. Neh. 4.7.

2. taken . . . to be wives: contrary to the law (Exod. 34.16; Dt. 7.1–3. Cf. Jg. 3.5f., where disobedience is acknowledged).

the holy race: the same phrase as that in Isa. 6.13 where it is thought to be dependent on post-exilic thought and usage. Cf. Neh. 9.2, 'seed of Israel' (translated 'Israelites' in RSV). The gravity of the situation is expressed through the use of the adjective 'holy' which looks back, unmistakably, to Dt. 7.6.

chief men: $s^e\bar{g}\bar{a}n\hat{i}m$; this is a word that occurs more frequently in the book of Nehemiah (RSV 'officials') than all other occurrences put together, and there it may be a synonym, more or less, for elder since Nehemiah does not use the Hebrew word for elder. In Ezek. 23.6 and Jer. 51.23 they are spoken of along with governors (or satraps). Here it is evidently used as a general word for leaders.

hand . . . foremost: i.e. they were ringleaders; this shows the seriousness of the problem.

3. rent: a common act of distress (2 Sam. 13.19), as also of mourning (Gen. 37.34).

pulled hair: only here as an act of grief; in Neh. 13.25 and Isa. 50.6 it is an act of violence. There is evidence, however, of baldness as a sign of grief and mourning (Lev. 21.5; Dt. 14.1).

sat appalled: it was a common thing to sit or squat for a length of time when engaged in some such solemn act. It was customary to sit or squat in worship (2 Sam. 7.18; Jg. 20.26; 21.2). (In Ps. 140.13 the verb—RSV has 'dwell'—could well be rendered 'worship'.) This act of Ezra's is comparable in some ways with the acted prophecies of the prophets; cf. Isa. 20. It was probably as much an act of worship as the prayer he offered in the evening, verses 5ff.

4. Ezra's solitary act became a corporate act of contrition; we may compare the way in which supporters rallied round Moses after the golden calf incident (Exod. 32.26).

returned exiles: 10.6 also limits the affair to those who had returned. This is one of the facts which show that the Chronicler's interest lay in the returned exiles; cf. verses 8, 13, 14, 15.

until the evening sacrifice: a division of the day; cf. 1 Kg. 18.29. This was an appropriate time for private or communal prayers, i.e. as the smoke of sacrifice went up, as was recognized also in later times; cf. Ac. 3.1. Ezekiel 46.3 shows that it was quite customary for the people to join in worship in their own way.

5. knees . . . hands: cf. 1 Kg. 8.38, 54.

EZRA'S PRAYER **9.6–15**

6. It is not certain how much attention to pay to the change of person from 1st singular in 6*a* to 1st plural in 6*b*. Perhaps we may envisage Ezra as conscious that he stands in a unique position, privileged to speak to God and therefore beginning on an intensely personal note, but at the same time identifying himself with the community and passing through a vicarious experience on their behalf.

7. kings of the lands: i.e. Assyrian (Neh. 9.32), Babylonian and Persian (Neh. 9.37). In later times when the passage was read in worship Greek and Roman kings would doubtless be counted in too.

8. a brief moment: this must refer to the period of restoration following the decree of Cyrus. In the view of a devout man like Ezra the century or more thus referred to was but a moment in God's time (cf. Ps. 90.4).

remnant: the Hebrew word used here does not mean those left over, but rather those who have escaped; cf. verse 14, where two words are used, the one meaning remnant, i.e. left over, and the other the word used here meaning escape; cf. also verse 15: it is the returned exiles who are meant by both words, i.e. they have escaped out of their exile and they are what remain of the Israelite people (cf. also Neh. 1.2).

a secure hold: literally a nail or tent-peg. It is probably the figure of the tent-peg that is in mind here since it would be used to pin down the nomad's tent and give security. One might also see in it a sense of tenure, of the right to be there, of belonging (cf. Jer. 7.2–7 where the right to belong is expressed in a different way). The implication is that restoration had proceeded so far that the people could feel settled and secure. In Isa. 22.23–25 the figure of the peg is that of a nail or hook in a wall on which so much is hung that it is wrenched out.

brighten our eyes: giving happiness or joy (cf. Prov. 29.13; Ps. 13.3; 19.8), and perhaps also confidence (1 Sam. 14.27).

reviving: lit. source of life, or, as we might say, new life; cf. next verse.

9. bondmen: subjects of an overlord. In Neh. 9.36 the same word is translated slaves.

steadfast love: this is not defined by the pronoun 'his' in Hebrew and the phrase could (and probably should) be understood to mean 'made the kings of Persia well-disposed to us', i.e. that *they* exercised the steadfast love towards the Jews; cf. 7.28.

reviving: this might be understood in two ways: either referring to the new life and fresh vigour that went into their rebuilding efforts, or to the 'sustenance' that made the building efforts possible, money and material.

protection: the Hebrew word (*gāḏēr*) is used of the fence or wall surrounding a sheepfold (cf. Num. 32.16, where it is the sign of peaceful occupation of the land) or bordering a path (Num. 22.24), and is therefore used figuratively here. The rendering of some earlier English versions, 'wall', gave rise to speculation about the city wall as being already built by this time and therefore supporting a date for Ezra later than Nehemiah, but the word is not properly used of a city wall and the wall of Jerusalem would not be described as **in Judea and Jerusalem.**

10. Ezra now turns to the immediate reason for his prayer.

11. **The land. . . :** this is not an exact quotation, nor is it from what we would call the prophets; it is rather a composite quotation from such passages as Exod. 34.16; Lev. 18.25, 27; Dt. 7.1, 3. Moses, however, was widely recognized as a prophet (Hos. 12.13; Dt. 18.15; 34.10; cf. Num. 12.6–8).

13. **a remnant as this:** lit. those who have escaped (or survived); cf. verse 8.

14. **no remnant, nor any to escape:** here both words are used (see verse 8), those who are left over, and those who escape. The idea of a remnant (cf. Isa. 11.11; 28.5f.; Jer. 31.7; 50.20) became an important concept after the exile and was used (especially by the Chronicler) to designate those who returned from Babylon.

15. **left a remnant that has escaped:** lit. we have been left over, escaped ones. **because of this:** i.e. the mixed marriages and their guilt.

COVENANT AND OATH TO DIVORCE FOREIGN WIVES 10.1–5

1. There is a further increase in the number of people who rally round Ezra; see 9.4.

before the house of God: they have clearly been in the Temple precincts all the time; cf. the reference to the evening sacrifice in 9.4–5. It was the natural place for such gatherings as this to take place.

2. **Shecaniah the son of Jehiel, of the sons of Elam:** we can scarcely expect to be able to identify this man whose name, meaning 'Yahweh has taken up his dwelling', is held by at least six different men, and who is not to be confused with the Shecaniah of 8.3, who was probably a Davidite, or the one in 8.5, who belonged to the family of Zattu. His father's name, Jehiel, is held by some eight or nine other men and is not to be identified with the Jehiel of 8.9, who belongs to the family of Joab. The family of Elam, a lay family, is mentioned in 2.7 and 8.7; 10.2, 26. Shecaniah seems to be acting here as a clear-minded spokesman of those who were zealous for purity of race.

hope: based on such a passage as Dt. 30.1–10.

3. **to put away:** lit. 'bring out'; it occurs only here and verse 19 as a verb for divorcing for which the usual verb is one meaning 'send away'. (In Dt. 24.1 the divorced woman is spoken of as 'going out' of the man's house.)

my lord: this translation, which is clearly right in the context, involves a slight change of pronunciation in Hebrew—'*aḏōnî* instead of '*aḏōnāy*.

tremble at: cf. 9.4.

4. your task: in virtue of his commission.

5. leading priests and Levites and all Israel: this could also be translated: 'the leaders (officials in 9.2) of the priests, of the Levites and of all Israel'. This seems preferable and would then be a proper move because (a) some of the leaders themselves were involved and (b) only through these could the rank and file be reached.

AN ASSEMBLY SUMMONED **10.6–8**

6. Jehohanan the son of Eliashib: in Nehemiah's time Eliashib was high priest (Neh. 3.1, 20). (Mention is made of a priest named Eliashib who was in charge of the chambers in Neh. 13.4, 7, but this is probably a different man from the high priest.) In Neh. 13.28 we read of Jehoiada the son of Eliashib, in Neh. 12.22f. of the line of succession—Eliashib, Joiada, Johanan, and Jaddua—and in Neh. 12.10, 11 of Jeshua, Joiakim, Eliashib, Joiada, Jonathan, and Jaddua. According to these therefore Jehohanan (once called Jonathan) was actually grandson of Eliashib. It looks as if the grandfather was high priest in Nehemiah's time and the grandson in Ezra's. The date, approximately, of Jehohanan's high priesthood is confirmed by the letter written to him in 410 B.C. by the Jews in Elephantine (Cowley, *Aram. Pap.*, No. 30). Both Eliashib and Jehohanan were fairly common names: Eliashib, 'May God restore', occurs three times in the list that follows, but otherwise occurs outside the books of Ezra-Nehemiah only in 1 Chr. 3.24 (seventh in succession in the Davidic line, and not a priest) and 24.12 (the leading figure of one of the twenty-four priestly courses). Jehohanan, 'Yahweh has been gracious', is borne by some fourteen different men (cf. 8.12). Jehohanan is not here called high priest, but it is almost certain that Ezra would go to no one of less rank.

spent the night: this is the reading of LXX in 1 Esd. 9.2 and involves only slight change in Hebrew from *wayyēlek* to *wayyālen*.

7. returned exiles: the implication is that these were the only Jews of any consequence (see on 9.4), and it is to these, called the congregation of the exiles in the next verse, that the Chronicler probably applies the term 'remnant'; cf. 9.14. (Haggai seems to use the term differently in 2.2, the same group of people being referred to in 2.4 as the people of the land.)

8. three days: cf. 8.32.

forfeited: the Hebrew word strictly means forfeit to God; in pre-exilic times, to ensure that such property was not kept in human use, it was destroyed (cf. Jos. 6.21), but in later times it became the property of the priests (Lev. 27.21; Num. 18.14; Ezek. 44.29). The property meant here is what we should call movable goods.

ASSEMBLY HELD AND ARRANGEMENTS MADE TO HANDLE THE PROBLEM **10.9–15**

9. Judah and Benjamin: cf. 1.5.

ninth month: Chislev; see note on 9.1.

open square: probably the Temple precincts; see verse 1.

heavy rain: which fell in the three winter months, Chislev, Tebet, and Shebet, roughly December, January, February.

10. the priest: see 7.6.

11. separate yourselves: see 6.21.

13. cannot stand: lit. have no strength to stand. Stand need not be taken literally; it has the force of remain.

14. officials: see 9.2.

15. Opposition was made by four men, but we are not told why. It may be that the opposition was directed only at the method adopted and not at the basic measure.

Jonathan the son of Asahel: is mentioned only here and there is no indication as to whether he was priest or layman. On the name Jonathan, see 8.6. This is the only post-exilic occurrence of the name **Asahel**, 'God has acted'; for pre-exilic use, see 2 Sam. 2.18; 2 Chr. 17.8; 31.13.

Jahzeiah the son of Tikvah: this again is the only mention of this man. The name Jahzeiah, 'May Yahweh see', is unique, and the name Tikvah, 'Hope', is found otherwise only in 2 Kg. 22.14.

Meshullam: this may be the same man as the one mentioned in 8.16—evidently one of Ezra's right-hand men; cf. Neh. 8.4.

Shabbethai the Levite: appears also as a leading man in Neh. 8.7. Whether the Shabbethai of Neh. 11.16 is to be identified with this one depends upon the dates assigned to Ezra and Nehemiah. The name does not occur otherwise, and seems to mean 'Born on the Sabbath'. Of these four, therefore, the first two are otherwise unknown while the last two are known to have been leaders—were their names used to give support to the opposition of the two unknown men?

A THREE-MONTH TASK **10.16–17**

16. Ezra . . . selected men: the adoption of the Greek text is clearly desirable; the Hebrew is ungrammatical and could only be rendered: 'And Ezra the priest, men who were heads of houses, were separated. . . .'

designated by name: their names are not set down here, so we are left to conjecture that the list appeared in Ezra's memoirs and that the Chronicler chose not to use it. If it had been given, the list would have answered the question, 'How many did he set apart?' He is not likely to have chosen one from each of the families mentioned in Ezr. 2. He may have followed tradition and chosen twelve, the representative tribal number.

How were the three months spent? There are 111 (or 113, see verse 38) names in the list that follows, and these would scarcely occupy the Jerusalem headquarters for three months: evidently much of the time was spent in sorting out the offenders in their own cities.

LIST OF OFFENDERS, PRIESTS, LEVITES, LAYMEN **10.18–44**

In the list that follows the four priestly families, Joshua the son of Jozadak and his brethren, Immer, Harim, and Pashhur, correspond with those in 2.36–39, except that the first is differently designated, namely, Jedaiah of the house of Joshua. The Levites are not divided into families. There are eleven lay families mentioned (whereas in 2.3–20 there are seventeen), but four of the eleven do not occur in chapter 2, namely, Harim, Binnui, Nebo, and the second Bani. Twenty-one of the names occur twice or more in the list. This reduces the number of different names to seventy-nine, nineteen of which occur only in this list.

18. Maaseiah: 'The work of Yahweh', also in verses 21, 22, 30. It is a common name.

Eliezer: also in verses 23, 31; this is another fairly common name, but only about half as frequent as Maaseiah; see 8.16.

Jarib: see 8.16.

Gedaliah: 'Yahweh is great'; there are five men of this name, the others are in Jer. 40.5; Zeph. 1.1; Jer. 38.1; 1 Chr. 25.3.

Jeshua the son of Jozadak: see 2.2, 36.

and his brethren: this suggests that there were wide ramifications of this family.

19. pledged: lit. gave their hand; cf. 2 Kg. 10.15, where it is a sign of a pledge or promise.

ram: the recognized victim for a guilt-offering (Lev. 5.14–19) where the sin was committed unwittingly. There is probably no need to press this point and think that the people did not know that they were contravening the law. It must be assumed that, although it is not repeated in the rest of the list, all the guilty men would be called upon to make the same sacrifice.

guilt offering: this was originally intended as compensation in cases where injury or damage was done whose value was assessable, but the term came to have a wider usage.

20. Immer: see 2.37.

Hanani: probably a shortened form of Hananiah, 'Yahweh has been gracious', a name which occurs in verse 28. There were six men of this name: (a) this one, (b) the one in verse 28, (c) the father of Jehu the prophet (1 Kg. 16.1), (d) the brother of Nehemiah (Neh. 1.2), (e) a chief musician (1 Chr. 25.4), and (f) another musician (Neh. 12.36).

Zebadiah: see 8.8.

21. Harim: see 2.39.

Maaseiah: see verse 18.

Elijah: 'Yahweh is (my) God'; also in verse 26. There are four men so named; the prophet, a Benjaminite (1 Chr. 8.27), and the two in this list. There seems to have been a tendency in post-exilic times to use the more familiar pre-exilic names; see on verse 23.

Shemaiah: also verse 31; see 8.13.

Jehiel: also verse 26; see 8.9.

Uzziah: 'Yahweh is (my) strength'; borne by three men in pre-exilic times, and by two in post-exilic times; this one and one in Neh. 11.4.

22. Pashhur: see 2.38.

Elioenai: 'To Yahweh are my eyes'; also in verse 27. There are three pre-exilic occurrences of the name, and three post-exilic, this one, verse 27, and Neh. 12.41.

Maaseiah: see verse 18.

Ishmael: 'May God hear'; only here in post-exilic times, and five times in pre-exilic times.

Nethanel: 'God has given'; only here and Neh. 12.21, 36 in post-exilic times. It was the name of seven men in pre-exilic times.

Jozabad: also in verse 23; see on 8.33.

Elasah: 'God has acted'; only here in post-exilic times. There were three men so named in pre-exilic times.

23. Jozabad: see verse 22.

Shimei: probably a shortened form of Shemaiah, 'Yahweh has heard'; also in verses 33, 38. There are only these three occurrences of the name in post-exilic times; before the exile sixteen men so named may be distinguished, seven of them being Levites.

Kelaiah: otherwise only in Neh. 8.7 and 10.10 (where the alternative form Kelita is used). Kelita may mean either 'Accepted' or 'Dwarf'. But see on Neh. 11.7.

Pethahiah: 'Yahweh has opened (the womb?)'; there were four men of this name, (a) this one, (b) 1 Chr. 24.16, (c) Neh. 9.5, and (d) Neh. 11.24.

Judah: the commonest use of this name is as that of the tribe and of the tribal ancestor of the tribe, the son of Jacob and Leah; otherwise it occurs only in 3.9, here, and Neh. 11.9; 12.8, 36. This post-exilic use of the name appears to be an intentional borrowing of an ancient name; cf. Benjamin in verse 32 and Amram in verse 34. The meaning of the name Judah is not known.

Eliezer: see verse 18.

24. Eliashib: also in verses 27, 36. On the name, see verse 6.

Shallum: also in verse 42; see 2.42.

Telem: 'Light'; only here.

Uri: probably a shortened form of Uriah, 'Yahweh is (my) light/fire'; only here in post-exilic times, and twice elsewhere.

25. Parosh: see 2.3.

Ramiah: 'Yahweh is high'; only here.

Jzziah: 'May Yahweh sprinkle'; only here.

Malchijah: 'Yahweh is (my) king/has become king'; also in verse 31. About eleven individuals are so named, mostly post-exilic.

Mijamin: if this is an original form of name it may mean 'In luck's way', but it has been thought to be a corruption of Benjamin (verse 32). All other instances are names of priests (1 Chr. 24.9; 2 Chr. 31.15; Neh. 10.7; 12.5, 17, 41). There are slight differences of spelling.

Eleazar: see 7.5.

Hashabiah: this name is taken from LXX in 1 Esd. 9.26. It avoids the repetition of

Malchijah in the same verse and from the same family, although it is not inconceivable that two members of a family should bear the same name. For the name,
see 8.19.

Benaiah: 'Yahweh has built'; also in verses 30, 35, 43. Eleven different men are
called Benaiah, the best known being David's captain (2 Sam. 8.18). The four in
this list are the only post-exilic occurrences.

26. Elam: see 2.7.

Mattaniah: 'The gift of Yahweh'; also in verses 27, 30, 37. This is a fairly common
name (twelve men), especially among Levites. It may be a family name in Neh.
11.22; 12.35, and perhaps elsewhere.

Zechariah: see 8.3.

Jehiel: see verse 21.

Abdi: probably a shortened form of Obadiah, 'Servant of Yahweh'; it occurs
otherwise only in 1 Chr. 6.44; 2 Chr. 29.12.

Jeremoth: 'Thick/Swollen'?; also in verses 27, 29. A fairly common name, being
that of twelve men.

Elijah: see verse 21.

27. Zattu: see 2.8.

Elioenai: see verse 22.

Eliashib: see verse 24.

Mattaniah, Jeremoth: see verse 26.

Zabad: possibly a shortened form of Zebadiah (verse 20), 'Yahweh has given';
also in verses 33, 43. The name of seven different men.

Aziza: 'Strong'; only here.

28. Bebai: see 2.11.

Jehohanan: see verse 6.

Hananiah: 'Yahweh has been gracious'; is a fairly common name; cf. Neh. 3.8,
30; 7.2.

Zabbai: possibly a shortened form of Zebadiah (see verse 27); elsewhere only
Neh. 3.20.

Athlai: (=Athaliah) see 8.7.

29. Bani: see 2.10.

Meshullam: see 8.16.

Malluch: also in verse 32. Six men are so named (1 Chr. 6.44; Ezr. 10.29, 32;
Neh. 10.4, 27; 12.2); but some of these may be family names. The name may
perhaps be regarded as a shortened form, with changed pronunciation, of a *melek*
('king') bearing name, such as Malchijah (verse 25).

Adaiah: 'Yahweh has bedecked himself/his servant'; also in verse 39. Eight men
are so named; cf. Neh. 11.5, 12.

Jashub: 'He will return', possibly a shortened form of a fuller unknown name.
Otherwise it occurs only in Num. 26.24 and 1 Chr. 7.1.

Sheal: 'Ask', occurs only here. Another reading is Yishal, 'May he ask'.

Jeremoth: see verse 26.

30. Pahath-moab: see 2.6.

Adna: 'Rapture', perhaps another form of Adin (2.15). Occurs only here and Neh. 12.15 (head of a priestly house).

Chelal: 'Completeness', occurs only here.

Benaiah: see verse 25.

Maaseiah: see verse 18.

Mattaniah: see verse 26.

Bezalel: 'In the shadow of God', otherwise only of the craftsman of Exod. 31.2, etc.

Binnui: see on 2.10, 40, 8.33.

Manasseh: 'Yahweh causes to forget (former troubles?)'; also in verse 33. Otherwise only (a) the older son of Joseph, and the tribe named after him, and (b) the son of Hezekiah, king of Judah (2 Kg. 20.21).

31. Harim: a family name; cf. Neh. 3.11, 10.5, which does not occur among the lay families in the list in chapter 2. See 2.39, where it is the name of a priestly family.

Eliezer: see verse 18.

Isshijah: 'May Yahweh forget (sins?)'; only here in post-exilic times, and only in 1 Chronicles in pre-exilic times, where it occurs as the name of five different men.

Malchijah: see verse 25.

Shemaiah: see 8.13.

Shimeon: a short form of a name like Shemaiah (8.13); apart from this man the name occurs only as that of the second son of Jacob and Leah (Gen. 29.33) and of the tribe (Num. 1.6, etc.), but in the form Simeon in English.

32. Benjamin: 'Son of luck/right hand'; (a) the younger son of Jacob and Rachel; (b) son of Bilhan (1 Chr. 7.10); (c) this one; (d) a wall-builder (Neh. 3.23); and (e) a priest (Neh. 12.34). This is perhaps another instance of revival of an ancient name; cf. verse 23.

Malluch: see verse 29.

Shemariah: 'Yahweh has kept'; also in verse 41. Otherwise only in 1 Chr. 12.5; 2 Chr. 11.19.

33. Hashum: see 2.19.

Mattenai: 'The gift of Yahweh'; also in verse 37; otherwise only in Neh. 12.19, a priest.

Mattattah: 'The gift of Yahweh'; only here.

Zabad: see verse 27.

Eliphelet: see 8.13.

Jeremai: only here; perhaps a short form of Jeremoth, verse 26.

Manasseh: see verse 30.

Shimei: see verse 23.

34. Bani: the name of a lay family in verse 29 and in 2.10. It is surprising to find a second family with the same name. There may be a scribal error here, Bani being written for Bigvai (2.14) or Bezai (2.17).

Maadai: only here, but compare Maadiah in Neh. 12.5 and Moadiah in Neh. 12.17, which may be fuller forms of the same name. The meaning is obscure: it could come from a root *yā'aḏ*, 'to meet', or a root *mā'aḏ*, 'to totter'. The first of these, with its possible hint at a meeting with Yahweh, is preferable.

Amram: 'Father's kin is tall'; occurs otherwise only as the father of Moses (Exod. 6.18, 20, etc.). It is a further example of the revived use of an ancient name; cf. verses 23, 32.

Uel: only here, but it may be a form of Joel (as some of the forms found in the versions, Lucianic LXX, Syr., suggest). If the Hebrew shows the correct form, it may mean 'Will of God'; Joel would mean 'Yahweh is God'.

35. Benaiah: see verse 25.

Bedeiah: only here; it may be a form of Obadiah, 'Servant of God'.

Cheluhi: only here and meaning obscure.

36. Vaniah: only here; meaning unknown. A somewhat similar name, *v-n-h*, occurs on a papyrus from Elephantine (Cowley, *Aram. Pap.*, No. 22, line 40).

Meremoth: see 8.33.

Eliashib: see verse 24.

37. Mattaniah: see verse 26.

Mattenai: see verse 33.

Jaasu: only here; possibly a short form of Jaasiel (1 Chr. 11.47), 'May God act'.

38. Of the sons of Binnui: this reading is suggested by that of 1 Esd. 9.34. The Hebrew has Bani, Binnui, which implies that further names from the family of Bani (verse 34) were intended. The correction is probably right for otherwise it would make a very long list of members of one family. Binnui occurs as a family name in Neh. 7.15. See 8.33.

Shimei: see verse 23.

39. Shelemiah: 'Yahweh has rewarded/completed'; the name occurs as that of four contemporaries of Jeremiah (Jer. 36.14; 36.26; 37.3; 37.13), of a Levite (1 Chr. 26.14), of a wall builder's father (Neh. 3.30), of a priest (Neh. 13.13), and of two men in this list (verse 41).

Nathan: see 8.16.

Adaiah: see verse 29.

40. Machnadebai, Shashai, Sharai: these names occur only in this verse and have no obvious meanings. The first, Machnadebai, cannot be satisfactorily explained as a Hebrew name form and it may be a corrupted form, the clue to a possible original being found in 1 Esd. 9.34. There LXX has 'of the sons of Ezora', which would in Hebrew be *mibb'nê-'azora*. This might be a form of the name Azzur, which occurs in Neh. 10.17 and is possibly a short form of a name like Azariah, 'Yahweh has helped'. The Greek is not, however, the safest of guides here, because the previous names do not closely match those in the Hebrew text. Further uncertainty is roused by the similar sounding names Shashai and Sharai (see on Neh. 11.8). They may resolve a badly corrupt text by supplying two forms that could be read as proper names, or they may be short forms of full names that cannot be confidently recovered. Sharai could perhaps be a short form of Sherebiah

(8.18), and Shashai has a parallel in the Elephantine documents (Cowley, *Aram. Pap.*, No. 49, line 1).

41. Azarel: 'God has helped'; the name occurs in post-exilic times only here, and Neh. 11.13; 12.36; and three times before the exile, in 1 Chr. 12.6; 25.18; 27.22.

Shelemiah: see verse 39.

Shemariah: see verse 32.

42. Shallum: see verse 24.

Amariah: see 7.3.

Joseph: probably a short form of Josiphia (8.10); elsewhere (a) the elder son of Jacob and Rachel, (b) a man of Issachar (Num. 13.7), (c) a son of Asaph (1 Chr. 25.2, 9), and (d) a priest (Neh. 12.14).

43. Nebo: this is the only certain occurrence of the name as a personal name, here a family name. Elsewhere it is a place-name; cf. 2.29. The name, if correct, may have some connection with the Babylonian god Nebo (Nabu).

Jeiel: see 8.13.

Mattithiah: 'Gift of Yahweh'; occurs here, in Neh. 8.4, and in 1 Chronicles (9.31; 15.18, 21; 16.5; 25.3, 21) where it is a Levite name.

Zabad: see verse 27.

Zebina: 'Bought'; occurs only here.

Jaddai: perhaps a short form of Jedaiah, 'Yahweh has known/cared for' (2.36). It occurs only here, but there is an alternative reading Iddo (or Jaddo), 'His beloved' (1 Chr. 27.21).

Joel: 'Yahweh is God'; is a fairly common name, being that of about fourteen men; cf. Neh. 11.9.

Benaiah: see verse 25.

44. In very few words the result of Ezra's marriage reform is set out. The second half of the verse is taken from 1 Esd. 9.36. The Hebrew text, literally translated, runs: 'and some of them were women and they put down children', which yields no meaning in the context. It is to be noted that whereas Ezra made the people divorce their wives, Nehemiah only extracted from them a promise not to continue the practice of mixed marriages (Neh. 13.25). The less rigorous measure of Nehemiah is the more likely to have been taken before the more rigorous measure of Ezra, and this may be regarded as one of the stronger arguments for the dating of Nehemiah before Ezra.

The book ends abruptly. One would expect a notice that the people pledged themselves in this matter—as did the priests, verse 19—and that a guilt-offering was sacrificed for them.

A further suggestion has been made, namely, that the day of fasting and confession followed by a covenant now recorded in Neh. 9.1–38a may have followed this investigation into the mixed marriages. There is striking similarity between Ezr. 10.11, which mentions making confession and separating from the people of the land, and Neh. 9.2, 'And the Israelites separated themselves from all foreigners, and stood and confessed their sins. . . .' It could, however, be argued that such a covenant is very much in place in Nehemiah's work and we may have to regard Neh. 9 as the conflation of the record of a day of confession and covenant in Ezra's time with the record of a similar day in Nehemiah's time.

THE BOOK OF

NEHEMIAH

NEHEMIAH

FIRST SECTION **1.1–6.19** THE RETURN OF NEHEMIAH AND
THE REBUILDING OF THE WALLS

Nehemiah's Return and Preparation **1.1–2.20**

REPORT ON THE STATE OF THE WALLS **1.1–3**

1. The words of: a reference to Nehemiah's memoirs (see Introduction, p. 32).
Nehemiah: 'Yahweh has comforted'; Nehemiah is mentioned in the O.T. only in
the book that bears his name, with the possible exception of Ezr. 2.2. He is mentioned in two books of the Apocrypha: in Sir. 49.13, where he is held in memory
for raising the walls and rebuilding ruined houses, and in 2 Mac. 1.18, 20ff.; 2.13,
where he is not only looked upon as the sole restorer of the Temple after the exile
but also as the founder of a library. Nehemiah is also the name of one of the wall-
builders, ruler of half Beth-zur (Neh. 3.16). The only other instance of the name is
in the list in Ezr. 2.2 and Neh. 7.7, where a Nehemiah is listed as one of those who
returned with Zerubbabel. This could be an otherwise unknown man named
Nehemiah, since others in the verse are equally unknown, but it could be an
anachronistic inclusion of Nehemiah's name among leaders of the restoration.
Hacaliah: a name of uncertain meaning; it may be a contracted form of the
Hebrew for 'Wait for Yahweh', but such a form, incorporating an imperative, is
contrary to normal proper-name formation in Hebrew. He is mentioned again in
10.1, but otherwise nothing is known of Nehemiah's father. The reference in 2.3, 5
to Nehemiah's fathers' sepulchres, if it be taken to mean his own immediate
ancestors as distinct from national ancestors, may imply a family of high standing.
Chislev: see 2.1, and cf. Ezr. 10.9.
twentieth year: i.e. of the reigning king, Artaxerxes I (465–425 B.C.), but the
omission of the king's name is unexpected and may be due to the date here being
editorial (see 2.1).
Susa: see Ezr. 4.9.
2. Hanani: see Ezr. 10.20. Does Nehemiah mean his own brother, or simply a
fellow Jew? The term 'brother' is used repeatedly in Deuteronomy to mean a
fellow countryman—a usage which would be familiar in Nehemiah's time since
Deuteronomy appears to have been the best-known law code in the days
immediately after the exile.
that survived, who had escaped exile: for the terms used here, see the notes on
Ezr. 9.8, 14f. The phrase is as ambiguous in Hebrew as it is in English: does it mean
people in Judah who had never been in Babylon and had thus 'escaped' exile, or
does it mean those who had escaped out of exile? The latter is the more probable

meaning, for when the Chronicler uses the word 'exile' ($\check{s}^e\underline{b}\hat{\imath}$), he means the *people* in exile, and it is clear throughout his writings that his interest lies mainly in the Jews who had returned from exile in Babylon.

What was the purpose of Hanani's journey? Were he and his companions officials or businessmen? The questions cannot be answered, but it is clear that they had not come specifically to report to Nehemiah about the state of Jerusalem. It is indicative of the regular traffic that there must have been between Palestine and Babylon.

3. The trouble and ruin mentioned here were almost certainly the result of a recent disaster. This may have been what is reported in Ezr. 4.23: 'they went in haste to the Jews at Jerusalem and by force and power made them cease'. This was done on instructions from the king following representations against the Jews to Artaxerxes (Ezr. 4.8–16).

by fire: much of the structure of the gates was of wood; see 2.8.

NEHEMIAH'S PRAYER 1.4–11

4. sat down and wept: see Ezr. 9.3, 4.

fasting: see Ezr. 8.21.

praying before the God of heaven: cf. Ezr. 10.1, which tells how Ezra prostrated before the Temple.

5. great and terrible: cf. Dt. 7.21; 10.17.

keeps covenant . . . : cf. Dt. 7.9; 1 Kg. 8.23; Neh. 9.32.

steadfast love: the quality of character and behaviour that honours a covenant or an obligation through thick and thin; cf. Ezr. 3.11.

6. confessing: Nehemiah joins the ranks of the great intercessors (cf. Moses, Exod. 32.31f.), and like Ezra (9.6) he identifies himself with the people.

8b–9. This is a conflate passage mostly based on Dt. 30.1–5.

9. to make my name dwell there: see Ezr. 6.12.

10. redeemed: a familiar word in the book of Deuteronomy (7.8; 9.26; 13.5; 15.15; 21.8; 24.18); in origin it means paying a ransom price, but it came to be used figuratively.

great power . . . strong hand: exactly as in Exod. 32.11; a more frequently used phrase is 'great power and outstretched arm' (Dt. 9.29; 2 Kg. 17.36; Jer. 27.5; 32.17), and the most often used is 'strong hand and outstretched arm' (Dt. 4.34; 5.15; 7.19; 11.2; 1 Kg. 8.42; 2 Chr. 6.32; Ps. 136.12; Jer. 32.21; Ezek. 20.33, 34).

11. this man: Artaxerxes.

NEHEMIAH HAS AUDIENCE OF THE KING AND RECEIVES PERMISSION TO RETURN 2.1–8

1. Nisan: was the first month of the year, hence this would be four months later than the time mentioned in 1.1, but it would also be at the beginning of another year according to normal Jewish reckoning in post-exilic times (following Persian usage), so that it ought now to be the twenty-first year of the king. Both 5.14 and 13.6 confirm that Nehemiah returned in the twentieth year; then how can 1.1 and 2.1 be reconciled? Some think that instead of twentieth in 1.1 we should read nineteenth and assume a scribal error, but it is not easy to see how a scribe could so misread. An alternative way is to suppose that there is here a revival of the practice from Solomon onwards until the exile of celebrating the new year in the seventh month (Tishri), using a sacred calendar alongside the secular one. Yet another possibility is that an editor added 1.1 and based his date in that verse on this reference but overlooked the fact that the earlier month was in the previous year. It would seem right to an editor to begin the book with a date; the omission of the king's name in 1.1 offers strong evidence of an editorial hand (see also 6.15).

Why did Nehemiah allow four months to pass? If he was waiting for a suitable occasion to approach the king it may be that at the new year the king celebrated either a birthday or a coronation anniversary. Requests would be more readily granted on such occasions (cf. Gen. 40.20; Est. 5.6; Mk 6.21–25).

2. afraid: knowing that the destruction had been officially inspired (see 1.3; Ezr. 4.23), Nehemiah may well have thought that he, a court official, was greatly daring in his request.

3. The non-mention of the name Jerusalem may have been deliberate to avoid rousing any dormant ill-feeling or suspicion.

4. So I prayed: this may be deemed indicative of the intense personal piety that crept in during the exile when personal religion thrived and when communal religion was necessarily nearly defunct. Nehemiah is shown as one who regularly resorted to prayer; cf. 4.4, 9; 5.19; 6.9, 14; 13.14.

6. the queen sitting beside him: the queen's presence may be meant to provide a witness, or to give evidence of their joint wish not to lose Nehemiah for too long a period; or Nehemiah may have been in her confidence and she ready to support him.

a time: no evidence is available about the length of time intended here. According to 5.14 he could have spent at least twelve years in Jerusalem, although it does not there say that he was in Jerusalem for the whole of the time that he held office as governor.

Nehemiah's journey became an authorized Persian commission, and the implication (5.14) is that he was appointed governor. Presumably the office was vacant. If it had been vacant for some time and if Sanballat had been discharging the functions of governor in addition to his control of Samaria, his jealousy might be readily accounted for.

7. letters: i.e. of safe conduct. There is a letter of this sort written in Aramaic in the fifth century and still extant (No. 6 in G. R. Driver, *Aramaic Documents*, 1957). It concerns provisions and is addressed to a number of local officers whose names are given, and it goes on: 'One named Nehtihur, my officer, is going to Egypt. Do you give him as provisions from my estate in your provinces every day two measures of white meal . . . give them these provisions, each officer of you in turn, in accordance with the stages of his journey from province to province until he reaches Egypt. . . .'

governors: the word used here (*peḥāh*) could be used at this time to mean both governors of provinces (satraps?) (cf. Tattenai, Ezr. 5.3; 6.7), and governors of lesser administrative areas (Sheshbazzar, Ezr. 5.14).

Beyond the River: see Ezr. 4.10.

8. Asaph, the keeper of the king's forest: this is the only mention of this man or of his office. The word translated forest is an Avestan loan-word strictly meaning enclosure (it has come into English as paradise). On the name, see Ezr. 2.41.

fortress of the temple: here the fortress (*bîrāh*) is spoken of in close connection with the Temple: there was probably only one such fortress in Jerusalem which served as protection for both city and Temple. It is just possible that the Tower of Hananel (3.1) could have served this purpose and have been so described. In 7.2 the fortress is spoken of without reference to the Temple and translated 'castle'. In 1.1 the same Hebrew word describes the city Susa and is translated 'capital', i.e. properly meaning fortress, the word could be used to describe either the fortress itself or the city dominated by that fortress. In 1 Chr. 29.1, 19 the Chronicler speaks of the Temple itself as a 'fortress', RSV 'palace' (*bîrāh*).

The detailed description of the rebuilding given in chapter 3 does not mention either the gate of the fortress or the house which Nehemiah was to occupy, but neither does it list Nehemiah and his men among the builders: possibly they repaired and rebuilt these.

hand of my God: see Ezr. 7.6.

NEHEMIAH'S ARRIVAL AND SANBALLAT'S DISPLEASURE 2.9–10

9. officers . . . horsemen: this indicates the high authority in which the king had placed him. Ezra 8.22 shows that it was not unusual for officials to have military escort for their journeys.

10. Sanballat the Horonite: Horonite could mean either (a) a man from Beth-horon, upper or lower, or (b) a man from the district of Hauran east of the sea of Galilee, or (c) a man from Horonaim in Moab. The name Sanballat is Babylonian (Sinuballit) and means 'Sin gave life'. It is pretty clear from Nehemiah's expulsion of his son-in-law (13.28) that he was not an Israelite. It is not certain therefore which of the three possible meanings of Horonite is applicable to him. He is the only man of this name in the O.T., but he is also mentioned on the Aramaic papyri (*A.N.E.T.*, p. 492; Cowley, *Aram. Pap.*, No. 30, line 29) in the statement: 'Delaiah and Shelemiah, the sons of Sanballat, the governor of Samaria.' Did he hold the governorship under the satrap of the province Beyond the River? The governorship of Samaria may well have been on a par with the governorship of Judah. He had an army at his command (4.2), and he could summon Nehemiah as an equal (6.2–5). The fact that his two sons had -ya (-iah) bearing names suggests that he was a Yahweh worshipper.

Tobiah the servant, the Ammonite: comes into the story also at 6.17 and 13.4–9. It is a Hebrew name and there are three other men so named; see Ezr. 2.60. The -iah termination may mean that he came from a Yahweh-worshipping family, although the fact that he is described as an Ammonite would tell against this. In

Dt. 23.3 Ammonites are singled out with Moabites as being unable to enter the assembly of Israel even to the tenth generation. Ammonite may be little more than a nickname, and it is possible to suppose that he may be identifiable with a member of the Tobiah family that could not trace its descent (Ezr. 2.60). He is described as 'servant', a word which more often than not in Hebrew means 'slave'. Was he a Persian official (a civil servant) in the territory of the Ammonites? Had he been a slave at the Persian court and earned the reward of some kind of office in his homeland? Or was Nehemiah mocking him? Whoever he was and whatever his background he appears in Nehemiah's memoirs as on equal footing with Sanballat; this may imply collaboration of Samaritans and Ammonites against Nehemiah. **displeased them greatly:** and they were not slow to act (verse 19).

NEHEMIAH MAKES A TOUR OF INSPECTION BY NIGHT **2.11–16**
There are three descriptions of the city walls and gates in Nehemiah, that of those parts which he inspected (2.13–15), that in the detailed list of the builders at work (3.1–32), and that which gives the routes of the dedication processions (12.31, 37–40). The details of these three more or less tally with each other, but there are difficulties in the way of reconstructing with confidence the actual line of the wall and the siting of some of its landmarks mentioned in these descriptions. In spite of much important archaeological discovery in recent years, we still have a very limited knowledge of the course of the wall in Nehemiah's time and of the position of its gates, corners, and towers, and for that reason we cannot always understand the meaning of the prepositions used in these descriptions, nor do we know for certain whether the description in chapter 3 was written down at the time or from memory some time afterwards; nor do we know whether some of the designations, e.g. 'the Angle', 'the projecting tower', were purely local names for features that had other names elsewhere.

It is not known for certain how large an area of city was enclosed by Nehemiah's walls. Recent excavation has shown that on the eastern side his wall was built on the ridge of the south-eastern hill, even though there had been building extending lower down the slope towards the Kidron gorge before his time (*B.A.*, XXVII (1964), pp. 34–52. It is now generally recognized, in spite of Josephus (*War*, V, iv, 1; *Ant.*, VII, iii, 1), that the south-east hill was the city of David, also known as Mount Zion. On the western side there are two possible lines for Nehemiah's wall. The more likely one runs along the central valley (the Tyropoeon valley), the Valley Gate being identified with the ruins found by Crowfoot in 1927 very nearly opposite the assumed site of the Water Gate due west of the spring Gihon. The size of the enclosed city at this point can be gauged by the fact that it is but one hundred yards across from one wall to the other. The other possible line runs along the western side of the south-west hill (identified by Josephus with Mount Zion), for it is known that during the monarchy the city did extend westwards to include this hill, and it is conceivable that Nehemiah followed the more recent limits of the city.

In spite of these possible alternatives, the descriptions in Nehemiah remain of the utmost significance because there is no comparable description of the topography of Jerusalem within the O.T. Elsewhere there are incidental references to some of the gates and the water sources, but no attempt at a comprehensive description of the outer wall.

Nehemiah left the city at the Valley Gate and went in an anti-clockwise direction to the Kidron gorge. It is not clear whether he retraced his steps from some point in that valley and re-entered the city at the Valley Gate or whether he made a complete circuit but did not register the individual points of progress (see verse 15).

11. three days: see Ezr. 8.15.

12. The inspection was made as quietly as possible, and for that reason he had few men with him and no beast other than his own. He was clearly aware of the fierce opposition that might be put up, opposition such as that which had resulted in the cessation of work on the walls not very long since (Ezr. 4.8–23). Surprise moves were his best weapon.

13. Inspection by night inside and outside the walls would be facilitated by the absence of gates, these being burnt down.

Valley Gate: mentioned also in 2.15; 3.13; 2 Chr. 26.9, where it is recorded that Uzziah built a tower there. The siting of this gate is uncertain: it could be either that discovered by Crowfoot in 1927 and situated on the west side of the south-east hill making an outlet into the central valley, the Tyropoeon, although that valley is nowhere clearly designated in the O.T.; or a gate, yet to be located, somewhere along the wall that ran round the south-west hill, possibly at the south-west corner where the wall would turn with the turn of the valley itself, the valley of Hinnom. As Nehemiah came out of the Valley Gate he turned southward or eastward (depending on where the gate is to be situated) in the direction of En Rogel.

to the Jackal's Well: the preposition is not a simple one in the Hebrew text and should probably be translated 'in the direction of'. Jackal's well is mentioned only here: the Hebrew word, *tannîn*, is translated 'serpent' in Exod. 7.9 and 'monster' in Jer. 51.34; either of these, or possibly 'dragon', would be better here (Jackal is *tan*, pl. *tannîm*). The most likely identification is with the modern *bir Eyyub*, the biblical En Rogel, below the southern end of the south-east hill. Near En Rogel was the stone *Zōḥelet*, the 'Serpent's Stone' (1 Kg. 1.9). To go towards En Rogel Nehemiah would leave the wall in a southerly direction into the valley of Hinnom.

Dung Gate: mentioned again in 3.13, 14; 12.31; it was probably at the south-west tip of the south-east hill, i.e. where the Tyropoeon valley begins to meet the Hinnom valley. An outlet from the city to the refuse dump in that valley might well be called Dung Gate: in Jer. 19.2 it seems to be called Potsherd Gate, possibly a local name.

14. Fountain Gate: since there were only two natural sources of water supply to the south-east hill in ancient times, the spring of Gihon on the eastern side and En Rogel to the south, and since the Water Gate clearly stood above Gihon, the main source of water, Fountain Gate, must be looked for near to En Rogel. It may be that spoken of in 2 Kg. 25.4 as 'the gate between the two walls, by the king's garden'; cf. also 3.15, 12.37.

the King's Pool: this was probably near the king's garden and served as its water supply. The king's garden lay in the Kidron gorge. If this is the proper identification it should not be confused with the lower pool (or old pool) (Isa. 22.8–11), or with the traditional pool of Siloam. The pool called 'the Pool of Shelah of the king's garden' in 3.15 is probably the lower pool or the (earlier) pool of Siloam. (The name 'pool of Siloam' seems to have been transferred to Hezekiah's reservoir at some time later than Nehemiah.)

no place for the beast . . . to pass: i.e. because of ruins.

15. valley: i.e. the Kidron.

and I turned back and entered: this implies that he did not at this time make a complete circuit of the walls and therefore a complete inspection. But it is possible to translate the Hebrew phrase 'and I re-entered', which would then allow the possibility of a complete circuit without specifying the individual points of progress.

16. officials: see on Ezr. 9.2.

that were to do the work: the Hebrew phrase, by usage, is capable of meaning 'those who would be responsible for the work'; cf. Ezr. 3.9, and also the description of Jeroboam in 1 Kg. 11.28 as 'industrious', i.e. one who could get a job done. Nehemiah would scarcely be talking to the ordinary workmen at this time.

RESOLVE TO BEGIN WORK AND MOCKERY FROM SANBALLAT AND HIS ASSOCIATES
2.17–20

18. hand of my God: see Ezr. 7.6.

for the good work: or, 'to good purpose'.

19. Geshem the Arab: in the Hebrew at 6.6 the form Gashmu occurs. The name could be identified with, or associated with, the name Geshem of a king of Kedar whose son's name, Cain, is inscribed in Aramaic on a silver vessel dedicated to an Arabian goddess. Another inscription mentions a Geshem together with the Persian governor of Dedan. The inscriptions are believed to date from the end of the fifth century B.C. (*B.A.*, XVIII (1955), p. 46). The name means 'Bulky', 'Stout'. **Sanballat** and his associates first tried intimidation by mockery.

20. Nehemiah, safe in the knowledge that he had the king's authority, could afford to ignore their charge that he was rebelling against the king, but they too would feel themselves to be on safe ground—had not their friends successfully sought the king's intervention not very long before (Ezr. 4.7, 8–23)?

portion: cf. the cry of revolt in 2 Sam. 20.1; 1 Kg. 12.16.

right: a claim that could be upheld by law.

memorial: some traditional standing, the outcome of loyal citizenship or outstanding duty performed and recorded.

DETAILS OF THE REPAIR WORK GIVING THE NAMES OF THE BUILDERS' LEADERS AND WHERE THEY WORKED 3.1–32

This is the most detailed specification of the wall of Jerusalem that is found in the Bible. It may be assumed that the record follows the line of the wall, not only piecemeal but in sequence. The description follows an anti-clockwise route round the city wall. In addition to the difficulty in locating every specified gate, tower, or stretch of wall, there are difficulties in establishing the meaning of some of the terms used and also of the implication of some of the prepositions. It may be noted here that on the west and north sides the sections repaired by the individual gangs are in general specified in relation to the several existing gates, while on the east, where Nehemiah seems not to have followed the previous line of wall but to have built on the ridge of the hill, the references are to private houses.

1. Eliashib: was the son of Joiakim son of Joshua the contemporary of Zerubbabel; cf. 12.10; Hag. 1.1; see Ezr. 10.6. His house is mentioned in verse 20. **Sheep Gate:** is mentioned also in verse 32; 12.39 (and Jn 5.2). It was probably at the eastern end of the north wall, as near the north-east corner as may be to allow room for the other named features on the north wall. It was not far from the Temple, and may have been near the sheep market, but whether that market was for sacrificial victims or not cannot be said. This may have been the gate called the Benjamin Gate before the exile; see Jer. 20.2; 37.13; 38.7; Zech. 14.10 (see also the note on verse 31).

consecrated: this is the only mention of consecrating while the work was being done and seems unlikely at this stage. A slight change (from *ḳiddᵉšûhû* to *ḳērᵉšûhû*) would enable us to translate 'laid its beams', which would be more in keeping with the context.

Tower of the Hundred: is mentioned again in 12.39, but is otherwise unknown. The next phrase, **as far as the Tower of Hananel**, is not attached by the conjunction and may therefore be in apposition and explanatory. The Tower of the Hundred may therefore be a popular name for the Tower of Hananel, which, according to Jer. 31.38 and Zech. 14.10, was the most northerly point of the city. The Hundred may refer to a military unit; cf. Dt. 1.15. Had this tower anything to do with the fortress of the Temple; see 2.8?

2. the men of Jericho: this may mean Israelites who could not be registered in well-established clans or families; cf. Ezr. 2.21–35. **Zaccur the son of Imri:** the only other Imri mentioned is a Judahite (1 Chr. 9.4). It is not clear whether Imri is here intended to be a family name rather than that of an individual; this is certainly the case with Pahath-moab and Harim in verse 11 and of Parosh in verse 25. The name Imri may mean 'tall' or 'eloquent', or it may be a short form of Amariah (Ezr. 7.3), or it may be an alternative form of Immer (Ezr. 2.37). Nothing further is known of this Zaccur, but it was not an uncommon name; see Ezr. 8.14.

3. sons of Hassenaah: see Ezr. 2.35.

Fish Gate: if this is the gate through which the merchants from Tyre brought in their fish (13.16), a suitable place for it would be the northern end of the Tyropoeon valley. In 2 Chr. 33.14 we are told that Manasseh 'built an outer wall to the city of David west of Gihon, in the valley, to the entrance by the Fish Gate, and carried it round Ophel'. Zephaniah 1.10 mentions it along with the Second Quarter, which was probably a northern extension of the city.

4. Meremoth the son of Uriah, son of Hakkoz: according to Ezr. 2.59, 61 (Neh. 7.61, 63) the sons of Hakkoz 'could not prove their fathers' houses or their descent'. They were priests (cf. 1 Chr. 24.10). Meremoth is probably the only man who can be shown to have shared in the work of both Ezra and Nehemiah. When Ezra came to Jerusalem he entrusted the silver and gold vessels to a priest, Meremoth son of Uriah (Ezr. 8.33). In Nehemiah's time Meremoth son of Uriah repaired two sections (3.4, 21). Meremoth is not a very common name (see note on Ezr. 8.33) and it is possible to identify these two, although there is no urgent necessity to do so. If Ezra returned nearly fifty years later than Nehemiah, then Meremoth, who in his youthful zeal had repaired two sections of wall, would be a suitable person in old age to appoint as treasurer. If they are not to be identified, then the one will be a later descendant in the same line.

Meshullam the son of Berechiah, son of Meshezabel: according to 6.18 his daughter married Jehohanan son of Tobiah (the Ammonite). Meshullam was a much-used name; cf. Ezr. 8.16. Meshullam seems to have repaired a second section, verse 30. **Berechiah** is probably a short form of Jeberechiah (Isa. 8.2), 'May Yahweh bless'. **Meshezabel** is one of very few Hebrew proper names that contain a participle; the root of the participle used here comes from Accadian through Aramaic, a fact which reflects the growing influence of Aramaic in postexilic times; cf. 6.10. The name means 'God is deliverer/delivering', and occurs only in this verse and in 10.21 and 11.24.

Zadok the son of Baana: both names are used for five or six different men; for Zadok, cf. verse 29 and Ezr. 7.2, and for Baana, cf. Ezr. 2.2 (Baanah): it is not possible to identify this Zadok with any other of the name.

5. the Tekoites: for repairs done by a town group, cf. verse 2, the men of Jericho. But unlike Jericho, Tekoa is not listed in Ezr. 2 (or Neh. 7). Were there none of those who had returned among its inhabitants, and was that why their nobles did not put their necks to the work? Did they distrust the leaders in Jerusalem? If it is meant as a sneer, it seems somewhat misplaced since the Tekoites also built a second section, verse 27.

Lord: i.e. God; the margin reading 'lords' would mean the leaders in Jerusalem and would include Nehemiah. It would not be inconsistent with Hebrew usage to translate it in the singular 'lord'; Nehemiah would then be meant.

6. Joiada the son of Paseah: apart from Joiada son of Eliashib (12.10, etc.), this is the only mention of a Joiada. It is a form of Jehoiada, 'Yahweh has known/cared for'. The father's name Paseah occurs as that of a Judahite in 1 Chr. 4.12 and as the family name of Temple servants in Ezr. 2.49. Since the Temple servants repaired elsewhere, verse 26, this Joiada was probably not one of them. Nothing more is known of him.

Meshullam the son of Besodeiah: on the name Meshullam, see verse 4 and Ezr. 8.16. This is the only mention of the name Besodeiah, which means 'In the counsel/friendship/intimacy of Yahweh'; cf. Ps. 25.14.

the Old Gate: this name is used only here and 12.39. There are at least four opinions on the meaning of the Hebrew: (a) as translated, but the grammar is against this since the word translated 'old' is an adjective and feminine and 'gate' before it makes it a genitive; (b) the Gate of the Old City, 'city' being understood as the feminine noun, which the feminine adjective qualifies—this will imply that there was a part of the city in Nehemiah's time which could be thought of as 'new' in distinction from the 'old'; (c) the Gate of *Jeshanah*, Jeshanah being a place on the Judah-Israel frontier (2 Chr. 13:19); and (d) by slight emendation (*ša‘ar ham-mišneh*) it can be made to mean the Gate to the Second Quarter (see note on verse 3 and cf. 2 Kg. 22.14). The gate was situated on the north-west corner of the city. In 12.39 one procession, moving clockwise, came to the Old Gate after passing the Ephraim Gate (not mentioned here), and in 2 Kg. 14.13 the Ephraim Gate is mentioned next to the Corner Gate: was the Old Gate the Corner Gate (but see verse 11)?

7. Melatiah the Gibeonite: this is the only use of the name Melatiah, which means 'Yahweh has set free/delivered'; from the reference to Gibeonite we may suppose that he had the men of Gibeon under him.

Jadon the Meronothite: Jadon possibly means 'Thin'; the name occurs only here (in 1 Chr. 27.30 there is a Jehdeiah the Meronothite). It looks as if Jadon stood in relation to the men of Mizpah as Melatiah did to those of Gibeon, in which case Meronoth, which is otherwise unknown, must be identifiable in some way with Mizpah. Mizpah means 'look-out point', and it is not surprising that several places should have been so named (cf. verses 15, 19).

who were under the jurisdiction of: the Hebrew literally means 'to (or, according to) the seat of': if 'seat' here means authority, then RSV is a natural enough paraphrase to bring out the meaning, but if it here means the place where the authority was exercised, then 'to the seat of' may designate that part of the wall which ran to the 'Residence' and which was repaired by the Gibeonites and the men of Mizpah.

province Beyond the River: see Ezr. 4.10.

8. Uzziel the son of Harhaiah: Harhaiah is of unknown meaning and occurs only here. Uzziel means 'God is (my) strength'; there are six men so named, of whom this is the only one in post-exilic times.

goldsmiths: the plural is ungrammatical after the single name. Syriac has 'one of the goldsmiths', similar to the phrase 'one of the perfumers' in the next clause, and this is probably right. Goldsmiths occur again in verses 31–2.

Hananiah: a fairly common name; see Ezr. 10.28. This is one of the few names in the chapter that are not further defined either by the father's name or the family name or by reference to the men who worked with them.

perfumers: in 1 Sam. 8.13 perfumers, cooks, and bakers are mentioned as trades for which daughters might be taken by the king.

restored: the same verb (*'āzaḇ*) as that translated 'help' at Exod. 23.5. The marginal reading 'abandoned' translates another and much commoner verb with the same spelling, but it is clearly not suited to the context.

Broad Wall: part of the wall lying between the Old Gate and the Tower of the Ovens (verse 11). The only other reference to it is in 12.38, where it lies between the Gate of Ephraim and the Tower of the Ovens. Was the wall at this point doubly reinforced for greater protection? A slight emendation (to read *ša'ar hā-rᵉḥōḇ*) would give 'the Gate of the Square'; according to 8.16 there was a square at the Gate of Ephraim.

9. Rephaiah the son of Hur: this is the only post-exilic use of either name, although both are used several times before the exile. Rephaiah means 'Yahweh has healed' and Hur appears to be an Accadian loan-name meaning 'Child'.

district: a word used in this way only in this chapter in biblical Hebrew; in 2 Sam. 3.29 and Prov. 31.19 it means 'spindle'. The ruler of the other half is mentioned in verse 12. To judge by the references to Mizpah in verses 15, 19 the territory designated 'district' may have been distinct from the town or city.

10. Jedaiah the son of Harumaph: the name Jedaiah occurs otherwise only in 1 Chr. 4.37 as the name of a Simeonite chief, and Harumaph only here. Jedaiah is spelt differently from the Jedaiah of Ezr. 2.36; the meaning is uncertain, but may perhaps be 'Yahweh has shown himself powerful'. Harumaph means 'Split-nose'.

opposite his house: as did several others, verses 23, 28, 29(30), all, except this one, being on the eastern side.

Hattush the son of Hashabneiah: for the name Hattush, see Ezr.8.2. Hashabneiah, perhaps meaning 'Yahweh has taken account of (me)', occurs only here and in Neh. 9.5, where it is the name of a Levite. It may be a fuller form of the name Hashabnah, 10.25, and perhaps also of Hashabiah, 3.17; see Ezr. 8.19.

11. Malchijah the son of Harim: two other Malchijahs occur in this list, one in verse 14, the son of Rechab, and one in verse 31, a goldsmith. See Ezr. 10.25 for the name. There was a Malchijah of the sons of Harim in Ezr. 10.31, one of those who had married foreign women. If Nehemiah and Ezra were shown to be contemporaries, these might be the same person, but they need not be identified if it be assumed that in one case Harim is a family name and in the other the father's name. On the other hand, Harim is a family name in every other place; see Ezr. 2.39.

Hasshub the son of Pahath-moab: Hasshub may be regarded as a shortened form of Hashabiah; see verse 10 and Ezr. 8.19. Another Hasshub occurs in verse 23; otherwise the name occurs only as a Levite name (Neh. 10.23; 11.15; 1 Chr. 9.14). Pahath-moab occurs elsewhere only as a family name (Ezr. 2.6; 8.4; 10.30; Neh. 7.11; 10.14); it may therefore be a family name here also.

another section: lit. a second section; this would naturally imply that these two men had already repaired one section, but there is no mention of it. Reference to 'another section' is made also in verses 19, 20, 21, 24, 27, 30; in two of these (verses 21 and 27), and a third (verse 24), if Binnui be read in verse 18, the men have already been named as repairing a previous section and the term can be taken at its face value. In this verse and in verses 19, 20, 30 it is unlikely that the term can have its face value, unless we assume that the text is so badly corrupt that at least four references, i.e. to the previous sections built in each of the four cases, have dropped out. A possible meaning is 'a further section', i.e. adjacent to the one just mentioned in verse 10.

Tower of the Ovens: Nehemiah is the only author to mention this tower by name. It may be the one Uzziah built at the Corner Gate (2 Chr. 26.9), in which case the suggested identification of the Old Gate with the Corner Gate (verse 6) would not stand. The ovens may have been the bakers' ovens situated in Bakers' Street (Jer. 37.21).

12. **Shallum the son of Hallohesh:** on the name Shallum, see Ezr. 2.42. Hallohesh is, in form, a participle and may mean 'Whisperer' or 'Snake-charmer', 'Magician'; it occurs again only in 10.24, and is doubtless a family name indicative, at least in origin, of the family trade.

ruler of half the district: cf. verse 9.

daughters: this is the only mention of women helping in the work. If he had no sons it would be natural for the daughters to help on an occasion like this, since they would inherit his name and property (Num. 36.8).

13. **Hanun:** 'Favoured'; is one of two wall-builders so named (verse 30), other-wise the name is used only of an Ammonite chief (2 Sam. 10.1–4; 1 Chr. 19.2–6).

Zanoah: 11.30, Jos. 15.34, lies in the lowland of Judah, south-west of Jerusalem.

Valley Gate: see 2.13, 15.

a thousand cubits: this must at the very least be regarded as a round figure; assuming nearly eighteen inches for the cubit, it gives us nearly 500 yards. About forty teams were at work in all, but it is quite clear that each team would not have repaired as great a length. One possibility is that this stretch of wall was in much less need of repair than most.

Dung Gate: see 2.13.

14. **Malchijah the son of Rechab:** see verse 11 for the name Malchijah. Three people are named Rechab, 'Rider', or 'Chariotry', in the O.T.: (a) the ancestor of the Rechabites (2 Kg. 10.15, 23; Jer. 35.6), (b) son of Rimmon a Benjaminite (2 Sam. 4.2), and (c) this one, who is otherwise unknown, but probably not a Rechabite in the technical sense.

Beth-haccherem: a town about 3 miles S. of Jerusalem; the name implies that it was a district of vineyards.

15. **Shallum the son of Col-hozeh:** for Shallum (Hebrew, *Shallun*), see verse 12; Col-hozeh is mentioned only here and in 11.5; it means 'Every seer' or 'Every one a seer' and suggests a family of seers.

Mizpah: see verse 7.

Fountain Gate: see 2.14.

the pool of Shelah of the king's garden: Shelah (*šelaḥ*) is to be equated with (or revocalized to) Shiloah (*šilōaḥ*)=Siloam (Isa. 8.6). The most likely identification of the pool of Siloam is with the 'lower pool' (Isa. 22.9), the present *birket-el-ḥamra*, to which the water from Gihon was led by an open canal. The name Siloam must at some stage later than Nehemiah have been transferred from this pool to the one made by Hezekiah for his tunnel conduit, which is the pool commonly meant by 'Siloam'. The pool of Shelah is described as 'of the king's garden' because it was adjacent to that garden and may have helped to supply water for the garden in addition to the King's Pool, 2.14.

the king's garden: was situated at the southern end of the Kidron gorge outside the city walls, access being given through the 'gate between the two walls' (2 Kg. 25.4). The king's wine presses, which were at the southernmost point of the city according to Zech. 14.10, may have stood by the city wall.

the stairs that go down from the City of David: it has already been said that the City of David was almost certainly situated on the south-east hill, as is clearly demonstrated by the several attempts to ensure its water supply in time of siege. During excavations by Weill in 1923–24 steps were discovered at the southern end of the hill which appear to have gone through a smallish opening in the city wall giving access to and from the city. See also 12.37.

16. Nehemiah the son of Azbuk: see 1.1 for the name Nehemiah. Azbuk occurs only here; if the name is similar in construction to Azgad (Ezr. 2.12), it may mean 'Buk is strong', Buk being taken as the name of a non-Israelite god otherwise unknown.

Beth-zur: lies some 13 miles S. of Jerusalem. The other half of Beth-zur is not included in this list; has it dropped out in transmission?

sepulchres of David: cf. 2 Chr. 32.33, 'tombs of the sons of David', and 2 Chr. 21.20, 'tombs of the kings': from 1 Kg. 2.10 we know that David was buried in the City of David. It is not possible to locate them more exactly.

artificial pool: probably the King's Pool, 2.14.

house of the mighty men: this may be the guard house (for the guard of the royal tombs?), or, being adjacent to David's Sepulchres, it may be a memorial to David's 'mighty men', his heroes.

17. Rehum the son of Bani: for the name Rehum, see Ezr. 2.2, and for Bani, Ezr. 2.10.

Hashabiah: see Ezr. 8.19.

Keilah: some 15 miles SW. of Jerusalem in the Shephelah; cf. Jos. 15.44; 1 Sam. 23.1.

for his district: it is to be assumed that few Levites had been deported to Babylon (see Ezr. 8.15) and that those left behind, with no official duties to perform, had accepted other duties: this one was officer for the district.

18. their brethren: either other Levites under the leadership of Bavvai, or the Jews from the other half-district of Keilah.

Bavvai: occurs only here; its meaning is unknown and the Greek transliterations vary. One of the latter, *benei*, supports the reading of two Hebrew MSS. and Syr., Bani. There is already a son of Bani among the builders, however, and it is thought that this may be an error for Binnui; cf. verse 24, where Binnui the son of Henadad occurs as building a second section. For the name Binnui, see Ezr. 2.10, 40; 8.33.
Henadad: see Ezr. 3.9.

19. Ezer: this may be a shortened form of Azariah (Ezr. 7.1); there are four other men in the O.T. with this name: (a) a Judahite (1 Chr. 4.4), (b) one of David's heroes (1 Chr. 12.10), (c) an Ephraimite (1 Chr. 7.21), and (d) a priest (Neh. 12.42).
son of Jeshua: does this mean of the family of Jeshua? In the previous verse Henadad is almost certainly to be regarded as a family name. Jeshua is a Levite family name in Ezr. 2.40 and possibly also in Ezr. 3.9.
ruler of Mizpah: i.e. of the town, cf. verse 15.
another section: see verse 11.
armoury: this is not otherwise known, but it is not inappropriate that it should be not far from the house of the mighty men, verse 16.
the Angle: this word (*miḳṣōaʿ*) is not the same as that (*pinnāh*) translated 'corner' in verses 31–32. The Angle seems to have been an identifiable part of the wall; cf. 2 Chr. 26.9 (where we are told that Uzziah built a tower there). There appears to be a further part of the wall called 'the Angle' mentioned in verses 24–25. The word may mean either escarpment or corner, but it is impossible to say which of the two is meant here. If it is a corner, then it may be a turn in the wall or it may be a place where an inner wall joins the outer wall.
20. after him: in the Hebrew a word meaning 'heated' stands next and is probably to be regarded as a dittograph of the word for 'repaired'.
Baruch: 'Blessed'; apart from Jeremiah's friend and secretary, this name occurs (a) as the name of a priest, here and 10.6 (a family name), and (b) as that of a Judahite layman, son of Colhozeh, 11.5.
Zabbai: a man of this name had a foreign wife (Ezr. 10.28); otherwise the name does not occur elsewhere. Another reading in Hebrew MSS. is Zaccai (see Ezr. 2.9).
another section: see verse 11.
house of Eliashib: for Eliashib, see verse 1 and Ezr. 10.6. Why was his house so far from the Temple? and why did not Eliashib build by his own house?

21. Meremoth: see verse 4.

22. priests: distinguished from those who assisted Eliashib (verse 1) by being described as 'men of the Plain'. The word for 'Plain' usually describes the Jordan valley on the west side of the river (Gen. 13.10f., 19.17; RSV has 'valley' in both), and this is apparently how the Syriac version understood it. However, the same word is used in 12.28 of land 'round Jerusalem' and is there translated 'circuit'. The same district is probably meant here.

23. Benjamin: in post-exilic times the name is that of (a) one of the sons of Harim who had married a foreign wife (Ezr. 10.32), (b) a wall-builder (here), and (c) a priest (Neh. 12.34).

Hasshub: see verse 11.

opposite their house: see verse 10: did they live together? or is the Hebrew word meant to be taken collectively? It was noted at the beginning of the chapter that along the east wall, where Nehemiah was apparently not following the previous line of wall, reference to position is given by private houses and not by gates or other points of the old wall.

Azariah: see Ezr. 7.1.

Maaseiah: see Ezr. 10.18.

Ananiah: only here, but Anan occurs in 10.26 and Anani in 1 Chr. 3.24, both being possible abbreviations of it. The name probably means 'Yahweh has answered (me)', but for that meaning the second *n* is unexpected; another possibility is to assume a root *'nn*, 'to meet face to face'; the name might then mean 'Yahweh has presented himself'.

   24. Binnui: see verse 18.

Angle: see verse 19.

   25. corner: this particular part of the wall went round (the) Ophel (see verse 27), and there may well have been a projecting part of the wall with projecting corners.

Palal: occurs only here; the name seems to be a short form of Pelaliah (11.12) meaning 'Yahweh has interposed/judged'.

Uzai: occurs only here; it may be a short form of a name like Azaniah (10.9), 'Yahweh has listened', but it could equally well be a short form of other names.

opposite the Angle and the tower projecting: it is not clear what part of the wall could be described as 'opposite the Angle'. The tower mentioned here may well have been built as a defence for the water supply at Gihon, the Water Gate being the next specified point. Remains of towers of different ages have been found along the eastern ridge, but cannot be confidently identified with the towers mentioned here.

upper house of the king: presumably an alternative residence for the king to be distinguished from that known as 'the house of David', 12.37.

court of the guard: also mentioned in Jer. 32.2.

Pedaiah: 'Yahweh has redeemed'; a name belonging to at least seven men; cf. 8.4, 11.7.

Parosh: the name of a family in post-exilic times; see Ezr. 2.3.

   26. temple servants living on Ophel: the conjectured change of text (from 'were living', RSV margin) is necessary if the phrase is to be retained here, but it occurs also in 11.21, where it is in a more likely context and it may have crept in here from that place. If we omit the phrase the text that remains is quite natural: 'After him Pedaiah the son of Parosh repaired to a point opposite the Water Gate. . . .'

Water Gate: the gate in the city wall nearest the spring Gihon. There was a large square in front of it used for gatherings (8.1).

projecting tower: was there a second tower, or is this a second reference to the same tower (verse 25)?

Note: The use of the term 'opposite' in this and the previous verse has led some to think that at this point the Temple wall came close to the city wall, and that the tower and the gate were on the Temple wall. On the other hand Nehemiah was in all probability building on a new line west of the previous wall and therefore these sections may well be described as opposite the (ruins of) the Water Gate and projecting tower.

27. Tekoites: see verse 5.
the great projecting tower: is this yet a third tower?
the wall of Ophel: Ophel was a mount forming a southern continuation of the Temple hill. The name simply means 'swelling' and can be applied, topographically, to what might otherwise be called an 'eminence'. 2 Kg. 5.24 speaks of one at Samaria (RSV 'hill'). 2 Chr. 33.14 shows it to have been distinct from the City of David and to have been walled in by Manasseh. That the Temple servants lived there probably implies proximity to the Temple. Cf. also 2 Chr. 27.3.

28. Above the Horse Gate: 'above' probably means 'north of'. 2 Kg. 11.16 might be thought to suggest that the Horse Gate was the entrance to the city for the particular use of palace traffic. According to Jer. 31.40 it was the easternmost point of the city towards the Kidron gorge.
priests: this is doubtless a third group, distinguishable from those in verses 1, 22.
own house: see verse 10.

29. Zadok: see verse 4, where another Zadok is mentioned as a wall-builder.
Immer: a priestly family; see Ezr. 2.37.
Shemaiah: see Ezr. 8.13.
Shecaniah: is this man to be identified with the father-in-law of Tobiah, 6.18? It is, however, a fairly common name (see Ezr. 8.3) and may here be a family name. There is a Shemaiah son of Shecaniah among the descendants of Jehoiachin in 1 Chr. 3.22, but there is no reason to identify them; this one is a priest.
keeper of the East Gate: this was the East Gate of the Temple (Ezek. 40.6, 10): Shemaiah was repairing part of the city wall and not the gate of the Temple of which he was keeper.

30. Hananiah: see verse 8 and Ezr. 10.28.
Shelemiah: see Ezr. 10.39.
Hanun: see verse 13.
Zalaph: 'Caper-plant'; the name occurs only here.
sixth: it is unusual to specify which son.
another section: see verse 11.
Meshullam: see verse 4 and Ezr. 8.16.
chamber: the word used here implies that this was one of the Temple chambers (cf. 13.5, 7; Ezr. 10.6).

31. Malchijah: see verse 11.
goldsmiths: see verse 8.
house of the temple servants: since the Temple servants lived on (the) Ophel

(11.21), this must refer to a house near the Temple that they occupied when on duty.

merchants: being near the Temple it is pertinent to ask whether these men engaged in the necessary business connected with the Temple services.

Muster Gate: this gate is not readily identifiable; there are three suggestions to note: (a) if the mustering is that of troops or guards it may be another name for the Gate of the Guard (12.39), (b) it may be the Benjamin Gate situated just south of the north-east corner of the city (Jer. 37.12f.; Zech. 14.10), and (c) it may be another name for the Sheep Gate (see verse 1). It is not certain that the word (*Hammipķāḏ*) does mean muster; in Ezek. 43.21 it means the appointed place where the sin-offering is to be burnt.

upper chamber of the corner: this seems to have been a well-known room on the wall. Possibly the wall widened at the corner and gave room for such a chamber. The word commonly means a roof chamber; cf. 1 Kg. 17.19, 2 Kg. 4.10f.

32. Sheep Gate: see verse 1.

OBSTACLES WHICH NEHEMIAH HAD TO FACE BOTH FROM OUTSIDE
THE COMMUNITY AND WITHIN IT **4.1–6.19**

TROUBLE-MAKING BY SANBALLAT **4.1–23**

1. Sanballat: see 2.10.

angry and greatly enraged: since rebuilding would help to make Jerusalem and Judah secure and independent and would tend to undermine his authority.

ridiculed: cf. 2.19 (there translated 'derided').

2. brethren: a word used frequently in Deuteronomy to mean fellow countrymen. It may not have quite so wide a meaning here, but it is certain to mean more than his immediate kinsmen and will include his associates in the administration of affairs.

army of Samaria: its presence indicates that this must have been an official assembly.

restore things: on 'restore' see 3.8. 'Things' implies the rebuilding of the walls and defences.

sacrifice: may mean either (a) will they make a foundation sacrifice? or (b) will they sacrifice in the belief that the job will be as good as done if God is propitiated?

finish up in a day: i.e. bring all their labours to a finish in one day as their zeal and the urgency of the situation demanded.

revive the stones: the burnt stones will have lost their goodness; will they put new life into them? Where will all the material come from?

3. Tobiah: see 2.10.

4. The memoir suddenly introduces a prayer for help against opposition: apparently Nehemiah refrained from answering their gibes. For the strong trust in God that underlies this resort to prayer, cf. 4.20; 5.15.

5. Do not cover their guilt: and thus treat it as negligible and not deserving punishment. Covering guilt is also tantamount to forgiveness; cf. Ps. 85.2 (Hebrew 'cover', RSV 'pardon'). This mood is fully in keeping with O.T. piety; cf. Jer. 51.63f.; Ps. 137.8f., and also the 'vindictive' psalms.

provoked thee: the pronoun is not expressed in the Hebrew and it may be that the original meaning was 'for they have made a show of anger before the builders'. If, on the other hand, it is right to supply the pronoun, it means that God feels his people's calamity.

6. While the ridicule was being cast on Nehemiah and his men, the builders got on so well with their work that they had the wall half-way up before Sanballat realized that he would have to take more drastic steps if he was to make successful opposition.

7. Sanballat was now joined by others: Arabs, i.e. Bedouin tribes dwelling to the south of Jerusalem and Judah (cf. Geshem the Arab, 2.19), the Ammonites from the east, and Philistines from the west, from Ashdod. The reference to Ashdod in 13.23f. suggests that Ashdod had become the principal Philistine city by this time. It is not clear whether the opponents were on Jewish territory or not, but verse 12 reads as if they were. The danger that these opponents saw was probably twofold: (a) they would lose any further chance of encroachment on Jewish territory; and (b) they might be pushed out of whatever territory they had gained if the Jews grew really strong; cf. Ezr. 9.1.

8. fight against: possibly with the success of the attack referred to in Ezr. 4.23 in mind, and thinking that their action would be upheld by the Persian king and authorities.

9–10. After meeting the external menace Nehemiah is faced with an internal one —failing spirits among the Jews.

10. Judah: i.e. the inhabitants of Judah. Disheartening rumours were probably spreading, or being spread by the enemies, among the people. The enemy taunts were taking effect.

11. The enemies trusted in the Jews' concentration and single-minded purpose.

12. lived by them: either on the outskirts of Jewish territory adjacent to these countries, or, the enemy had encroached on that territory and Jews were still living there.

ten times: i.e. time and time again.

they live: this is a necessary change (reading yēšᵉḇû for tāšûḇû) demanded by the sense: the Hebrew 'you return' can yield no meaning in the context.

they will come up: this addition (yaʿᵃlû), also demanded by the sense, is made on the evidence of LXX and Syriac.

13. The uncertainty in the Hebrew text continues into this verse. The verse begins with 'So I stationed', which is repeated half-way through the verse (but translated once only by RSV). If the first verb were emended to wᵉʿāmᵉdû, 'and they will station themselves', we get an easy description of what was expected to happen: 'they will come up against us and will station themselves on the lowest levels behind (i.e. on the other side of) the wall in open places. So I stationed the people. . . .' This avoids repetition of the verb 'I stationed', or ignoring it as RSV does, and makes the existence of open places more natural outside the wall than inside.

14. nobles and . . . officials: see 2.16; Ezr. 9.2.

great and terrible: see 1.5.

15. It is typical of Nehemiah's memoir that he acknowledges the help that comes from God.

16. Vigilance could not be relaxed; the relief implied in verse 15 could only be regarded as temporary.

my servants: Nehemiah probably means all the men at work, but the Hebrew word (*na'ar*) is a flexible one; cf. its use in verse 23; 5.10, 16; 13.19 (= 'servants').

17. RSV is to be preferred to RV in taking the first clause with verse 16. It was natural for the porters, being more mobile and in better position to ward off attack, to have their weapons to hand.

laboured on the work: this must be understood to mean attending to the load they were carrying.

18. trumpet: anticipating verse 20.

20. Instruction in case of emergency. Nehemiah evidently expected to be able to reach the danger-spot quickly and early enough to give warning.

Our God will fight: see on verses 4, 15.

21. till the stars came out: an extra long day; the usual time to stop being sunset (Dt. 24.15; Mt. 20.1–12).

23. my servants: see verse 16; here the word is used in the narrower sense of his own personal staff.

the guard: probably meaning those posted as such in verse 22, but it could mean a Persian guard allotted to Nehemiah as governor.

in his hand: this emendation is clearly preferable to the corrupted Hebrew text. Another suggested emendation, much closer to the Hebrew, is 'kept his right hand on' (reading *hêmîn* for *hammayim*).

FINANCIAL PROBLEMS WITHIN THE COMMUNITY 5.1–19

Although no mention of it has been made so far, this chapter shows that Nehemiah had been appointed governor (verse 14). There appear to be three separate complaints. As the text at present stands they are: (a) the extremity of the need for food (verse 2), (b) mortgaging land and houses for food (verse 3), and (c) selling children into slavery to pay the king's tax on fields and vineyards (verses 4, 5). Another way of taking the text (see below for details) reshapes these complaints in this way: (a) giving their children into pledge to buy food (verse 2), (b) mortgaging property to buy food (verse 3), and (c) mortgaging fields and vineyards to pay the king's tax (verse 4). In this way verse 5 becomes a summary of the plight of all three groups.

2. This, as worded, is not really a complaint and there is nothing in the Hebrew text for 'with'. It is possible that the word now translated 'many' is miswritten for a word meaning 'pledging' (reading '*ōrᵉbîm* for *rabbîm*), the word which, in verse 3, is translated 'mortgaging'. They were losing their daily earnings by concentrating on the building of the wall and they had to raise money somehow. If this slight change is accepted the verse may be translated: 'We are giving our sons and daughters as pledges so as to buy grain to eat and keep ourselves alive.' This is now a genuine complaint. Such pledging of children was probably not a new thing: treatment of Hebrew slaves had been regulated by law; cf. Exod. 21.2; Dt. 15.12.

3. The second group had property but, because of the 'famine' produced by lack of workers on the land while the wall-building was in progress, were obliged to mortgage their property to pay for their food.

4. A third group complained of the burden of the king's tax. The present form of the Hebrew text has the two words translated by 'our fields and our vineyards' at the end of the verse unattached. RSV has supplied the preposition 'upon'. This assumes that the king's tax was a kind of land tax, but it could have been any other kind of tax intended for payment into central funds in addition to the taxes that would be levied to meet the satrap's requirements for local purposes. One recension of LXX (the Lucianic) takes the unattached words with 'we have borrowed money'; this seems to be preferable, and it demands no more than the supplying of a preposition as does RSV's rendering. We may then translate: 'We have borrowed money on our fields and vineyards to pay the king's tax.'

5. If the reconstruction suggested in the previous verses (2 and 4) is justified, this verse can be treated, not as part of what the third group said, but as a summary of the situation in which all three groups find themselves.

it is not in our power: lit. 'it is not according to the strength of our hand'.

6. Nehemiah's anger at this plight is natural enough.

7. took counsel with myself: self-reliance was one of Nehemiah's strong points; cf. 2.11ff. It was demanded of him by the situations he had to face.

the nobles and the officials: see 2.16. This verse identifies them with the people called Jewish brethren in verse 1, but in the next verse their victims are also called Jewish brethren, it being a flexible term.

exacting interest: it is possible that the word refers not to interest on money loans but to pledges of persons against loans; this would be in keeping with the nature of the first complaint.

held a great assembly: but an assembly is out of place here; what Nehemiah was doing was giving the leaders a piece of his mind, and the word here translated 'assembly' can be connected with an Arabic root and bear the meaning 'rebuke', hence: 'I gave them a severe rebuke.'

8. bought back: as urged in the law (Lev. 25.47f.).

that they may be sold to us: implying 'and they will have to be bought back by us'.

10. Nehemiah is admitting that he and his kinsmen have been no less guilty than the other leaders and that he is willing to discontinue immediately.

11. hundredth: it is not certain what can be meant; so far there has been no mention of what might be termed a percentage interest, families and lands have been pledged. The Hebrew word may be a corruption of a word meaning 'what is taken from' (reading *mass'aṭ* for *m^e'aṭ*), i.e. the gain or income from the pledged and mortgaged lands. (The only way to interpret hundredth to give sense is to assume that it means a hundredth per month, i.e. 12 per cent.)

12. the priests: to witness or administer the oath.

of them: i.e. the people concerned. Nehemiah took this step to ensure that they would not regret their decision and go back on their word.

13. shook out my lap: a gesture comparable with an acted prophecy to actualize the spoken word. The 'lap' was the fold of the garment which served in lieu of a pocket.

Amen: cf. the use of 'Amen' in the recital of curses in Dt. 27.15–26; cf. also Neh. 8.6, where it is used in an act of praise.

the people: presumably the Jewish brethren of verse 1 are meant here.

14. twentieth year to the thirty-second year: i.e. 444 to 432 B.C. This verse implies that he spent the whole of the twelve years in Jerusalem, but it is not at all certain that he did do so and it is difficult to imagine that when asked to set a time in 2.6 he could have said it would be twelve years. 13.6 would tend to confirm a long stay. This is the first intimation that Nehemiah was governor. (See also on 13.4.)

food allowance: this would be a statutory charge on the province. When Nehemiah couples his brethren with him he may mean his own near kinsmen or he may be using the word in a wider sense to include those fellow Jews who were in attendance on him. The latter is the more probable.

15. former governors: nothing is known of these since the time of Zerubbabel.

besides: the Hebrew text does not yield a clear meaning here: the word properly means 'after' and not 'besides'. The Vulgate seems to have read, or understood, 'for one day' (*l^eyôm 'eḥāḏ* for *'aḥar*). If we were to accept this reading, and in addition read the preposition that stands before 'food'—untranslated in RSV—as 'tribute' (reading *b^elô* for *b^e*) we could translate: 'and took from them tribute of food and wine, forty shekels worth in silver per day'.

forty shekels of silver: some idea of the value of this amount can be seen from 2 Sam. 24.24, where we learn that David paid fifty shekels for Araunah's threshing floor and the oxen, and from 2 Kg. 6.25 that in time of siege and famine an ass's head cost eighty.

because of the fear of God: because of his true religious fervour; cf. 4.4, 20.

16. There is no mention of any actual building work done by Nehemiah; his time may have been taken up in supervision and in diplomatic work. Since he bought no land his men would be all the more free to help in the wall building (but see note on 2.8).

17. Nehemiah seems to have made himself personally responsible for feeding 150 of the people who worked on the wall. Also he was called upon to entertain diplomatic visitors from outside Judah. These visitors could have included Jews of the dispersion, who could equally well be said to come from the nations round about.

18. Contrast the lavishness of Solomon's provisions as recorded in 1 Kg. 4.23.

19. Cf. 4.4, 15, 20; 5.15.

FURTHER ATTEMPTS BY SANBALLAT AND HIS ASSOCIATES TO TRAP NEHEMIAH AND MISREPRESENT HIM 6.1–9

1. doors in the gates: i.e. the city remained partially defenceless.

2. Tobiah is not mentioned here, but the omission is probably an accidental one. He is mentioned in verse 1, although without the designation 'the Ammonite', and he takes part in the further plot in verses 10–14.

Ono: 27 miles or so NW. of Jerusalem; it lay on the extreme edge of Judah. If, as is not unlikely, Samaria, Ashdod, and Judah had in the past disputed its ownership, it may have been regarded as neutral territory.

one of the villages: this translates *bakkᵉpîrîm*, which could also be treated as a proper name 'in Hakkephirim'; this would still mean one of the villages, but would be a more grammatical rendering of the Hebrew. Ono was virtually midway between Samaria and Jerusalem, and Nehemiah would not only be more than a day's journey from Jerusalem but would be about as far from the city as he could be while remaining on Judean soil. Did they expect the work to come to a standstill in his absence?

harm: we are not told what they contemplated: to capture him? or to assassinate him? to intimidate him? or to give opportunity for an armed attack on the city?

3. great work: important and of first priority.

4. four times: stresses the urgency of their desire to lure Nehemiah out of the city.

5. open letter: charging Nehemiah with treason and ensuring that the charge would be known among his servants and fellow countrymen, and he might feel under the necessity of answering it not only among his own men but also in person to his adversaries.

6. Geshem: see 2.19. Why should Geshem's word mean so much? Perhaps because as an Arab he stood outside the Israelite race and was a stronger and impartial witness.

7. Throughout Israelite history, as is clear from the record both in Kings and in Chronicles, the prophets played an important part in the setting up of kings. If this accusation was founded on fact it may mean that some men in Judah were looking upon Nehemiah as a possible Messianic king, just as men had looked upon Zerubbabel. There is no evidence of Nehemiah's tribal or family connections, so we cannot tell whether he was in the Davidic line or not.

There is a king: Nehemiah is meant.

let us take counsel: presumably Sanballat is here posing as Nehemiah's friend.

8. With a clear conscience, and perhaps with a letter of appointment from the king in his possession, Nehemiah dismisses the charge as groundless.

9. O God: this is added in the English to make sense. LXX, however, instead of the imperative 'strengthen thou' has a 1st person form; if we adopt this we need not add a helping word and may translate: 'and now I strengthened my hands', i.e. 'I got on with the job with renewed energy'.

ATTEMPT TO DRAW NEHEMIAH INTO THE TEMPLE AND PUT HIM IN THE WRONG **6.10–14**

10. Shemaiah: see Ezr. 8.13. Although his father's and his grandfather's names are given, it is not possible to identify this man more closely.
Delaiah: see Ezr. 2.60.
Mehetabel: occurs only here as a man's name: it is participial in form (see 3.4) and means 'God is doing good/one who does good'.
shut up: the word originally meant under the protection of the family, but in usage it came to mean any situation in which a man was 'protected' and therefore held or detained—a ritual limitation. Here it probably means that Shemaiah could be in his own house or in the Temple but not otherwise free. The part this limitation plays in the narrative is probably to make a plausible excuse to get Nehemiah into the Temple precincts. In doing so he would be usurping the prerogative of the priests and putting himself in the wrong. Violating the Temple was punishable by death according to biblical law (Num. 18.7). Nehemiah's answer in the next verse shows him to be aware of this.

11. such a man as I: in this place Nehemiah is probably speaking of himself as governor and leader of the community rather than as a man of such character as not to seek safety in flight.
what man such as I: here he is speaking of himself as a layman.
could go: it was not strictly possible for a layman to enter the sacred Temple; this is therefore to be preferred to the margin reading 'would go into the temple to save his life', which implies that he could go but will not.

12. The fact that Shemaiah had set himself up as a prophet and asked Nehemiah to do a thing he knew to be wrong roused his suspicions and he saw through it.

13. evil name: Nehemiah seems to be acting generously in saying this, for if he had gone into the Temple it might well have precipitated serious trouble between him and the priests.

14. No-adiah: on the name, see Ezr. 8.33. Nothing more is known of this person. The mention of a prophetess here suggests either that the affair with Shemaiah involved more people than Shemaiah himself, or that there were other similar attempts to involve Nehemiah. We would have expected mention of Shemaiah by name in this verse.

THE WALL FINISHED IN SPITE OF THE INTRIGUE OF TOBIAH **6.15–19**

15. wall . . . finished: this probably does not include the doors; see 6.1 and 7.1.
Elul: the sixth month according to post-exilic reckoning.

fifty-two days: a strikingly short time, amounting to not quite nine weeks, allowing for the probability that they did not work on the sabbaths. Nehemiah seems to have moved quickly in everything that he did—assuming that this was still the same year in which he returned from Babylon. The months so far mentioned are: Chislev, the ninth month, when the news from Jerusalem arrived, Nisan, the first month of the following year (see note on 2.1), four months later when he asked for permission to return, and now Elul six months later in the same year. This must have been a crowded six months, what with preparations for the journey, the journey itself (which took Ezra the best part of four months, Ezr. 7.9), the preparations for building the wall and then the actual building.

16. afraid: marg. 'saw'; either reading is possible (i.e. either *wayyîrᵉʾû* or *wayyir'û*). It is more in keeping with Nehemiah's character to say that the nations were afraid.

fell: this is a mild reaction, especially if they were afraid. With change of one consonant (*wayyippālēʾ* for *wayyippᵉlû*) the meaning would be: 'it was a wonderful thing in their sight', i.e. well-nigh impossible.

17. Tobiah is in touch with Jewish nobles, some through marriage, and is able to continue his attacks on Nehemiah through letters to them, and, more-over, keep himself well informed of the situation in Jerusalem by their letters to him.

18. bound by oath: this doubtless means more than the mere fact of marriage connection and may imply trade or commercial agreements.

Shecaniah the son of Arah: is not otherwise known. There were other men named Shecaniah; cf. Ezr. 8.3, 5. Arah is a family name; see Ezr. 2.5.

Jehohanan: see Ezr. 10.6.

Meshullam: see Ezr. 8.16.

19. The correspondence kept Nehemiah on tenterhooks.

Note: The description of the way in which the rebuilt walls were dedicated by formal processions is to be found in 12.27–43.

SECOND SECTION 7.1–73 SPARSE POPULATION OF JERUSALEM AND LIST OF THE PEOPLE OF ISRAEL WHO HAD RETURNED

APPOINTMENT OF OFFICERS IN JERUSALEM AND ANXIETY ABOUT THE SPARSE POPULATION 7.1–4

1. the singers, and the Levites: these, strictly speaking, have nothing to do with the finishing of the walls and the setting up of doors. Gatekeepers were properly wanted. These two words may be a gloss added to Nehemiah's memoir by the Chronicler, who may have had 13.22 in mind, where the Levites were to keep the gates on the sabbath.

2. my brother Hanani and Hananiah: since the end of the verse describes the character of one man only, it looks as if 'and Hananiah' is a slightly altered dittograph of 'my brother Hanani'. The castle is mentioned in 2.8, but there translated 'fortress'. Hanani is a short form of Hananiah; see Ezr. 10.20, 28.

3. to them: this either means Hanani and Hananiah (if we retain the full Hebrew text of verse 2) or the gatekeepers.

still standing guard: marg. Hebrew obscure; the obscurity in the Hebrew lies in the ungrammatical connection of this phrase, which simply says 'while they were standing', and in the fact that the pronoun has no obvious antecedent. It is probably to be understood as an impersonal construction, i.e. 'men', and the 'standing' may then refer to the rest period at midday when the heat was too great to work: the gates were to remain shut during the siesta.

4. The situation mentioned here caused Nehemiah so much concern that he brought into the city a tenth of the population of Judah. This is described in 11.1. The need to review the population for this purpose enabled the editor to introduce the list in verses 6–73a.

DECISION TO ENROL BY GENEALOGY **7.5**

5. God put it: in deliberate contrast to the numbering of the people by David which, according to the Chronicler (1 Chr. 21.1), was at Satan's instigation; cf. 2 Sam. 24.1.

enrolled by genealogy: to repopulate the city Nehemiah would want to be able to draw representatives from all the clans and families and thus spread the burden as widely as possible.

And I found: this and what follows to the end of the verse may be an editor's insertion to introduce the list which follows and which he took to be a list of those who returned from exile, but which is more probably a list compiled after they had settled down (see Ezr. 2). The references to those who lived in towns, verses 25ff., make it unlikely that the list would have served Nehemiah's purpose, that is, if we press the intention to enrol by genealogy.

the book of the genealogy of those . . .: the phrase is ungrammatical in Hebrew, made so, possibly, by putting in 'of the genealogy' to link verse 5a with what follows. (The grammatical construction of the Hebrew would be eased if *hityaḥēś* were read instead of *hayyaḥaś*, i.e. 'I found the book of enrolment-by-genealogy of those who came up . . .'.) In other words, there is a bad join in the narrative at this point and what we would expect to be told is that the register was obtained and the entries made.

LIST OF THOSE WHO RETURNED **7.6–73a**

(*Note:* This is virtually a copy of the same list as in Ezr. 2, and comments are made here only where Nehemiah differs significantly from Ezra in other respects than numbers which have already been mentioned in the comments there.)

7. Azariah: Ezra has Seraiah. On the name see Ezr. 7.1.

Raamiah: Ezra has Reelaiah. Raamiah means 'Yahweh has thundered' or 'Thunder of Yahweh' and occurs only here. Cf. Raamah (Gen. 10.7).

Nahamani: is not in Ezra. The name occurs only here and probably is similar in meaning to the name Nehemiah, i.e. 'Yahweh has comforted (me)'.

Mispereth: Ezra has Mispar; both forms occur only in these lists.

Nehum: Ezra has Rehum. The name Nehum occurs only here and may be a short form of Nehemiah.

15. Binnui: Ezra has Bani. On Binnui, see Ezr. 2.10, 40; 8.33.

24. Hariph: Ezra has Jorah; see 10.19, and on the name, Ezr. 2.18.

25. Gibeon: this name does not occur as a personal or family name, but only as a place-name. In the Nehemiah form of the list, therefore, the place-names begin here and not with Bethlehem as in Ezr. 2.21. Ezra has a personal name, Gibbar.

28. Beth-azmaveth: Ezra has the shortened form, Azmaveth; see on Ezr. 2.24.

33. the other Nebo: Ezra has Nebo. There appears to be no reason for thus distinguishing Nebo; 'the other' may have crept in from the next verse. Ezra introduces here 'The sons of Magbish, one hundred and fifty-six'. In a comparable list in Neh. 10.14–27, the names Nebai and Magpiash occur next to each other (verses 19, 20) and these are so much like Nebo and Magbish as to suggest that (a) Neh. 7.33 may originally have had both names, and (b) that in Ezr. 2.29, 30 they may be family names and not place-names.

48. Hagaba: of which Hagabah (Ezr. 2.45) is but an alternative spelling in English. Ezra adds: 'the sons of Akkub, the sons of Hagab'.

Shalmai: Ezra has Shamlai.

52. Besai: after this Ezra adds 'the sons of Asnah'.

54. Bazlith: Ezra has Bazluth.

57. Sophereth: Ezra has Hassophereth—a difference due to the addition of the definite article in Hebrew.

Perida: Ezra has Peruda.

59. Amon: Ezra has Ami.

61. Addon: Ezra has Addan.

65. the governor: see Ezr. 2.63.

67. two hundred and forty-five: Ezra has two hundred, but see next note.

68. This verse has been supplied from Ezr. 2.66. It has obviously dropped out of the Hebrew text (and has been inserted in the margin of some mss.) by accident, but it looks as if the scribe who was responsible for overlooking it wrote in verse 67 the total for this verse in place of the total given in Ezr. 2.65. (It should be noted that the numeral stands at the end of the verse in Hebrew in each case.)

70–72. As in Ezra (2.68, 69) the list closes with a record of gifts. There are some similarities in the two records, but whatever their common origin they have each been adapted to the circumstances for which the lists were used by the editor, in Ezra to record offerings for the building of the Temple and here to record offerings for 'the work' which, in the circumstances, can only mean the rebuilding of the wall. It is difficult to see what the priests' garments have to do with wall-building, although they may be said to have some remote connection with re-establishing the Temple (Ezr. 2). Probably, like the list of names, this record was already in existence for some purpose now unknown and the editor used it to serve his own purpose on these two occasions and made only the most obviously necessary changes each time.

73a. This half-verse seems to have no direct bearing on Nehemiah's situation and is probably to be regarded as part of the source material which the editor has retained without adaptation, except that, if it be due to the editor and not a later scribe, there is no mention of Jerusalem and its vicinity as there is in the parallel verse in Ezr. 2.70. The mention first of **some of the people** and then of **all Israel** seems to demand reference to Jerusalem as well as **their towns**. It could perhaps be argued that Jerusalem is not mentioned deliberately, since in Nehemiah's day it was sparsely inhabited.

73b. This, as it now stands, is properly introductory to chapter 8, and this fact is accepted by the RSV paragraph division. On the other hand, 8.2 places the bringing of the law before the assembly on the first day of the seventh month, thus leaving no time for the people to assemble from their towns to Jerusalem for it. Since the same statement about assembling in Jerusalem in the seventh month occurs also in Ezr. 3.1, it may be taken to be part of the material which the editor borrowed and adapted to his purpose. If for the moment we accept it as an intended sequence in Nehemiah's affairs, it was less than a week after the completion of the wall on the twenty-fifth day of the sixth month, and we shall have to suppose that the problem of repopulating Jerusalem was shelved for the time being in favour of the reading of the law. However, the probability is that the reading of the law did not immediately follow the building of the wall and that we need not look for sequence here. In any case, the reading of the law was part of Ezra's story and not Nehemiah's. The sequence of events in Nehemiah's story is broken at this point and is not resumed in the narrative until 11.1.

THIRD SECTION **8.1–10.39**   THE READING OF THE LAW BY EZRA:
A FAST AND A COVENANT

SOLEMN READING OF THE LAW **8.1–8**

1. gathered: thus making an assembly such as is spoken of in Lev. 23.24 as proper for the first day of the seventh month.

Water Gate: see 3.26.

told Ezra . . . to bring: this does not demand the assumption that Ezra had a new book of the law with him (see Ezr. 7.14). The consciences of the people had doubtless been stirred, and Ezra, in virtue of his training and office, let alone his present commission, was clearly the right man to handle the book of the law.

2. women: it was customary for women and children to be brought along on such solemn occasions; cf. Dt. 31.12; Jos. 8.35; 2 Kg. 23.2.

with understanding: there was a strong recognition of the necessity not to take the reading of the law for granted. For the idea of understanding as important, cf. verse 7 and Ezr. 8.16.

first day of the seventh month: the year is not given, but if we are right to dissociate this chapter (and perhaps the following chapter) from the sequence of events in Nehemiah's time, it will probably be the year of Ezra's return, the sequence of events in that year being: fifth month, arrival; seventh month, reading of law; ninth month, marriage problems. This was a suitable date for reading the law, first because of the holy convocation (the Hebrew word for convocation being the same as that for 'reading' in Neh. 8.8) ordained for that day in Lev. 23.24, and second because Dt. 31.10f. enjoins the reading of the law once in seven years during the feast of booths, i.e. the fifteenth to the twenty-second of the seventh month. Verses 13-18 make the dependence on Deuteronomy fairly clear. In view of this it may be said that the date given here is liturgically apt, even if it cannot be confirmed as a sound historical one.

3. early morning . . .: while they were fresh. Ezra could not get through the whole law (if that was his intention) in a morning, but the subsequent narrative shows that (a) on the next day he expounded some of it to the leaders (verse 13), and (b) it was read each day throughout the feast (verses 13-18).

and those who could understand: as used here the phrase seems to imply a different group from the men and women, but in 10.28 they appear to be identified. It is another instance of the Chronicler's insistence on understanding the law.

4. pulpit: this is the only time the Hebrew word, which normally means 'tower', is used of a pulpit. The details given here, the pulpit, the opening of the book in sight of the people, the standing, etc., are either the model on which subsequent synagogue practice and usage were based, or was itself modelled on already (*c.* 300 B.C.) existing usage.

It is not clear why there should be thirteen men (who might be priests, see below) named here and thirteen Levites mentioned in verse 7. In the Hebrew text there are six on the right and seven on the left, but in 1 Esdras there are seven on the right and six on the left, an Azariah being inserted among those on the right and Meshullam being omitted from those on the left. To omit both names, Azariah from the Greek and Meshullam from the Hebrew, would produce an even six on either side; this would be appropriate, the two together equalling the tribal number, but two sevens would not be out of keeping with Hebrew tradition, seven being the most common round number.

Mattithiah: probably a post-exilic name; it occurs several times in 1 Chronicles, where it is a Levitical name, and otherwise only here and Ezr. 10.43.

Shema: this name occurs otherwise only in Chronicles; it may be a short form of Shemaiah (Ezr. 8.13).

Anaiah: 'Yahweh has answered'; occurs only here and 10.22.

Uriah: if this man was identical with the Uriah of 3.4, 21 then he was a priest, but the identity is most uncertain and cannot be made if Ezra can be shown to be later than Nehemiah, for the father of a man active in Nehemiah's time was not likely still to be able-bodied in Ezra's time. See Ezr. 8.33 for the name.

Hilkiah: a fairly common name, especially for priests; see Ezr. 7.1.

Maaseiah: see Ezr. 10.18.

Pedaiah: see 3.25.

Mishael: 'Who is what God is?'; a name that occurs elsewhere only as (a) that of a cousin of Moses (Exod. 6.22), and (b) that of Daniel's companion (Dan. 1.6).

Malchijah: see 3.11 and Ezr. 10.25.

Hashum: see Ezr. 2.19.

Hashbaddanah: occurs only here; it may be a mixture of two names, Hasshub (see 3.11) and Baddanah (cf. 1 Chr. 7.17, Bedan), a name of uncertain meaning.

Zechariah: see Ezr. 5.1; the name occurs too frequently to be distinctive.

Meshullam: see Ezr. 8.16; also a very frequently used name.

What kind of men were these? Not one of them can be identified with certainty as either priest or Levite. Since verse 7 lists thirteen Levites the probability is that these are either priests or, less likely, leading laymen (although verse 13 does show that laymen had a place at readings of the law).

5. stood: cf. 9.3.

6. blessed the LORD: perhaps with such words as now stand at the end of Ps. 135.

Amen: see 5.13.

lifting up their hands: cf. Ps. 134.2; Ezr. 9.5.

bowed: cf. Gen. 18.2; 19.1.

7. Jeshua: see Ezr. 2.2, 36.

Bani: see Ezr. 2.10.

Sherebiah: see Ezr. 8.18.

Jamin: otherwise only (a) a son of Simeon (Gen. 46.10), and (b) a Judahite (1 Chr. 2.27). The name means literally 'Right hand' but may also carry the meaning 'Luck'; it is probably a short form of Benjamin (Ezr. 10.32).

Akkub: see Ezr. 2.42.

Shabbethai: see Ezr. 10.15.

Hodiah: 'Yahweh is splendour'; (a) the name of a Judahite in 1 Chr. 4.19, (b) of Levites in Neh. 8.7; 9.5; 10.10, 13, and (c) of a 'chief of the people', 10.18.

Maaseiah: see verse 4.

Kelita: see on Kelaiah in Ezr. 10.23.

Azariah: see Ezr. 7.1.

Jozabad: see Ezr. 8.33.

Hanan: see Ezr. 2.46.

Pelaiah: 'Yahweh has acted wonderfully'; only here and 10.10.

to understand: see verse 2.

8. read . . . clearly: it is difficult to picture exactly what was being done. Ezra had read some of the book (verse 3), and now apparently the Levites read more of it and expounded what they read. Did they expound to the people split up into several groups, and is that what is meant by 'in their places' in verse 7? We are told nothing of what the thirteen men named in verse 4 did. What sort of exposition was it? Did they give the meaning in the vernacular Aramaic? The word translated 'clearly' basically means 'separated' or 'split up', which is what they would have to do if they gave comments or translation section by section. Neh. 13.24 shows how urgent had become the need for interpretation of what was read in Hebrew. The part played here by the Levites is similar to that represented in 2 Chr. 17.7–9. It has been suggested that the first verb of the sentence should be read in the singular 'he (i.e. Ezra) read', and then they (the Levites) interpreted or taught. This would make a natural sequence.

CELEBRATION OF A HOLY DAY 8.9–12

9. Nehemiah: there has been no mention of Nehemiah so far in this narrative about reading the law, and it is unlikely that he would be first mentioned only at this point if he had been a leading figure as governor at that time. This is to be regarded as an editor's (the Chronicler himself ?) addition when the order in which the narrative ran made Ezra and Nehemiah contemporaries. The verb 'said' is singular in Hebrew which would be natural if there were one named subject (Ezra) accompanied by Levites, but it is unnatural with the two names. On **governor,** see Ezr. 2.63.

taught: the verb is the same as that translated 'helped to understand' in verse 7.
this day is holy: see on verse 2 and cf. Lev. 23.24.
weep: the part read by Ezra and the Levites must have been denunciatory and have contained threats of punishment (such as those found in Lev. 17–26 and Deuteronomy). Weeping was a normal way of showing contrition and sorrow; cf. the 'Bochim' incident (Jg. 2.1–5).

10. the fat: the Hebrew word, connected by root with the ordinary word for fat or oil, means delicacies, extra tasty food. Leviticus 2.1–3 and 6.21 show how high a place oil occupied in food preparation.
sweet wine: the word occurs only here of a drink; otherwise it is used of a lover's speech (or kisses) (Ca. 5.16). To what does it refer here? Possibly either spiced wine (cf. Prov. 9.2, 5), or new wine (cf. Isa. 49.26; Jl 1.5, 3.18).
send portions: in accordance with Deuteronomic law, 14.29; 16.10; 26.12.
the joy of the LORD: not the Lord's joy in them, but theirs in him, a joy to which expression was given by the festival, but also a joy that was stimulated by it. 1 Chr. 16.27 links strength and joy as this passage does.

12. the words: the reading and expounding of the law.
Note: The way in which verses 10–12 speak of the celebration of this feast bears comparison with the way in which Purim was to be celebrated (Est. 9.19).

CELEBRATION OF THE FEAST OF BOOTHS 8.13–18

Details of the feast of booths are to be found in Lev. 23.33–36, 39–43; Num. 29.12–39, and Dt. 16.13–15. No recognition of the list of offerings in Num. 29 is made here.

13. second day: the second day of the month. The feast would begin on the fifteenth day of the month, so there was practically a fortnight for preparation.

the heads: presumably there was an inkling that some part of the law concerning the seventh month needed to be put into practice and these men would have to be consulted and share in the decision since their families were involved.

to study: the Hebrew verb may mean 'to get a full insight into the implications of the words'—as we might say 'their relevance to the contemporary situation'.

14. See especially Lev. 23.40–43 and Dt. 16.13–15.

15. publish and proclaim: there is no specific reference to this in the law, but Lev. 23.2, 4 could be regarded as a sufficient command.

bring branches: it should be noted that there is no reference to fruit here (cf. 2 Mac. 10.6) as there is in Lev. 23.40, but in later times, at least, they carried fruit of some sort (cf. Josephus, *Ant.*, III, x, 4).

16. Water Gate: see 3.26.

Gate of Ephraim: a gate which opened towards the north-west, i.e. towards Ephraim. It is mentioned in 12.39; 2 Kg. 14.13; 2 Chr. 25.23, but is not mentioned in chapter 3. Was it an alternative name for one of the other gates? If so, it is not known which.

17. returned from the captivity: this is fully in keeping with the Chronicler's point of view, namely, that these virtually constituted the true Israel (see Introduction, p. 13). Leviticus 23.42 says that participants must be native Israelites.

from the days of Jeshua: i.e. since the wilderness period.

had not done so: this overlooks the statement in Ezr. 3.4 that the Jews celebrated the feast shortly after the first return, but see note there.

18. read: this agrees with Dt. 31.10–13, where it is laid down that the law should be read at the feast of booths every seventh year. The construction is probably an impersonal one as if to say, 'there was a reading from the book'; it was not necessarily Ezra who read.

solemn assembly: another possible meaning of the word is 'closing ceremony' (cf. Lev. 23.36, where it is a celebration held on the eighth day).

It is to be noted that, although the preceding narrative shows some dependence on Lev. 23.33–43, there is no recognition here of a day of Atonement, which should take place on the tenth day of the seventh month (Lev. 23.27). It might be claimed that the fast day which took place on the twenty-fourth day of this month (9.1) left no room that year for a celebration of a day of Atonement. Another view is that Ezra was at cross-purposes with the Temple authorities and withheld sanction for celebration of the day of Atonement. Its existence could scarcely have been ignored when details about the feast of booths were read. It could be held that *in practice* the community at this time still held more to the Deuteronomic law than any later form.

FURTHER READINGS ON A DAY OF FASTING 9.1–5

It is clearly the intention of the narrative as it now stands, and probably as the Chronicler intended, to let this day of fasting come within the work of Ezra. This is probably right at bottom, but it is not necessarily to be regarded as following immediately on the reading of the law. It may be that its proper place was following upon the settlement of the marriage question. See note on verse 2.

1. twenty-fourth day: the seventh month seems to have been a favourite month for fast days: there was the day of Atonement on the tenth, there was a fast day for which men from Shechem, Shiloh, and Samaria were coming to Jerusalem on the day after Gedaliah's murder (Jer. 41.4, 5), and there was one known to Zechariah (Zech. 7.5). Fasting was an act of humiliation before God; it was a time for self-mortification (Ezr. 8.21; 10.6).

sackcloth: a common sign of mourning and confession.

earth: cf. 2 Sam. 1.2; 15.32, a sign of abnegation and also of transitoriness (Gen. 3.19; Ps. 146.4).

2. the Israelites: lit. the seed of Israel, cf. 'holy seed' in Ezr. 9.2 (RSV 'holy race') and Isa. 6.13.

separated . . . foreigners: this exclusiveness was one of the marks of the piety and religious outlook in post-exilic days; cf. Ezr. 6.21. The reference here has to be understood as having no immediate connection with the mixed marriages problem (and in any case, according to the present arrangement of the text the marriage problem had already been faced and settled). Out and out foreigners may be intended. But the phrase strongly echoes that used in Ezr. 9.1, and this chapter if divorced from its present context might be taken as the sequel to Ezr. 10. The date would then be the first month (Ezr. 10.17) and not the seventh.

stood: either in the square in front of the Water Gate, as in 8.1, or in the forecourt of the Temple.

3. read: either Ezra or the Levites would do the reading.

a fourth of the day: is this the same length of time as from early morning until midday, 8.3?

worshipped: lit. bowed down to, or did obeisance to.

4. stairs of the Levites: possibly a structure made for the occasion, as was Ezra's pulpit, 8.4.

Jeshua: see Ezr. 2.2, 36.

Bani: see Ezr. 2.10.

Kadmiel: see Ezr. 2.40; 3.9.

Shebaniah: a name that, apart from 1 Chr. 15.24, occurs only in Nehemiah—as a Levite name in 9.4, 5; 10.10, 12, and as a priestly name in 10.4; 12.14. In form it is a Yahweh-bearing name with the perfect tense of the verb *š-b-n*, whose meaning is not known. The fact that in Nehemiah some MSS. have Shecaniah suggests some confusion of the two names; see on 12.3.

Bunni: occurs here, in 11.15 (a Levite) and in 10.15 (a lay 'chief'). It is probably a short form of a name compounded of Yahweh and *bānāh*, 'has built', such as Benaiah; see also Ezr. 2.10.

Sherebiah: see Ezr. 8.18.

Bani: a second occurrence of the name in the same list gives rise to the feeling that it might be read as Binnui (as Syr. does). The names Bunni, Bani, and Binnui were liable to confusion with one another and also with $b^e n\hat{e}$, 'sons of'. LXX has 'sons of' in each case. For the name Binnui, see Ezr. 2.10, 40, 8.33.

Chenani: occurs only here; it is probably a short form of a name meaning 'Yahweh has made firm'.

cried: the verb strictly means cried for help; cf. Ps. 107.6.

5. The list of Levites given here has five names in common with verse 4: Jeshua, Kadmiel, Bani, Sherebiah, and Shebaniah. If it was intended to be a repetition of the same list, it is surprising to find as many as three names out of the eight changed; moreover, if it had been the same list it would probably not have been repeated. The new names are Pethahiah (see Ezr. 10.23), Hodiah (see 8.7), and Hashabneiah (see 3.10). Bunni and Chenani are the only names in either list that do not occur in other lists of Levites (Ezr. 10.23; Neh. 8.7; 10.9–13). The two groups here perform different functions; those in verse 4 seem to be professional petitioners and those in verse 5 professional chanters.

Stand up and bless: with this ascription of praise, cf. Ps. 106.48; 1 Chr. 16.36.

Blessed be: this is what Syr. has, and that version also apparently takes the words 'from everlasting to everlasting' with this and not with the preceding clause. It is illogical to exhort the people to stand up and bless from everlasting to everlasting. Syriac is altogether to be preferred to the Hebrew, which has 'from everlasting to everlasting; and let them bless . . .'.

PRAYER TO GOD, WITH A REVIEW OF THE NATION'S HISTORY **9.6–37**

6. And Ezra said: if these words, borrowed from LXX, were in the original text their removal from the present form of the text may have been due to the feeling, engendered perhaps by Lev. 16.21, that it was a high-priestly prerogative to utter a confession, but their removal might have been due to a desire to attribute chapter 9 to Nehemiah. Such a prayer could have been uttered by an individual or by the group of eight Levites. It may have been a well-known liturgical prayer. Examples of similar prayers, some with historical reconstructions as here, may be seen in Ps. 78, 105, 106; Lam. 5 in verse, and in Ezr. 9.6–15; Dan. 9.4–19; Bar. 1.15–2.10 and Sir. 36.1–17 in prose. Verse 6 echoes Dt. 10.14.

heaven of heavens: a superlative (cf. song of songs), meaning the very centre of heaven.

host of heaven: either the stars (cf. Gen. 2.1) or the angel army (1 Kg. 22.19; Ps. 103.20f.; 148.2).

7. Ur: Gen. 11.31.

Abram . . . Abraham: Gen. 17.5; the first form probably means 'Father (a divine appellative) is high', and the second 'Father of a multitude'.

8. find his heart faithful: echoes Gen. 15.6, where the words 'he believed' come from the same root as faithful does here.

covenant: Gen. 15.17–21.

Canaanite . . .: the six names listed here occur in Gen. 15, where four others are also listed. Five of the six occur in Ezr. 9.1.

10. signs and wonders: Exod. 7.3; Dt. 6.22; Jer. 32.20.

a name: cf. Isa. 63.12, 14; Jer. 32.20; Dan. 9.15.

11. Cf. Exod. 14.21, 22; 15.4, 5, 19.

12. Exod. 13.21f.; Num. 14.14.

13. Exod. 19f.; Dt. 4.

14. Exod. 31.13–17; Ezek. 20.12.

15. Exod. 16.4; Ps. 78.24; 105.40.

sworn: lit. lifted up thy hand; cf. Num. 14.30.

16. they and our fathers: the 'and' must be regarded as explanatory; 'they' are our fathers.

17. leader: this is based on Num. 14.4 (where RSV has 'captain').

Egypt: this is the reading of some Hebrew MSS. and LXX. The majority of Hebrew MSS. have *miryām*, 'their rebellion'. The Hebrew phrase could be translated: 'they resolved in their rebelliousness to return to their slavery'.

ready to forgive . . .: Exod. 34.6f.; see on Ezr. 3.11; Neh. 1.5.

18. Cf. Exod. 32.

20. good Spirit: cf. Ps. 143.10. Contrast the bad spirit in 1 Sam. 16.14–16. For the gift of the spirit, see Isa. 63.11; Num. 11.17.

21. Cf. Dt. 8.4; 29.5.

22. Cf. Num. 21.10–35; Dt. 29.7f.

didst allot to them every corner: this is a forced meaning since, strictly speaking, 'to them' is the direct object of the verb 'allot'. The word *pē'āh* may be connected with an Arabic cognate meaning 'spoils', and the phrase will then mean 'didst allot them as spoils of war'.

23. stars: cf. Dt. 1.10; Gen. 15.5; 22.17; Exod. 32.13.

24. subdue: Dt. 9.3.

Canaanites: this is the term for the pre-Israelite inhabitants of Palestine commonly used by the J writer; E and D use Amorite.

25. fortified cities: Dt. 1.28; 9.1.

rich land: Num. 13.20.

houses . . . cisterns: Dt. 6.11.

fat: Dt. 32.15.

26. killed thy prophets: 1 Kg. 18.4, 13; 19.10, 14; 2 Chr. 24.21.

27. give them into the hand of: Jg. 2.14.

saviours: the judges were either called saviours (Jg. 3.9, 15), or were said to save (Jg. 2.18; 6.14, etc.).

28. had rest . . . did evil again: Jg. 3.11, 12, 30; 4.1; 6.1.

many times . . . thy mercies: LXX has a simpler and perhaps preferable form: 'and thou didst deliver them according to thy great mercies'; cf. the phrase in verse 31; cf. also Ps. 106.43, 45.

29–30. Cf. 2 Kg. 17.13f.

29. acted presumptuously: cf. verses 10 (where the verb is translated 'acted insolently') and 16.

by the observance of which a man shall live: cf. Lev. 18.5; Ezek. 20.11.

31. Cf. verse 28.

make an end of: Jer. 4.27; 5.10, 18; cf. also Lev. 26.44.

gracious and merciful: cf. verse 17.

32. Now therefore: Dan. 9.15; Bar. 2.11.

great and mighty and terrible: cf. 1.5; Dt. 7.21.

kings of Assyria: this reference may be intended to take the reader back to Shalmaneser III (858–823 B.C.) or perhaps only to Shalmaneser IV (727–722 B.C.), followed by Sargon II and Sennacherib and then including the Babylonian and Persian kings up to the date of writing; see Ezr. 6.22.

33. just: cf. Ezr. 9.15.

35. Cf. Dt. 28.47.

36. slaves: cf. Ezr. 9.9, where RSV has 'bondmen'.

Note: A comparison of the wording of this chapter and that of the passages referred to above on which it is dependent shows a great deal of close verbal agreement.

DECISION TO MAKE A COVENANT **9.38**

38. In the Hebrew text this is numbered as the first verse of chapter 10: this is a much better position, for it introduces the making of a covenant such as is described in chapter 10. By its position chapter 10 must be intended to set out a covenant which Ezra was instrumental in making. It is not inconceivable that Ezra did feel it necessary to make a covenant with the people after the marriage question was disposed of, and this verse could be regarded as a relic of the original introduction to that covenant. On the other hand, a covenant would also be very much in place in Nehemiah's work if it preceded the reforming measures which he put in hand (chapter 13). Whether Ezra or Nehemiah, or both men independently, established a covenant, there is little doubt that chapter 10 describes a declaration of allegiance to the law that is independent of the reading of the law described in chapter 8. In many ways the covenant in chapter 10 is more in keeping with Nehemiah's work than with Ezra's, and if it could be shown that both men set up a covenant, we should have to suppose that the record of Ezra's covenant was suppressed after chapter 9 in favour of Nehemiah's covenant (chapter 10).

Levites and . . . priests: the same order occurs in 2 Chr. 19.8; 30.21.

set their seal to it: this is a paraphrase of the Hebrew, which may be rendered lit. 'at the sealing' or 'on the sealed thing (document)'.

LIST OF SIGNATORIES (OR WITNESSES) **10.1–27**

There seem to be three parts to the record: the first, 9.38–10.27, is the act of entering into a firm covenant (*'ᵃmānāh*) by the officials and signatories; the second, 10.28–29, is the adjuration and oath made by the rest of the people to share in the *'ᵃmānāh*; and the third, 10.30–39, giving the terms of the *'ᵃmānāh*.

1. **Those who set their seal:** lit. 'on the sealed things'; but it is not clear why the plural is used here and the singular in 9.38.

Nehemiah: see 1.1, and for **governor**, see 8.9; Ezr. 2.63. Unless it is assumed that the list of names that follows is a purely arbitrary list, we may regard it as a genuine list of the men and families (see below) who were involved in the covenant, foremost among them being Nehemiah himself. This would support the suggestion that the covenant belongs to Nehemiah's work and should be regarded as independent of the law reading. (If it was the Chronicler's intention to include the covenant in Ezra's activity, it is unlikely that he was responsible for including this list of names which has no reference to Ezra; see Introduction, pp. 28, 34 and 38.) **Zedekiah:** 'Yahweh has been righteous/acted rightly'; this is the only use of the name in post-exilic times. His name may have been placed next to Nehemiah's because he held some official position, secretary perhaps.

2. Of the twenty-one priestly names that follow in verses 2–8, six occur neither in 12.1–7 nor in 12.12–21 (which are comparable lists), and a seventh occurs in 121–7 but not in 12.12–21. The six that occur only here are **Pashhur, Malchijah, Obadiah, Daniel, Baruch, Meshullam,** and the seventh that is not in 12.12–21 is **Hattush.** It may also be noted that there is a Shebaniah in 10.4 and 12.14, but Shecaniah in 12.3 probably due to scribal error. Comparison of the names in verses 2–8 with those in 12.12–21 shows that they are family names and the implication is that the contemporary head of the family (or presumably an accredited representative) could sign or seal in the name of the family. This being so, the absence of any particular individual name is without undue significance. The fact that there are twenty-one names here raises the possibility that an original form of the list might have contained twenty-four names representing the twenty-four priestly courses or family divisions of priests (finally listed in 1 Chr. 24.1–19). On the other hand, the several lists of the priestly families that have been handed down to us (1 Chr. 24.1–19; Neh. 10.2–8; 12.1–7, 12–21) show much variety in the names (see above) and do not appear to include all of the four (or five) families named in Ezr. 2.36–39: Joshua, (Jedaiah), Immer, Pashhur, and Harim.

In the present list, if Amariah were shown to be the full form of the name Immer, though this is not at all certain, Bilgai to stand for Bilgah, and Shebaniah for Shecaniah, then there are eight names in this list which occur also in 1 Chr. 24, i.e. **Amariah**(Immer), **Malchijah, Shebaniah**(Shecaniah), **Harim, Abijah, Mijamin, Maaziah,** and **Bilgai**(Bilgah). Of the priestly families in Ezr. 2.36–39, this list contains three only, i.e. **Amariah**(Immer), **Pashhur,** and **Harim.** If dates could be confidently assigned to these lists, we might be in a position to discover whether family names could vary from one generation to another, and whether, while the 'divisions' or 'families' remained constant, the names varied. In view of the prominence given to the family of Joiarib in 1 Chr. 24.7 and of the connection of the Maccabees with that family (1 Mac. 2.1; 14.29), it is thought that that form of the list may be as late as the Maccabean age, but this cannot be proved, and in any case Joiarib is found, though not in so prominent a position, in Neh. 12.1–7 and 12–21. But we must not overlook the possibility of a different explanation of the changing names of families in these lists. There may have been many more priestly families than the twenty-four included in the service rota, amongst whom there would be rivalry for promotion to membership of the twenty-four. The families included in the twenty-four priestly divisions may therefore have changed from time to time when families were able to displace their rivals from the list.

Seraiah: a well-known priestly name in post-exilic times; see Ezr. 2.2.

Azariah: see Ezr. 7.1.

Jeremiah: a common priestly name; cf. 12.1, 12, 34. Its meaning is uncertain; it may come from the root *r-m-h* giving either 'May Yahweh throw down' or 'May Yahweh deceive', both being very improbable, or from the root *rûm*, 'May Yahweh raise up'.

3. Pashhur: see Ezr. 2.38.

Amariah: see Ezr. 7.3.

Malchijah: see 3.11 and Ezr. 10.25.

4. Hattush: see Ezr. 8.2.

Shebaniah: see 9.4.

Malluch: see Ezr. 10.29.

5. Harim: see 3.11 and Ezr. 2.39.

Meremoth: see 3.4 and Ezr. 8.33.

Obadiah: see Ezr. 8.9.

6. Daniel: see Ezr. 8.2.

Ginnethon: only here and 12.16. In 12.4 the slightly shorter form Ginnethoi occurs. The meaning is not certain, but may have something to do with 'garden' (Hebrew *gan*).

Baruch: see 3.20.

7. Meshullam: see Ezr. 8.16; 10.15; Neh. 3.4. Although it is one of the names common to associates of both Ezra and Nehemiah, it is a too frequently used name to be of value in identification.

Abijah: 'Yahweh is Father'; apart from this instance and 12.4, 17, the name belongs to pre-exilic times.

Mijamin: see Ezr. 10.25.

8. Maaziah: a name that occurs otherwise only in the list in 1 Chr. 24.18. The name means 'Yahweh is a stronghold'. In 12.5 it appears to be replaced by Maadiah, and in 12.17 by Moadiah.

Bilgai: only here; presumably a short (or hypocoristic) form of Bilgah 12.5, 18, and may mean 'Cheerfulness', i.e. how one would feel after a blessing from Yahweh.

Shemaiah: see Ezr. 8.13.

9. Jeshua the son of Azaniah: this is the only mention of Azaniah, 'Yahweh has listened', but see note on Uzai, 3.25. The designation of this Levitical house by a second name is probably made to distinguish this Joshua from Joshua son of Jozadak of priestly descent (Ezr. 10.18). See also Ezr. 2.2, 36; Neh. 8.7.

Binnui of the sons of Henadad: see 3.18, 24, and Ezr. 2.10, 40; 3.9.

Kadmiel: see Ezr. 2.40; 3.9.

10. Shebaniah: see 9.4.

Hodiah: see 8.7.

Kelita: see 8.7 and Ezr. 10.23.

Pelaiah: only here and 8.7.

Hanan: see 8.7 and Ezr. 2.46.

11. Mica: probably a short form of Micaiah meaning 'Who is like Yahweh? See 12.35. The name occurs as that of a son of Mephibosheth (2 Sam. 9.12), and also of a Levite in Neh. 11.17, 22.

Rehob: otherwise only as an Aramaean name (2 Sam. 8.3, 12). Possibly a short form of Rehabiah (1 Chr. 23.17), 'Yahweh has set free/in a wide place'; cf. Ps. 31.8.

Hashabiah: see 3.17; Ezr. 8.19.

12. Zaccur: see 3.2 and Ezr. 8.14.

Sherebiah: see Ezr. 8.18.

Shebaniah: see 9.4.

13. Hodiah: see 8.7.

Bani: see Ezr. 2.10.

Beninu: only here. If the text is correct the name would mean 'our son', but it is widely felt that a name like Chenani (9.4) or Bani (Ezr. 2.10) or Binnui (Ezr. 8.33), all shown elsewhere to be possible Levite names, may have stood here originally.

14–27. In the list of lay families in verses 14–27, the first part (verses 14–19a) follows very closely the first part of the list in Ezr. 2, namely verses 3–19, there being at least fourteen names in common (counting **Adonijah** and **Adonikam** as alternative names for the same family), with a possible fifteenth if **Hariph** be read in Ezr. 2.18 for Jorah, twelve of them, from **Pahath-moab** to **Hezekiah**, apart from one transposition and one substitution, in the same order. Further, the next three names, **Anathoth, Nebai**, and **Magpiash**, seem to be developed from the (place?) names in Ezr. 2.23, 29, 30, Anathoth, Nebo, and Magbish. From **Meshullam** (verse 20) to the end of the list (verse 27), **Baanah**, there are a further twenty-three names that are not found in Ezr. 2, but of which some are found as family names elsewhere, for instance, **Meshezabel** (3.4), **Hallohesh** (3.12), **Hashabnah** (3.10, Hashabneiah), **Anan** (3.23, Ananiah), **Harim** (3.11), and **Baanah** (3.4). This increase in the number of families listed may indicate an increase in the actual number of separate families between the time when the list in Ezr. 2 (=Neh. 7) was compiled and the time when the present list was drawn up. There may have been a splitting up of some of the larger families.

14. Parosh: see Ezr. 2.3.

Pahath-moab: see 3.11 and Ezr. 2.6.

Elam: see Ezr. 2.7.

Zattu: see Ezr. 2.8.

Bani: see verse 13 and Ezr. 2.10.

15. Bunni: see 9.4.

Azgad: see Ezr. 2.12.

Bebai: see Ezr. 2.11.

16. Adonijah: 'Yahweh is lord'; the name occurs for two men elsewhere, (a) the fourth son of David (1 Kg. 1.5), and (b) a Levite (2 Chr. 17.8). In Ezr. 2.13 the name Adonikam, 'The lord has risen up', is given instead.

Bigvai: see Ezr. 2.2.

Adin: see Ezr. 2.15.

17. Ater: see Ezr. 2.16.

Hezekiah: see Ezr. 2.16.

Azzur: probably a short form of Azariah, 'Yahweh has helped' (Ezr. 7.1); it occurs otherwise only for the father of Hananiah (Jer. 28.1) and the father of a prince of the people (Ezek. 11.1) (in each case it may be a family name and not the father's name).

18. Hodiah: see 8.7.

Hashum: see Ezr. 2.19.

Bezai: see Ezr. 2.17.

19. Hariph: meaning either 'Autumn' or 'Sharp/keen'; occurs only here and 7.24 (Ezr. 2.18 has Jorah).

Anathoth: this name occurs only here and in 1 Chr. 7.8 (a Benjaminite). Its use here may be directly due to the inclusion of Anathoth in Ezr. 2.23, where it was presumably intended as a place-name but was understood by the editor of this list as a personal name. The -oth ending is probably hypocoristic, and the name may mean 'Anath's man', Anath being a Canaanite goddess.

Nebai: only here; the meaning is unknown. Possibly this too, like Anathoth, is due to a mistaking of the place-name Nebo in Ezr. 2.29. See note on 7.33.

20. Magpiash: only here and meaning unknown. Here also there may be a mistaking of the place-name Magbish in Ezr. 2.30.

Meshullam: see verse 7.

Hezir: only here and in the list of priestly families in 1 Chr. 24 (verse 15). The word means 'pig'; it is presumably a nickname.

21. Meshezabel: see 3.4.

Zadok: see 3.4.

Jaddua: the name occurs only here and 12.11, 22. It is probably a short form of Jedaiah (Ezr. 2.36) or Joiada (Neh. 3.6), both meaning 'Yahweh has known/cared for'.

22. Pelatiah: 'Yahweh has rescued'; only here in post-exilic times, and otherwise only Ezek. 11.1, 13; 1 Chr. 3.21; 4.42.

Hanan: see verse 10 and Ezr. 2.46.

Anaiah: only here and 8.4.

23. Hoshea: this is the only post-exilic use of the name; but cf. Hoshaiah 12.32, of which this is probably a short form—'Yahweh has saved'. In form the name is identical with that of the prophet Hosea.

Hananiah: cf. 3.8 and Ezr. 10.28.

Hasshub: see 3.11.

24. Hallohesh: only here and 3.12.

Pilha: 'Mill-stone'; only here.

Shobek: 'Overpowering', 'Victor'; only here.

25. Rehum: see Ezr. 2.2.

Hashabnah: only here; but see 3.10. It is probably a short form of Hashabneiah, 'Yahweh has taken account of (me)'.

Maaseiah: see 3.23 and Ezr. 10.18.

26. Ahiah: 'Yahweh is brother/my brother'; only here in post-exilic times, but frequent before the exile.

Hanan: see verses 10, 22 and Ezr. 2.46.

Anan: only here; probably a short form of Ananiah, 'Yahweh has answered me'; but see 3.23.

27. Malluch: see Ezr. 10.29.

Harim: see 3.11 and Ezr. 2.39.

Baanah: see Ezr. 2.2.

THE PEOPLE TAKE AN OATH TO SHARE IN THE COVENANT **10.28–29**

28. The rest of the people: those who were not leaders or family heads and were not among those at the sealing.

temple servants: see Ezr. 2.43.

separated themselves: see Ezr. 6.21.

understanding: see 8.3.

29. a curse: the Hebrew word strictly means an adjuration which would be couched in some such terms as 'a curse be upon so-and-so'; cf. 1 Sam. 14.28.

to walk . . . to observe and do: if the list of names in verses 1–27 were shown to be an editorial addition, then these infinitives could be regarded as dependent on the phrase 'make a firm covenant' in 9.38.

DETAILS OF THE COVENANT, TO OBSERVE THE LAW, KEEP THE SABBATH, AND PAY
   THE REGULAR DUES **10.30–39**

30. not give our daughters: cf. the problem of mixed marriages faced by Ezra (Ezr. 9, 10) and by Nehemiah (Neh. 13.23–28). The form of words is similar to that in Dt. 7.3. If, as seems most probable, this covenant belongs to the work of Nehemiah it was most likely made shortly after the marriage reforms, otherwise it blindly ignores the fact that mixed marriages did exist. It may be wondered if the Chronicler, in placing this part of Nehemiah's work immediately after the reading of the law and the holding of a fast day in Ezra's time, suppressed an account of a similar acceptance of obligation to the law made by Ezra which would not be out of place after a reading of the law.

31. sabbath day: Nehemiah found it necessary to tighten up the observance of the sabbath (13.15–22); cf. Jer. 17.19–27; Am. 8.5. Many of the traders were non-Jews (13.16) who would not be very willing to observe the Jewish sabbath.

holy day: for instance, the first and seventh days of the Passover and the first and eighth days of the feast of booths (Exod. 12.16; Lev. 23).

forgo the crops: for the fallow year, see Lev. 25.2–7 and Exod. 23.11 (where the same term as is used here is translated 'let it (the land) lie fallow').

exaction of every debt: cf. Dt. 15.1–3.

32. charge . . . for the service: the decrees made by Cyrus, Darius, and Artaxerxes (Ezr. 6.3–5, 7–9; 7.20–22) were intended to cover running-costs as well as initial building expenses, but this sort of subsidy cannot go on unconditionally for ever. 2 Chr. 24.6 speaks of the 'tax levied by Moses . . . on the congregation of Israel for the tent of testimony', and Exod. 30.11–16 sets down the law of a half-shekel offering by each male Israelite twenty years old and upward for the service of the tent of meeting. Both these passages may represent a slightly later time than that of the present covenant: Exod. 30.11–16 is regarded as a supplementary addition to the Priestly Code and Chronicles may have been written as late as the third century B.C.

33. showbread: lit. 'the bread of the arrangement-in-rows'; this is the Chronicler's term (1 Chr. 9.32; 23.29; 2 Chr. 13.11) for what is elsewhere called the 'bread of the Presence' (1 Sam. 21.6, etc.). Instructions for setting the bread in rows are found in Exod. 40.23 and Lev. 24.8. The showbread was set 'before' or 'in the presence of' God in two rows of six loaves each and was renewed every sabbath day. By this time it was *in fact* but a continuation of a very ancient practice of setting food before the deity, but *in meaning* it was both a reminder to men of the presence of God and a token gift by men to God of that which was a daily necessity.

continual cereal offering: i.e. the grain that accompanied the morning and evening sacrifice of flesh; cf. Num. 28.1–8.

continual burnt offering: the animal sacrifice morning and evening. It is not clear why the cereal-offering is mentioned before the burnt-offering, as it also is in Ezek. 45.13, 15, but it may be that the cereal-offering was steadily assuming a greater significance in the ritual.

sabbaths . . . new moons . . . appointed feasts: the offerings for these are set out in Num. 28.9–31; 29.1–39.

holy things: these were normally voluntary gifts of animals for peace-offerings (Num. 29.39; cf. 2 Chr. 29.33), but their handling probably involved some public cost, and in any case, there were some compulsory peace-offerings (Lev. 23.19) which would be at public expense.

sin offerings: these were public offerings on most festival days (Num. 28.15, 22; Lev. 4.13–21).

all the work of the house of our God: this is a comprehensive phrase which would cover any administrative charge not so far listed.

34. Casting lots was a common way of making decisions between one person and another, or one thing and another (Lev. 16.8–10; Jos. 14.2; 18.10; 1 Sam. 10.19ff.).

wood offering: this and 13.31 are the only places where a wood-offering (*kurban*) is mentioned. Leviticus 1.17 briefly mentions the wood and in 6.12f. it says that a priest shall keep the wood replenished every day to prevent the fire from going out. It was a plain necessity; cf. Gen. 22.3, 6, 7, 9.

as it is written in the law: as has just been noted the law speaks of the burning of the wood but not of its provision. We may perhaps see here the building up of detailed laws supplementing what was written in the Pentateuch; they were finally written down in the Mishnah. *Taanith* (iv, 5) lists days on which the wood was carried by respective families, and Josephus (*War*, II, xvii, 6) refers to the feast of wood-carrying. It may have been the king's prerogative in pre-exilic times to supply the wood from the royal forests. It is known that Cambyses discontinued the practice in Egypt of supplying Egyptian temples.

35–36. first fruits: for the first fruits from the ground, see Exod. 23.19; 34.26; Dt. 26.1–10, and for first fruits of fruit, Num. 18.12f.; cf. Lev. 19.23–25; and of sons, Num. 18.15f.; but the latter were redeemable on payment of five shekels at sacred standard (Exod. 13.13; 34.20); for first fruits of herds and flocks see Num. 18.17; Dt. 12.6.

37. coarse meal: cf. Num. 15.20; Ezek. 44.30.

and our contributions: the term means what is raised from the main bulk and set aside as a gift for sacred purposes. It is, however, the odd member of the list, for in all the other cases it is the first that is to be brought to the priests (grammatically, 'first' must be taken to govern all the other items, for obviously only a first of the fruit, etc., was to be brought), but it would be strange for only a first part of that which is *all* for sacred use should be brought to the priests. The word is not found in LXX and should probably be regarded as a gloss. (It is arguable that if the priests took the first of the contributions the rest would be consumed by the worshippers, which is implied in Dt. 12.6, 7, 17f.)

to the Levites the tithes: cf. Num. 18.21; Lev. 27.30. Here the Levites are not only the recipients of the tithe but they are responsible for its collection. In other places the responsibility rests on the individual to bring it to the Temple (Am. 4.4; Mal. 3.10; Dt. 14.23f.; 2 Chr. 31.12). There was always likely to be difficulty in the collection of tithes.

There were, according to these verses, four different kinds of gift to the sanctuary and the priests—(a) first fruits(*bikkūrîm*), (b) first part(*rē'šît*), (c) contributions (*t^erûmôt*), and (d) tithes(*m^{eʿ}aśś^erîm*).

rural towns: the Hebrew literally means the towns of our labour or cultivation, i.e. where we do our tilling.

38. the priest: not the high priest, but a representative of the priesthood must be present in the rural towns when the Levites are collecting the tithes.

tithe of the tithes: the priestly part of the tithes as laid down in Num. 18.26.

39. contribution: see verse 37. Here it is used widely to include first fruits, tithes, and tithe of tithes; cf. Num. 18.24ff.

It may be noted that there is no mention in these verses of a tithe of herds and flocks, as there is in Lev. 27.32. The two practices cannot be reconciled and belong to different periods. The tithing of cattle may be a later adaptation in the interests of the priesthood.

The references given above will show that the terms of this covenant are not taken exclusively from any one part of the Pentateuch, and from this we may infer that the whole Pentateuch was already known in Palestine before it was publicly read by Ezra and accepted by the people in congregation.

FOURTH SECTION 11.1–13.31 SOCIAL AND RELIGIOUS REFORMS

DECISION TO MOVE A TENTH OF THE PEOPLE TO JERUSALEM 11.1–2

1. The decision to move some of the population into Jerusalem should clearly follow 7.4. At first sight 7.5 seems to herald such a move, but serves in fact only to introduce a list in the remainder of that chapter which has little or nothing directly to do with the problem.

lived: could also mean 'settled' and would then imply that the leaders took the first step.

cast lots: see 10.34.

2. willingly offered: probably over and above the one in ten mentioned in verse 1, but it could mean those who willingly acted on the decision by lot.

SUNDRY EXTRACTS FROM REGISTERS 11.3–12.26

SETTLERS IN JERUSALEM 11.3–19

We should now expect a list of those chosen by lot (and of those who volunteered), but instead we find lists of settlers both in Jerusalem and in outlying towns in Judah. The first such list is in verses 3–19 and gives heads of families settled in Jerusalem. The same list occurs, with some differences, in 1 Chr. 9 2–18. Although it is not just the list expected, it cannot be said to be entirely out of place here because it does give a list of heads of families resident in Jerusalem *after* Nehemiah's reform. It was probably based on a document in the Temple or state archives and may be regarded as genuine, at least such of it as has not suffered in transmission. If that is so, then the editor of 1 Chr. 9.2ff., who is probably to be distinguished from the Chronicler and given a later date, either based his list on it or borrowed the same list from the archives. The former is probably the more likely in view of the apparent dependence of 1 Chr. 9.2 on Neh. 11.3. Nehemiah 11.3 refers to people living in towns outside Jerusalem, a reference that comes into its own in verses 25ff., where such residents are mentioned. 1 Chr. 9.2 repeats part of the verse, but has no subsequent mention of those who live in the towns (with one exception, verse 16). Some significant differences between the two lists will be noted in the comments.

3. temple servants: see Ezr. 2.43.

descendants of Solomon's servants: see Ezr. 2.55.

4. Athaiah: only here; 'Yahweh has shown himself pre-eminent'; cf Uthai in Ezr. 8.14.

Uzziah: see Ezr. 10.21.

Zechariah: see Ezr. 5.1; 8.3.

Amariah: see Ezr. 7.3.

Shephatiah: see Ezr. 2.4.

Mahalalel: a name occurring only in Gen. 5.12ff.; 1 Chr. 1.2 and here. The name is compounded of a noun and a participle—'God is one who illuminates/flashes light'; see also on 3.4.

Perez: 'Breach'; only here and verse 6 in post-exilic literature. Perez was one of the sons of Judah (Gen. 38.29), and the name is used in the O.T. only for him and the family named after him. Occasionally, as here, we find a man identified by more than his father's name or his family's name: in Neh. 3.4 both Meremoth and Meshullam are more closely identified by the mention of their father and their grandfather (unless this latter be the family name). Ezra was given a full genealogy in Ezr. 7.1 (now shortened by loss of names in transmission) going back to Aaron. Here, as with Ezra, there was evidently a sense of importance attaching to the name or the situation, as with other names that follow, which induced the compiler to retain a full genealogy. The names given for the successive members of the family of the sons of Perez in 1 Chr. 9.4 are completely different from those given here. Only the first name in 1 Chr. 9.4, Uthai, is recognizable as a form of Athaiah, and presumably this change in pronunciation of the first name brought to the mind of the 1 Chr. 9 editor the genealogy of a man of that name in his own generation which he substituted for the genealogy which now appears in Neh. 11.4.

5. Maaseiah: see 3.23 and Ezr. 10.18.

Baruch: see 3.20.

Colhozeh: see 3.15.

Hazaiah: only here; meaning 'Yahweh has seen'.

Adaiah: see Ezr. 10.29.

Joiarib: see Ezr. 8.16.

Zechariah: see Ezr. 5.1, 8.3.

the Shilonite: a better form would be that of Syr., which has 'the Shelanite', thus connecting with Shelah another son of Judah (Num. 26.20). For this list 1 Chr. 9.5 has: 'And of the Shilonites: Asaiah the first born and his sons'. Asaiah is an obvious shortening or corruption of Maaseiah, first born is a slight alteration of the name Baruch and 'his sons' is all that remains of the rest.

1 Chr. 9.6 includes the family of another son of Judah, Zerah. A descendant of Zerah is mentioned in verse 24; this indicates that the family of Zerah was still existent at the time the list was compiled and that the editor of 1 Chr. 9 has preserved material that has doubtless been lost from Nehemiah's list.

6. This reference to the family of Perez jumps back to verse 4. The fact that a total is given for the family of Perez and not for that of Shelah is further evidence that the list here has lost some items and details by the accidents of copying at some time.

7. Sallu: this name occurs otherwise only in 1 Chr. 9.7 and Neh. 12.7, and possibly also, in the form Sallai, in Neh. 11.8; 12.20. It is perhaps to be connected with the Arabic root *sala'a*, 'pay back quickly', but the significance of a name with such a meaning is not obvious.

Meshullam: see Ezr. 8.16; 10.15; Neh. 10.7.

Joed: 'Yahweh is witness', occurs only here; 1 Chr. 9.7 has Hodaviah.

Pedaiah: see 3.25.

Kolaiah: a name that occurs only here, Jer. 29.21, and LXX in Ezr. 10.23 (Kelaiah). It is probably another pronunciation of the name Kelaiah for which a natural meaning cannot be found. Kolaiah may mean 'The voice of Yahweh'.

Maaseiah: see verse 5.

Ithiel: 'With me is God'; occurs only here and, if the text is sound, Prov. 30.1.

Jeshaiah: see Ezr. 8.7.

The Benjamin line is not traced back to an immediate descendant of Benjamin as is the Judah line to the sons of Judah: this may well be because of the chequered history of Benjamin; cf. Jg. 19–21. In 1 Chr. 9.7 only the first two names given in this verse, Sallu and Meshullam, appear and there follows 'son of Hodaviah, son of Hassenuah', which seems to be a slightly different form of 'Judah the son of Hassenuah' in Neh. 11.9. But, besides omitting what stands between these names (Meshullam and Judah) in Nehemiah, the 1 Chronicles record has three other families from Benjamin—Ibneiah, Elah, and Meshullam. This makes it fairly clear that the Nehemiah list has another lacuna, and ought to have more than one family for Benjamin, for otherwise, nine hundred and twenty-eight (verse 8) is a large number for one family. The two names Gabbai and Sallai in verse 8 may be a scribe's attempt to fill the gap (see below).

8. after him: i.e. after Sallu, but the formula is not used with the other names and it is not easy to see why it should be used here. One recension of LXX (the Lucianic) has 'and his kinsmen' (reading *wᵉ'eḥāw* instead of *wᵉ'aḥarāw*) which may well be right.

Gabbai: only here; in late (post-biblical) Hebrew the word means 'tax-gatherer'.

Sallai: elsewhere only the name of a priest (Neh. 12.20). It may be a variant form of the name Sallu, verse 7. These two names are not readily intelligible here, for, apart from the unexpected 'after him' that introduces them, they lack a conjunction and they are so like sounding as to suggest an imaginative insertion of two names. Similar like sounding names are to be found in 12.20, Sallai, Kallai, and in 12.36, Milalai, Gilalai, and with these we may compare Muppim and Huppim in Gen. 46.21, Huppim and Shuppim in 1 Chr. 7.15, and Shashai, Sharai in Ezr. 10.40. It may be that they are an attempt to put meaning into a corrupt text. 1 Chr. 9.9 has 'and their kinsmen according to their generations', and in verse 14 of this chapter we find 'and their brethren, mighty men of valour'. Something comparable must have stood here originally, but some further reference to families of Benjamin is also expected; see p. 189.

9. Joel: see Ezr. 10.43.

Zichri: is a fairly common name, of some twelve individuals, three others being Benjaminites (1 Chr. 8.19, 23, 27). It is probably a short form of Zechariah, 'Yahweh has remembered'.

their overseer: i.e. of the Benjaminites, but if Judah was second over the city, was Joel first over the city as well as being overseer of the Benjaminites? The Hebrew, in spite of some awkwardness in phrasing, could yield the meaning 'was over the second quarter of the city'; cf. 2 Kg. 22.14. If this is contemporary with 7.2, then, according to the present form of text there, there were already two men in charge of the city.

Judah: see Ezr. 10.23.

Hassenuah: only here; Ezr. 2.35 speaks of a very large family of Senaah, a place-name presumably, and Neh. 3.3 records that the sons of Hassenaah built the Fish Gate. In form the name means 'The hated one'.

10. Jedaiah: this name is spelt differently in Hebrew from that in 3.10; for this one see Ezr. 2.36.

Joiarib: see Ezr. 8.16. According to 1 Chr. 24.7 there was a high priest named Joiarib from whom the Maccabees claimed descent, 1 Mac. 2.1.

Jachin: presumably a shortened form of Jehoiachin, 'May Yahweh make firm'. The name occurs also as that of the head of a priestly family in 1 Chr. 9.10; 24.17; otherwise it is the name of a Simeonite (Gen. 46.10). But, since it stands in a genealogy where the normal term is 'son of', it is highly probable that it is an error for 'son of' (i.e. *ben* instead of *yākîn*) and such a change of text would yield a longer type of genealogy here, as one would expect alongside others in this chapter.

11. Seraiah: see Ezr. 2.2; 1 Chr. 9.11 has Azariah (Ezr. 7.2).

Hilkiah: see Ezr. 7.1.

Meshullam: see Ezr. 8.16; 10.15.

Zadok: see 3.4, 29 and Ezr. 7.2.

Meraioth: this name seems to have been limited in use to descendants of Aaron (1 Chr. 6.6ff.; 6.52; Ezr. 7.3 (q.v.); cf. 1 Chr. 9.11; Neh. 12.15).

Ahitub: see Ezr. 7.2.

12. who did the work of the house: this can mean either, the normal work of a priest, implying that not all priests were active, or, the supervision of work done by others; cf. Ezr. 3.9. The former is more likely.

Adaiah: see verse 5 and Ezr. 10.29.

Jeroham: 'May he find compassion'; is the name of some nine individuals.

Pelaliah: only here; 'Yahweh has interposed/judged'; cf. Palal, 3.25.

Amzi: possibly a shortened form of Amaziah, 'Yahweh has acted strongly'; the name occurs otherwise only in 1 Chr. 6.46 (a Levite).

Zechariah: see Ezr. 5.1; 8.3. These last three names are not in 1 Chr. 9.12.

Pashhur: see Ezr. 2.38.

Malchijah: see 3.11; Ezr. 10.25.

13. Amashsai: only here; it is not a readily intelligible form and may be an error for Amasai, 'Yahweh has carried' (a priest of that name is found in 1 Chr. 15.24). 1 Chr. 9.12 has Maasai.

Azarel: see Ezr. 10.41; 1 Chr. 9.12 has Adiel.

Ahzai: only here in this form; it is probably a shortened form of Ahaziah, 'Yahweh has grasped', which occurs only as the name of two kings, that of Israel (1 Kg. 22.40) and that of Judah (2 Kg. 8.24). 1 Chr. 9.12 has Jahzerah.

Meshillemoth: only here and 2 Chr. 28.12 (an Ephraimite); 1 Chr. 9.12 has Meshullam, son of Meshillemith. The name may be a form of Meshelemiah (1 Chr. 9.21), 'Yahweh is one who makes complete'.

Immer: see Ezr. 2.37.

14. Zabdiel: 'Gift of God' or 'God has given'; elsewhere only 1 Chr. 27.2.

Haggedolim: this, though treated as one, is scarcely a proper name. In form it is masculine plural of the adjective 'great' with the definite article, i.e. 'the great ones'. Does it refer to the high priests, or is it an error for such a name as Gedaliah (Ezr. 10.18) or Giddel (Ezr. 2.47, 56)? The statement about Zabdiel is not in 1 Chr. 9.13.

15. Shemaiah: see 3.29 and Ezr. 8.13.

Hasshub: see 3.11.

Azrikam: '(My) help has risen up'; elsewhere only 1 Chr. 3.23; 8.38; 9.14, 44; 2 Chr. 28.7.

Hashabiah: see Ezr. 8.19.

Bunni: see 9.4. 1 Chr. 9.14 has Merari, and since, according to Ezr. 8.19, Hashabiah was 'of the sons of Merari' it might be the original reading.

16. Shabbethai: see Ezr. 10.15.

Jozabad: see Ezr. 8.33.

over the outside work: if this is the same Jozabad as that named in Ezr. 8.33, then the outside work was probably not fabric, as comparison with verse 22 might suggest, but external business matters. The name Jozabad is common enough, however, not to demand identity of the two men. There is nothing in 1 Chr. 9 to correspond with this verse.

17. Mattaniah: see verse 22 below, and Ezr. 10.26.

Micah: see 10.11.

Zabdi: probably a short form of Zabdiel, verse 14; in 12.35 the corresponding name is Zaccur, and in 1 Chr. 9.15 it is Zichri. Otherwise Zabdi occurs only in Jos. 7.1; 1 Chr. 8.19; 27.27.

Asaph: see Ezr. 2.41. If Asaph was in *fact* Mattaniah's great-grandfather, we may assume that he was an individual member of the *family* of Asaph who happened to bear the same name as that of the first head of the family, but it seems very likely that in some places 'son of' must have the same force as 'of the sons of'='of the family of' (see note on 12.16) and that this is one such case; see also 12.35. This will mean that here, contrary to the usual practice in Ezra-Nehemiah (cf. Ezr. 7.7), the singers are included among the Levites.

the leader to begin the thanksgiving in prayer: lit. 'as head of the beginning would offer thanksgiving in prayer'. Instead of 'beginning' the Lucianic LXX has 'praise' (*t^ehillāh* instead of *t^ehillāh*), which is more in keeping with the tradition which associated Asaph with Temple-singing (1 Chr. 15.16–20) and with Psalms (Ps. 50, 73–83).

Bakbukiah: elsewhere only 12.9, 25. A Bukkiah belongs to the Hemanite family (1 Chr. 25.4, 13), and it may be that they are simply different forms of the same name—the name of a family within the Hemanite group. The -iah ending may be a hypocoristic one, and not, as so often in Hebrew proper names, a contracted form of the divine name, since Bakbuk (Ezr. 2.51) means 'flask' and the name 'Yahweh is (my) flask' would be very unlikely to be used.

second among: i.e. to Mattaniah; cf. 12.25 where his name appears immediately after Mattaniah's. In 1 Chr. 9.15 instead of 'and Bakbukiah the second among his brethren' we find 'and Bakbakkar, Heresh, Galal'.

Abda: elsewhere only 1 Kg. 4.6. In 12.25 the name Bakbukiah is followed by that of Obadiah, which 1 Chr. has in 9.16. Abda is probably a shortened form of Obadiah (Ezr. 8.9).

Shammua: elsewhere only 12.18; Num. 13.4; 2 Sam. 5.14. 1 Chr. 9.16 has Shemaiah, 'Yahweh has heard', of which Shammua is doubtless a short form.

Galal: only here and 1 Chr. 9.15, 16; the name may mean 'Tortoise'.

Jeduthun: the chief of one of the three choirs (1 Chr. 16.42). 'Son of' here should probably be taken to mean 'of the family of', as in the case of Asaph. The meaning of the name is not known.

18. This verse, closing the list of Levites and standing before verse 19, which speaks of gatekeepers, shows that by this time Levites were reckoned separately from gatekeepers. The list may therefore be dated later than that in Ezr. 2 (=Neh. 7), where gatekeepers are still apparently reckoned among the Levites. Instead of this verse, 1 Chr. 9.16 has 'and Berechiah the son of Asa, son of Elkanah, who dwelt in the villages of the Netophathites'; which is scarcely right, because they could not at the same time dwell in Jerusalem.

19. Akkub: see 8.7 and Ezr. 2.42; this is probably a family name, as it is in Ezr. 2.42, contrary to the usage of the rest of this chapter, where the names are those of heads of families.

Talmon: see Ezr. 2.42. This is presumably another family name, and we would therefore expect mention of the third family of gatekeepers, that of Shallum, as in 1 Chr. 9.17 (cf. Ezr. 2.42, Neh. 7.45).

SOME FURTHER REMARKS ABOUT SETTLEMENT **11.20–24**

21. temple servants: see Ezr. 2.43ff.

Ophel: see 3.26.

Ziha: see Ezr. 2.43. Ziha is a family name; the family therefore seems to be responsible for leadership. For a family group in authority, see Ezr. 3.9.

Gishpa: occurs only here; it may be a corrupt or variant form of Hasupha, who is listed along with Ziha in Ezr. 2.43 (=Neh. 7.46).

22. Uzzi: see Ezr. 7.4.

Bani: see Ezr. 2.10.

Hashabiah: see Ezr. 8.19.

Mattaniah: see verse 17 and Ezr. 10.26.

Mica: see 10.11.

Asaph: see verse 17.

If we compare this verse, where Uzzi is great-grandson of Mattaniah, who was son of Mica of the family of Asaph, with verse 17 where Mattaniah son of Micah (of the family of Asaph) must clearly be regarded as a contemporary of Uzzi, we gain the impression that within three generations there were two men named Mattaniah son of Mica(h). It became a common enough practice from the second century B.C. onwards for grandsons to bear their grandfather's or father's name.

over the work of the house of God: the translation gives the impression that this (in contrast with one way of taking verse 16) means the internal work, preparation for rituals, etc., but the preposition in Hebrew ($l^e ne\underline{g}e\underline{d}$) cannot readily mean 'over'. It normally means 'in front of', and may here have the meaning 'in respect of'; the 'work' will then be the worship in the Temple; cf. 1 Chr. 9.13, 'the work of the service of the house of God'.

23. command: perhaps referring to the tradition given by the Chronicler in 1 Chr. 15.16ff.; but it is not clear that the king mentioned here would naturally mean David; it might mean the contemporary king, i.e. Artaxerxes, as it does in verse 24.

them: either the Levites or else the singers who are the subject of the next clause.

settled provision: the same Hebrew word in 9.38 is translated 'firm covenant'; the idea of fixity is basic in the root (from which 'amen' comes). This, then, is a permanent regulation governing their duties.

24. Pethahiah: see Ezr. 10.23.

Meshezabel: see 3.4.

Zerah: probably a short form of Zerahiah (Ezr. 7.4), 'Yahweh has shone forth/risen'. Seven different people in the O.T. are called by this name, but here Zerah son of Judah and Tamar (Gen. 38.30) is clearly meant (see verse 5) and is the family name.

Judah: see Ezr. 10.23.

at the king's hand: this would suggest that he was Jewish resident at court for Jewish affairs; cf. Ezr. 7.12 (although it may not have been the same office; Ezra was a priest but this man may have been a layman).

TOWNS OCCUPIED BY JEWS OF JUDAH AND BENJAMIN **11.25-36**

This list is comparable with the similarly constructed list in Ezr. 2.21-35 (=Neh. 7.25-38), where, after a full list of families, there follows a list of towns and the number of their inhabitants. Here only the towns are given and not the number of inhabitants. The lists, however, are not comparable in detail, for of the thirty-two places listed here ten only occur in Ezr. 2 and all of those in territory occupied by Benjaminites—Geba, Michmash (Michmas), Aija (Ai), Bethel, Anathoth, Nob (Nebo), Ramah, Hadid, Lod, and Ono. (None of the seventeen towns listed here as occupied by Judahites occurs in Ezr. 2.) It is not evident from the names in the list upon what principle the compiler based his collection. A majority of the places, but by no means all, were border-towns, and this may indicate that the Jews were beginning to reoccupy towns taken over by the neighbours who encroached on their territory during the exile.

25. Kiriath-arba: the older name of Hebron; it lay some 20 miles S. of Jerusalem. Its mention is surprising because it must already have been firmly in Edomite possession, where it remained until Maccabean times (1 Mac. 5.65). The Edomites almost certainly moved in during the exile.

Dibon: only mentioned here (and is not to be confused with the Dibon in Moab, Num. 21.30). It may be the same place as that called Dimonah in Jos. 15.22.

Jekabzeel: name found only here, but probably the same as Kabzeel (Jos. 15.21; 2 Sam. 23.20; 1 Chr. 11.22).

26. Jeshua: mentioned only here.

Moladah: Jos. 19.2; 15.26; 1 Chr. 4.28, a place not identified with certainty, but probably lying well south of Jerusalem and traditionally allotted to Simeon.

Beth-pelet: only here and Jos. 15.27 in this form, but in 2 Sam. 23.26 a man from Beth-pelet is called 'the Paltite'.

27. Hazar-shual ('fox enclosure'): mentioned in Jos. 15.28 and 1 Chr. 4.28.

Beer-sheba: often cited as the southern limit of Jewish territory in Palestine.

28. Ziklag: according to Jos. 15.31, a Ziklag was assigned to Judah, and in Jos. 19.5 to Simeon, while in 1 Sam. 27.6 it was a town in Philistine territory which David was allowed to occupy. It probably became Israelite in David's time, and then at a later date there came to be two traditions about its allocation.

Meconah: name occurs only here.

29. En-rimmon: in Simeon's territory (Jos. 19.7). In Jos. 15.32 it has been separated into two names, Ain and Rimmon.

Zorah: cf. Jos. 15.33. It was a town in the territory which the Danites occupied in Samson's time (Jos. 19.41, Jg. 13.2).

Jarmuth: also in Jos. 15.35; it lies between Hebron and Lachish.

30. Zanoah: see 3.13.

Adullam: famous as David's centre in his outlaw days (1 Sam. 22.1; 2 Sam. 23.13; cf. Jos. 12.15; 15.35).

Lachish: cf. Jos. 10.3; 15.39. It became the base of Assyrian operations (2 Kg. 18.14).

fields: Lachish was evidently not large enough to have its dependent villages (daughters), but not so small as to be mentioned without any outlying district.

Azekah: cf. Jos. 10.10; 15.35.

valley of Hinnom: usually designated 'of the sons of Hinnom'; it lay off the south-west corner of Jerusalem and formed a boundary between Judah and Benjamin (Jos. 15.8). See on 2.13.

31. Geba: a levitical city (Jos. 21.17), about 10 miles N. of Jerusalem.

Michmash: see Ezr. 2.27 (Michmas).

Aija: so spelt only here, but is probably the same as Aiath (Isa. 10.28) and Ai (Ezr. 2.28).

Bethel: see Ezr. 2.28.

32. Anathoth: see Ezr. 2.23.

Nob: this is probably the ancient priestly city (1 Sam. 21.1; 22.19); it is named in Isa. 10.32 as a place on the route of the invading Assyrian army.

Ananiah: only here, possibly the modern Beit Hanina 4 miles NNW. of Jerusalem.

33. Hazor: at least six places are so called: (a) Jabin's city (Jos. 11.1), (b), (c), and (d) three places in the Negeb (Jos. 15.23, 25), (e) this one in Benjaminite territory (in 2 Sam. 13.23 there is mention of a Baal-hazor on the border of Ephraim and Benjamin which may be the same), and (f) an Arabian place (Jer. 49.28).

Ramah: meaning 'the height', a name given to several places. This is probably *er-Ram* 5 miles N. of Jerusalem; see Ezr. 2.26.

Gittaim: also mentioned in 2 Sam. 4.3 but not identifiable.

34. Hadid: see Ezr. 2.33.

Zeboim: also mentioned in 1 Sam. 13.18 and to be distinguished from Zeboiim (Gen. 14.2) near Sodom.

Neballat: mentioned only here.

35. Lod: i.e. Lydda, modern Ludd, 11 miles SE. of Joppa.

Ono: see Ezr. 2.33 and Neh. 6.2.

craftsmen: probably craftsmen in wood, since it was not far to Joppa where wood was imported from Lebanon (Ezr. 3.7; 2 Chr. 2.16).

36. Levites . . . Benjamin: was this to ensure adequate teaching throughout the territory? There may have been a shortage of Levites in some territories owing to the downgrading among their ranks in exilic and post-exilic times.

PRIESTS AND LEVITES WHO CAME UP WITH ZERUBBABEL 12.1–9

Of the twenty-two priestly names given in verses 1–7, twenty-one occur in verses 12–22 as family names (**Hattush** being the only name not repeated); see note on 10.2. It is a reasonable assumption therefore that this list was originally intended to give the names of twenty-two family groups whose heads of family are listed in verses 12–21, but as now written (verses 1–7) is meant to be the list of individual priests in the time of Joshua and (verses 12–21) of those in the time of Joiakim together with their families. This and the following lists were presumably taken from the same source as that in chapter 11, namely the Temple or state archives, but we cannot tell how far it has been adapted by the editor. The eight names (assuming **Maadiah** to stand in the place of Maaziah (10.8), **Rehum** (see on Ezr. 2.2) in the place of Harim (10.5; 12.15), and **Ezra** to be another form of

Azariah (10.2)) that are commented on below, verses 3–7, did not occur in 10.2–8. Six of these eight names occur at the end of the list, the first, **Joiarib**, being attached with 'and' (not translated in RSV), as also in verse 19. This 'and' is the only one in the list of names and suggests that the six names were added by an editor at some time. If it be assumed that the list in 10.2–8 was up to date in Joiakim's time (as implied in Neh. 12.12), i.e. at about 500 B.C. (Joiakim being son of Joshua, Neh. 12.10), then these added families, replacing names that have now fallen out of use and keeping the number near the recognized twenty-four (1 Chr. 24.7–18), must be regarded as an attempt to bring the list up to date in Nehemiah's time. This naturally throws the reference to 'those who came up with Zerubbabel' in 12.1 out of gear, at least that is how we would look at it, but the Hebrew historian of those days felt no serious difficulty in telescoping events and generations.

If these are to be thought of as family groups, as demanded by verses 12–21, then comparison with the names in Ezr. 2.36–39 makes it conceivable that these are sub-families together comprising the four main groups—Jedaiah-Jeshua, Immer, Pashhur, and Harim. It is not possible, with the uncertainty over changing names of some of the families, to reconstruct the list so as to bring the number up to twenty-four—assuming it to have been the original intention to list twenty-four names (see note on 10.2). One obvious name that might be supplied is that of Pashhur which is found in Ezr. 2.38 and in Neh. 10.3 but is absent from chapter 12. (Names that occurred in 10.2–8 are not listed below.)

3. Shecaniah: the other two lists have Shebaniah, which may have stood here originally. For Shecaniah, see Ezr. 8.3, 5, and for Shebaniah, Neh. 9.4. The alteration in the name may have been due to the fact that Hattush is given as a close descendant of Shecaniah in 1 Chr. 3.22, and knowledge of this may well have led a scribe to write Shecaniah for Shebaniah immediately after the name of Hattush.

4. Iddo: only here and verse 16 as the name of a priestly family, unless Iddo grandfather of Zechariah the prophet (Ezr. 5.1) is also a family name, and therefore perhaps the same family (see verse 16).

6. Joiarib: see 11.10 and Ezr. 8.16.
Jedaiah: see Ezr. 2.36. (The name has a different spelling in Hebrew from Jedaiah in 3.10.)
7. Sallu: see 11.7.
Amok: 'Deep' (Wise?); only here and verse 20.
Hilkiah: see 8.4 and Ezr. 7.1.
Jedaiah: see verse 6.
8. With this list of Levites, or Levite families, in verses 8f., compare the lists in Ezr. 2.40–42; Neh. 8.7; 10.9–13; 12.24–26. Since these two verses seem to break the connection between verses 7 and 10, it looks as if the source from which the editor obtained the lists in this chapter did not contain them. The editor may have based this list of Levites on such lists as those mentioned above.
Jeshua: see Ezr. 2.36, 40.

Binnui: see Ezr. 8.33.

Kadmiel: see Ezr. 3.9.

Sherebiah: see Ezr. 8.18.

Judah: see 11.9 and Ezr. 10.23. Is this to be regarded as an alternative form for Hodaviah (or vice versa)? See on Ezr. 2.40.

Mattaniah: see 11.17, 22 and Ezr. 10.26.

in charge of the songs: see 11.17.

9. **Bakbukiah:** see 11.17.

Unno: a name otherwise found only in 1 Chr. 15.18, 20, where it is spelt Unni. It is possibly a short form of Anaiah (8.4), 'Yahweh has answered'.

GENEALOGY OF HIGH PRIESTS FROM JOSHUA TO JADDUA **12.10-11**

This list may be regarded as a continuation of that found in 1 Chr. 6.3-15, which ends with Joshua's father Jehozadak. The continuation was evidently thought to be necessary because verses 12-21 are set in the time of Joiakim who succeeded Joshua, and it thus brings the line of priests to two generations beyond the point at which 1 Chr. 6.14 ends.

10. **Jeshua:** see Ezr. 2.2.

Joiakim: 'May Yahweh set up/establish'; apart from this high priest (also verses 12, 26) the name occurs only as the name of the son of Josiah (2 Kg. 23.34).

Eliashib: see Ezr. 10.6.

Joiada: see 3.6.

11. **Jonathan:** 'Yahweh has given'; Jonathan was quite a common name, three others occurring in this chapter, verses 14, 18, 35. In verse 22 the name Johanan (=Jehohanan) stands in the same place in the list as Jonathan does here. Either Jonathan here is a scribal error for Johanan, which is very likely owing to the occurrence of the name Jonathan in three other places in this chapter, or Jonathan and Johanan may have been brothers and Jonathan may have held the high priesthood for a short while only. There is no doubt at all that whatever view is taken of the name Jonathan here, the name Johanan should also stand between Joiada and Jaddua, as is shown by verses 22f. and Ezr. 10.6. Other men named J(eh)ohanan, 'Yahweh has been gracious', occur in 12.13, 42; 6.18; Ezr. 8.12; 10.28.

Jaddua: for the name, see 10.21. This and verse 22 are the only references to this high priest in the O.T. According to Josephus he was still in office in Alexander's time. The inclusion of his name in this list gives some indication of the date of the compilation of Ezra-Nehemiah.

HEADS OF PRIESTLY HOUSES IN THE TIME OF JOIAKIM **12.12-21**

The twenty-one families listed here are all named in verses 1-7, although with some slight differences in the forms of some names—Rehum/**Harim**, Shecaniah/**Shebaniah**, Meremoth/**Meraioth**, Ginnethoi/**Ginnethon**, Mijamin/**Miniamin**, Maadiah/**Moadiah**, Sallu/**Sallai**. If the names in verses 1-7 have to be regarded as those of individuals (which is improbable), then we should have to assume that they became family names before this list was compiled, or that the author is saying, in effect, 'the contemporary priestly head who now stands where *so-and-so* stood is *so-and-so*'. But the list should be taken as a repetition of that in verses 1–7, repeated for the purpose of giving the names of heads of families. For the family names (not included in the following notes), see the notes on 10.2–8 and 12.1–7. As in verses 1–7, so here, it may be asked if the list at one time contained twenty-four names to correspond with the twenty-four priestly courses.

12. Meraiah: only here; the name possibly means 'Rebel'.
Hananiah: see Ezr. 10.28.
13. Meshullam: see Ezr. 8.16; 10.15.
Jehohanan: see note on verse 11.
14. Jonathan: see verse 11.
Joseph: see Ezr. 10.42; this is the only priest of this name mentioned.
15. Adna: see Ezr. 10.30.
Meraioth: this seems to be either an error for, or (less probably) an alternative form of, Meremoth (10.5; 12.3).
Helkai: only here; probably a short form of Hilkiah (Ezr. 7.1).
16. Zechariah: see Ezr. 5.1; it is possible that this man is to be identified with the prophet who is called son of Iddo in Ezr. 5.1; 6.14, and son of Berechiah son of Iddo in Zech. 1.1. In both cases Iddo can be taken as the family name; see verse 4, and cf. note on 11.17.
Meshullam: see Ezr. 8.16.
17. Zichri: see 11.9; only here as a priest's name.
of Miniamin: there should be the name of an individual to follow this, but it is not recoverable.
Piltai: only here; probably a short form of Pelatiah (10.22), 'Yahweh has rescued'.
18. Shammua: see 11.17.
Jehonathan: see verse 11.
19. Mattenai: see Ezr. 10.33.
Uzzi: see 11.22.
20. Kallai: only here: the meaning is unknown; it could be a shortened form of a name not recorded, but its similarity in sound with Sallai makes it plausible to suggest that a scribe has guessed a name to fill a gap; see 11.8.
Eber: only here as a priest's name; four other men are so named (Gen. 10.24; 1 Chr. 5.13; 8.12, 22). The name may be connected with the word 'Hebrew', but some mss. read '*ebed*, 'servant'.
21. Hashabiah: see 3.10; Ezr. 8.19.
Nethanel: see Ezr. 10.22.

HEADS OF LEVITICAL HOUSES **12.22–26**

22. As for the Levites: but the reader has to wait until verse 24 for the names of Levitical heads of houses; what follows here and in verse 23 seems to have little connection with the context, nor does it seem to be a complete statement in itself.

Possibly the original form said that the record of priests was also to be found in the Book of the Chronicles.

Eliashib, Joiada, Johanan, and Jaddua: see verse 11.

Darius the Persian: if it is assumed that this king was contemporary with the last-named high priest, Jaddua, he will be Darius III (336–330 B.C.).

23. the Book of the Chronicles: official annals, but not to be confused with the canonical books of Chronicles, although the title is the same.

24. Hashabiah: see 3.10; Ezr. 8.19.

Sherebiah: see Ezr. 8.18.

Jeshua: see Ezr. 2.2, 36, 40.

son of: but Jeshua was not the son of Kadmiel; this should probably be read either as Bani (Jeshua, Bani, Kadmiel) (cf. 8.7), or as Binnui (Jeshua, Binnui, Kadmiel) (cf. 10.9; 12.8). On Bani, see Ezr. 2.10, and on Binnui, Ezr. 8.33.

Kadmiel: see Ezr. 2.40; 3.9.

commandment of David: cf. 1 Chr. 15.16–24; 16.4–6, 41f.; 25.1, 6.

watch corresponding to watch: cf. 1 Chr. 26.16.

25. The first three names of this verse appear to belong to the Levites because (a) elsewhere when gatekeepers are mentioned they begin with Shallum (for which Meshullam here is to be taken as a variant form) (cf. Ezr. 2.42; 1 Chr. 9.17), and (b) Mattaniah, Bakbukiah, and Obadiah (assuming Abda to be a variant form of Obadiah) are Levites in 11.17 (cf. 12.8, 9). Either we must put a full stop after Obadiah and count them among the Levites, or assume that these, being singers (12.8, 9), were also gatekeepers.

Mattaniah: see 11.17, 22 and Ezr. 10.26.

Bakbukiah: see 11.17.

Obadiah: see Ezr. 8.9.

Meshullam: see Ezr. 8.16. Here it may be another form of the name Shallum, see above (cf. Ezr. 2.42).

Talmon: see Ezr. 2.42.

Akkub: see Ezr. 2.42.

26. in the days of: the time references in this verse seem to contradict that of verse 22, but this may be due to the composite nature of the section. Nehemiah and Ezra are clearly regarded here as contemporaries.

PROCESSION OF DEDICATION OF THE WALLS 12.27–43

The completion of the walls is recorded in 6.15 and this section should be regarded as the immediate sequel: it is not clear why it is placed here, so far from the account of the building of the walls.

28. sons of the singers: i.e. members of the singers' guilds.

Netophathites: 1 Chr. 9.16 records that Berechiah the son of Asa son of Elkanah dwelt in the villages of the Netophathites. He was a Levite and probably one of the singers. Netophah is listed in Ezr. 2.22.

29. Beth-gilgal: only here, but is probably the same as Gilgal (a well-known early Israelite settlement east of Jericho).

Geba: see 11.31.

Azmaveth: see Ezr. 2.24 (called Beth-azmaveth, 'House of Azmaveth', in Neh. 7.28).

30. purified: the predominant emphasis in post-exilic times was on purity and separation from things regarded as unclean.

31. upon the wall: i.e. to walk along the top of it (see below).

and went in procession. One went: this rendering, which gives the obvious sense of the verse, strictly involves a slight change in the text (possibly reading *wᵉhā'aḥaṭ hōleḳeṭ*, 'and the one went in procession', for *wᵉtahᵃlūḵōṭ*, 'and processions'). We are not told where the starting-point was; a possible place might be the Valley Gate (2.13, 15; 3.13) from which Nehemiah began his inspection. The two processions went in opposite directions and joined up at the Temple, having left the wall at the nearest convenient point for the Temple.

Dung Gate: see 2.13; 3.14.

32. after them: the pronoun has no antecedent—it must be understood to mean the members of the procession as it formed.

Hoshaiah: 'Yahweh has saved'; occurs only here and Jer. 42.1; 43.2 (where the name is mentioned simply as that of the father of an Azariah).

33. Azariah: see Ezr. 7.1.

Ezra: see 12.1 and Ezr. 7.1.

Meshullam: see Ezr. 8.16.

34. Judah: see Ezr. 10.23.

Benjamin: see Ezr. 10.32.

Shemaiah: see Ezr. 8.13.

Jeremiah: see 10.2.

It is not said whether these are priests or laymen, but since seven priests are named in verse 41 as accompanying the other procession with trumpets, these too are probably priests. Some of the names are shown elsewhere to be possible priestly names.

35a. priests' sons: this implies that the heads of priestly families just named (if that interpretation is sound) were accompanied by members of their families to sound the trumpets. We may assume therefore that when verse 41 ends with the words 'with trumpets' it will imply that the second procession also was accompanied by priests' sons with trumpets.

35b. Zechariah . . . Asaph: in this genealogy of Zechariah it may be assumed that **Mattaniah** was the contemporary name of the family that ultimately derived from Asaph; other references suggest that Asaph could still be in use as the family name (11.17). For Mattaniah as a family name, see 11.17, 22, where Mica(h) and Zabdi are alternative forms of Micaiah and Zaccur; for Asaph, see 11.17 and Ezr. 2.41. The other names are all fairly common ones: for **Zechariah,** see 12.16; for **Jonathan,** see 12.11; for **Shemaiah,** see Ezr. 8.13; for **Mattaniah,** see Ezr.

10.26; for **Micaiah**, see Neh. 10.11; 11.17, 22; for **Zaccur**, see 3.2. For instances of longer genealogies, see Ezr. 7.1; Neh. 11.4. The reason for the longer list here may be the popularity of the name Zechariah and the need to distinguish this one from others of the same name.

36. Shemaiah: see Ezr. 8.13.

Azarel: see 11.13 and Ezr. 10.41.

Milalai, Gilalai, Maai: these three names occur only here and may have become like-sounding through faulty transmission or imaginative insertion; see 11.8. Milalai could be taken as a short form of a name such as Milalaiah, 'Yahweh has spoken', Gilalai as another form of Galal (11.17), and Maai as a shortened form of Maadiah (12.5) or Maaziah (10.8).

Nethanel: see Ezr. 10.22.

Judah: see 11.9; Ezr. 10.23. This man may be a descendant of the Levite musician, Judah, mentioned in 12.8.

Hanani: this is not Nehemiah's brother. A musician named Hanani is listed for David's time in 1 Chr. 25.4, 25. For the name, see 1.2.

musical instruments: according to 2 Chr. 29.25 these were cymbals, harps, and lyres.

and Ezra: added to Nehemiah's memoirs by the editor, who regarded Ezra and Nehemiah as contemporaries (see Introduction, p. 28).

37. at: but they were *on* the wall (see verse 31) and this would be better taken to mean *over*, i.e. they went over the Fountain Gate and then over the stairs (3.15) and so on to the Water Gate.

Fountain Gate: 2.14; 3.15.

house of David: see 3.25.

Water Gate: 3.26. Here the procession left the wall, apparently, and found the nearest way to the Temple.

38. to the left: this translation involves a slight change in the Hebrew text from $l^e m \hat{o}' l$ to $l i \dot{s}^e m \hat{o}' l$.

Tower of the Ovens: see 3.11. (Early editions of RSV inadvertently retained 'furnaces' from RV.)

Broad Wall: see 3.8.

39. Gate of Ephraim: see 8.16.

by: in each case this should be *over* or *above*, see verse 37.

Old Gate: 3.6.

Fish Gate: 3.3.

Tower of Hananel . . . Tower of the Hundred: 3.1.

Sheep Gate: 3.1.

Gate of the Guard: mentioned only here; it may be another name for Muster Gate (3.31). The last phrase of the verse is not in two of the principal manuscripts of LXX (A & B) and may be a gloss.

40. I and half of the officials: this begins the description of the membership of the second procession.

41. Eliakim: 'May God establish/set up'; occurs only here in post-exilic literature. It was the name of two persons before the exile, Hezekiah's prefect in the palace (2 Kg. 18.18) and the king Eliakim=Jehoiakim (2 Kg. 23.34; 24.1).

Maaseiah: see Ezr. 10.18.

Miniamin: another form of Mijamin, see Ezr. 10.25.

Micaiah: cf. verse 35.

Elioenai: see Ezr. 10.22.

Zechariah: see verse 16.

Hananiah: see Ezr. 10.28.

42. Maaseiah: see above.

Shemaiah: see Ezr. 8.13.

Eleazar: see Ezr. 8.33.

Uzzi: see 11.22.

Jehohanan: see note on verse 11.

Malchijah: see Ezr. 10.25.

Elam: see Ezr. 2.7

Ezer: see 3.19.

Jezrahiah: 'May Yahweh shine forth/arise' (cf. Zerahiah, Ezr. 7.4); only here and 1 Chr. 7.3 (RSV Izrahiah) a man of Issachar.

43. sacrifices: probably not 'burnt' offerings but 'peace' offerings which were shared by the people in a communion meal; cf. Exod. 32.6.

joy: the verb and noun occur five times in this verse: cf. the joy at the laying of the Temple foundations (Ezr. 3.13).

ORGANIZATION AMONG THE LEVITES **12.44–47**

44. On that day: this phrase occurs also at the beginning of chapter 13. It probably does not mean on the very day on which the walls were dedicated, nor is there any obvious time-reference in the paragraphs preceding the dedication of the walls to which it might refer back. It must be taken as a general reference to some time within the period of Nehemiah's governorship, a time when the walls were repaired, Jerusalem reinhabited, and tithing brought up to full standard, so that the people were full of joy and enthusiasm both towards God (verse 43) and towards the priests and Levites (verse 44). The verse suggests some form of regulating the channels for receiving the first fruits and tithes, and hints at regional control—'according to the fields of the towns', i.e. wherever there were lands in cultivation.

45. purification: cf. verse 30 and the detailed laws for ritual cleanness in Lev. 11–15.

command of David: referring specifically to the singers; cf. 2 Chr. 8.14.

46. Asaph: appointed by David (1 Chr. 16.5). On Asaph, see 11.17 and Ezr. 2.41.

47. set apart: lit. sanctified, so that only priests and Levites and their families could use it.

ACTING UPON THE LAW OF RACIAL PURITY 13.1–3

1. On that day: cf. 12.44; here it may mean little more than 'on a certain day' (thus to become 'that day'), when the lesson was read on which they now act. The reading of Scripture was an integral part of synagogue practice and may have come into use during or soon after the exile.

Ammonite or Moabite: see Dt. 23.3–6.

2. Repeats the gist of Dt. 23.4f. and alludes to Num. 22–24.

3. separated: how far did they go at this time? Presumably they took steps to prevent the children of mixed marriages from sharing in any way in the religious observances; it would seem well-nigh impossible to eradicate all such descendants from ordinary citizenship.

NEHEMIAH CLEANSES THE TEMPLE ROOM PREPARED FOR TOBIAH 13.4–9

Not only does this resume the personal narrative of Nehemiah, it gives also a specific instance of the purification involved in verses 1–3.

4. Eliashib the priest: this man is usually identified with the high priest of that name (3.1, 20; 13.28), but it seems unlikely for a high priest to have been appointed over the chambers of the Temple. This is probably a different Eliashib. See Ezr. 10.6 for the name. Meremoth appears to have held a similar kind of office (Ezr. 8.33). **connected with:** lit. was near to. Tobiah is presumably the same man as Tobiah the Ammonite, the slave; see 2.10. It is not clear what the relationship was, but according to 6.18 Tobiah was well connected in Israel, and possibly Eliashib was connected with either Shecaniah son of Arah (Tobiah's father-in-law) or Meshullam son of Berechiah (father-in-law of Tobiah's son Jehohanan). Advantage had apparently been taken of Nehemiah's absence from Jerusalem and Judah to bring Tobiah into the Temple room. There is some uncertainty, however, about Nehemiah's movements. Could he have stayed away from court for a full twelve years? Or would he have been given a twelve-year leave of absence when asked to state a time (2.6)? Verse 6 implies (a) a return to the king in the thirty-second year (Nehemiah had originally come to Jerusalem in the king's twentieth year) and (b) a request, after a lapse of time, to go back to Jerusalem. The uncertainty lies chiefly in deciding where he was from the time of the dedication of the wall to the thirty-second year of the king's reign. 5.14 could imply a twelve-year stay in Judah, but need not mean more than the exercise of a twelve-year governorship.

5. large chamber: see 10.38, 39 for mention of the store-chambers. Such personal occupation of the room would (a) cut across Nehemiah's arrangements for the orderly handling of tithes, etc., and (b) give Tobiah central headquarters from which he could continue to work against Nehemiah's influence and against his effort to secure racial purity.

6. king of Babylon: is probably to be regarded as a thoughtless Jewish designation of the king of Persia.

9. cleansed: i.e. ritually, see 12.45.

chambers: adjacent ones as well as that immediately concerned.

10. portions: evidently the tithes mentioned in 10.38.

who did the work: see on 11.12; here it is probably used in a general sense with no suggestion of being supervisors.

each to his field: strictly speaking the Levites had no holdings (Dt. 14.29; 18.1; Num. 18.20, 23f.), but Dt. 18.8 suggests that some at least had some private property or income. This would be almost a necessity for such Levites as were left behind during the exile and had no Temple duties or dues. This could explain why the next verse says that the Temple was forsaken; it was so of necessity.

13. treasurers: an additional office to that in 12.44 where collectors are intended; here distributors are meant.

Shelemiah: in 3.30 a Shelemiah is named as father of a wall-builder, and this might be the same man. Two other men named Shelemiah are mentioned in Ezr. 10.39, 41 as laymen who had married non-Israelites.

Zadok the scribe: or secretary; see on Ezr. 7.6. Two wall-builders were named Zadok, 3.4, 29, but they cannot be more closely identified.

Pedaiah: see 3.25.

Hanan: a Levite name in 8.7 and 10.10; also in Ezr. 2.46.

Zaccur: see 3.2.

Mattaniah: see 11.17, 22, 12.35.

14. Remember me: cf. 4.4, 20; 5.15, 19; 13.22, 31.

my good deeds: this is the plural (with pronoun) of the word elsewhere translated 'steadfast love', and here means the deeds which were impelled by that quality which will accept an obligation and honour it, come what may; cf. 1.5.

15. on the day when they sold: i.e. the Sabbath.

16. Men of Tyre: resident in Jerusalem and representatives of Tyrian fish and other companies. Their wares would probably come into the city either through the Fish Gate or the Gate of Ephraim (3.3; 8.16).

18. Did not your fathers: cf. Jer. 17.19–27.

19. began to be dark: lit. 'became shadowy', but there is no preposition for 'at' in the Hebrew and 'gates' might equally well be taken as the subject of the verb (which is plural), and in that case the verb could be connected with an Aramaic root *ṣᵉlal*, 'be clear', i.e. 'When the gates of Jerusalem became clear before the Sabbath. . . .'

no burden: presumably *bona fide* visitors might enter.

20–21. To have allowed the merchants to do this would (a) create noise and disturbance at the city wall with other attendant disadvantages, and (b) tempt the townsfolk to go out to them.

22. purify: thus regarding the protection of the Sabbath as much a sacred duty as any of those in the Temple itself.

Remember: cf. verse 14.

MIXED MARRIAGES: OATH NOT TO CONTINUE THE PRACTICE 13.23–27

23. One of the terms of the covenant recorded in chapter 10 was the decision not to take foreign women as wives, 10.30.

Ashdod: once one of the five Philistine cities but now incorporated in the Persian empire.

Ammon and Moab: cf. verse 1.

24. Foreign speech would alienate them from the Law and the synagogue.

25. Apart from showing his anger in typical Oriental fashion, all that Nehemiah felt able to do was to prevent recurrences of the practice in the future. This contrasts with Ezra's policy of divorce (Ezr. 9, 10).

26. Cf. 1 Kg. 11.1–8.

NEHEMIAH EXPELS SANBALLAT'S SON-IN-LAW 13.28–29

28. Jehoiada: see 3.6; 12.10.

Eliashib: 3.1, 20; 12.10. It is not clear whether 'high priest' refers to Jehoiada or to Eliashib, i.e. whether this took place while Eliashib was high priest or afterwards. See also 13.4; Ezr. 10.6.

Sanballat the Horonite: see 2.10.

I chased him from me: he must have refused to co-operate. The Hebrew phrase implies that Nehemiah would not have him in his company. The name of the expelled priest is not given, but he may have been a brother of Jehohanan and named Jonathan (see 12.11, 23). Priests (and this one was in the direct line of the high priesthood) had to be extra careful in marriage (Lev. 21.14) and take only an Israelite girl (LXX limits further: only a Levite girl). The crime was worsened by the fact that Sanballat had shown himself an uncompromising political enemy of Nehemiah. Josephus has his own version of this incident (*Ant.*, XI, viii, 2ff.) and connects the building of the Samaritan temple with this expulsion, but places it in the time of Alexander. Nehemiah obviously felt confident of his standing with the king, and of his duty both to God and to his fellow Jews, so to act against a fellow governor's son-in-law.

SUMMARY OF NEHEMIAH'S GOOD WORK 13.30–31

31. wood offering: see 10.34.

first fruits: see 10.35.

Remember me: cf. verses 14, 22.

Thus the so-called 'memoirs' end in a way that exhibits its purpose, namely, to ensure that Nehemiah has a memorial before men and God that shall do justice to his achievements on his people's behalf (see Introduction, p. 33).

INTRODUCTION TO
THE BOOK OF
ESTHER

INTRODUCTION TO ESTHER

1. THE STORY

Briefly the story runs like this: the Persian king Xerxes held a feast and in the course of it ordered his queen Vashti to appear before the princes to exhibit her beauty. On her refusal to do so the king made a public example of her and later put in her place Esther, the cousin and adopted daughter of a Jew named Mordecai. Mordecai had at one time been instrumental in saving the king's life, but he fell foul of the court favourite Haman who, to avenge the insult, obtained permission to kill all Jews and to appropriate their belongings. This, as determined by lot (*pûr*), was to happen on the thirteenth of Adar. Esther, instructed by Mordecai, undertook to intercede for her people and arranged a banquet to which she invited both the king and Haman. Haman, basking in this favour, planned to have Mordecai hung on a gigantic gallows he had prepared for him. But it so happened that the king spent a restless night and caused the book of memorable deeds to be read to him. He heard the record of Mordecai's former service and learnt that no reward had been made to him. He sent for Haman and consulted him, without naming either the person or the deed, as to how such a service should be rewarded. Haman, thinking that he himself was to have the reward, suggested a suitable one, whereupon the king commanded Haman to make the appropriate honour to Mordecai in person. Haman, thus made to suffer the gall of having to pay the highest honour and respect to his most hated enemy, was beside himself with frustration, but before he could resolve on what to do he was summoned to Esther's second banquet. There Esther made her petition on behalf of the Jews and disclosed Haman as the instigator of the plot. In the king's temporary absence from the hall Haman threw himself at Esther's feet to plead with her, but the king came in and, mistaking the nature of the gesture, cried out, 'Will he even assault the queen in my presence in my own house?' Haman was condemned to be hung on the gallows prepared for Mordecai, and the latter was given Haman's house and position and the Jews were allowed to defend themselves against any they should find armed and massed to attack them on the thirteenth of Adar. Seventy-five thousand people were massacred. The two following days were decreed as festival days to be known as the Days of Purim.

2. DATE

If we are to take the book at its face value we are to think of a time extending from the first deportation of Jews in 597 B.C., when Mordecai was among those deported (2.5, 6), to the time of King Xerxes (presumably Xerxes I, 485–465 B.C.). This means that the action took place at very least 112 years after Mordecai's deportation (Mordecai became grand vizier in Xerxes' twelfth year, i.e. 124 years after deportation) and makes him far too old a man for this to be at all likely. There is no other historical information in the book which can be justifiably claimed as giving any clear indication of the date of writing. Apart from Xerxes, none of the characters in the book are known to be historical figures; indeed it is known only that Xerxes had a wife named Amestris (Herodotus, VII, 114; IX, 112), but there was not a wife named Vashti or Esther. We are forced to the conclusion that the author deliberately projected his book on to this early post-exilic period, but telescoped the period, as was not unusual with Jewish writers, so that it could come within the compass of one man's life. There are other things besides the name of Xerxes' wife that are clearly unhistorical. 1.1. mentions 127 provinces—seven more than the figure given in Dan. 6.1. There were in fact never more than twenty-nine. It is improbable that a Jew would ever have occupied the second place in the Persian kingdom (Nehemiah comes nearest to this) or that a Jewess would become queen. Again, who would plan a vindictive attack on the Jewish residents and then allow eleven months to elapse before its execution, or, when the tables were turned, who would expect the Jews to wait patiently until the thirteenth of Adar? These things do not belong to true history but to fiction and when we read the book as a historical novel moving steadily towards its culmination in the holding of two days' festival to celebrate the reversal of Jewish fortunes and the cruel massacre of thousands of Gentiles (in 9.16 the figure is given as 75,000) we see

how artfully the author tells his story, bringing out his own strong
interests, primarily the political ascendancy of his own (Jewish)
race and the degradation of the Gentiles. Of genuine religion he
shows little or no sign, and does not even mention the name of
God; the nearest he comes to it is the reference to help arising from
'another quarter' for the Jews (4.14).

It is feasible to infer that the choice of the thirteenth of Adar as
the day of the massacre and the fourteenth and fifteenth as the days
of the Purim festival was deliberately made so that the first should
coincide with Nicanor's day (1 Mac. 7.49; 2 Mac. 15.36), the day
on which Nicanor fell in battle before Judas in 161 B.C. 2 Mac. 15.36
is the first distinct reference to the Purim festival ('Mordecai's day')
and is to be dated early in the first century B.C. Thus, sometime
between 160 and 100 B.C. seems to be indicated for the time of
writing. A closer definition of the latest possible date may perhaps
be made on the basis of the statement in 11.1 of the Additions to the
Book of Esther (see below) that the book had already been translated into Greek by Lysimachus by the fourth year of Ptolemy and
Cleopatra: this could be Ptolemy VIII giving 112 B.C. or Ptolemy XII
giving 76 B.C. This is supported in general by the language of the
book, which shows affinities with the Hebrew of the late books of
Chronicles, Ecclesiastes and Daniel and could well have been
written by one who normally used Aramaic. There are also several
Persian words in the book and the majority of the proper names are
Persian; this throws it, at very least, well into the Persian period.
Ben Sira, whose book is generally thought to have been written at
about 180 B.C., makes no mention of either Esther or Mordecai,
although either or both of them would have made useful additions
to his list in chapters 44–50.

A time shortly after 161, when the Jews were flushed with the
temporary success of their revolt against the religious oppression of
Antiochus Epiphanes and were therefore prone to exaggerated
racial pride and at the same time harboured ill-will against the
Gentiles, would seem appropriate. We need not wonder at Luther's
words about the book and its heroine: 'I am so hostile to the book
and to Esther that I wish they did not exist at all; for they Judaize
too much and have much heathen impropriety' (*Tischreden*, Weimar

ed., XXII, 2080). On the other hand, there was little likelihood at that time of any threat of massacre by Gentiles comparable with that envisaged in Esther. If the book is not regarded as history in any strict sense, this is by no means a serious consideration since it is then only to be taken as part of the elaboration of the novelist. In any case, there seems no need to press this point as far as to seek a possible place of origin where such a massacre might be a real danger. Those who do think it can be located find the province of Persis north-east of the Persian Gulf a likely place. It showed a strong spirit of independence and was the home of a very zealous, almost fanatic Zoroastrianism which might well turn on the Jews at slight provocation.

3. SOURCES OF MATERIAL FOR STORY

A historical novel need have little more basic fact than the names and approximate historical setting of the chief characters, but there may well be much more source material that need not be regarded as fact and yet which may have been borrowed from folk-lore by the author and not be the product of the author's own imagination. It is well known that stories are told about public figures, popular or unpopular ones, which may or may not be founded on fact but which nevertheless are handed on to subsequent generations. The author of Esther may have found stories of this kind ready to hand for inclusion in his own story. It has been suggested that while 'the Book of the Chronicles of the kings of Media and Persia' (10.2) may not be a factual title—it too closely resembles the titles to the Books of the Chronicles of the kings of Israel and Judah—it might hint at the existence of some Jewish literature, midrashic in character, that covered the years of the Persian domination and could be used as a source by historical novelists.

There is also the possibility that the author based his book on popular myths. This turns on how much significance can be attached to the proper names. Mordecai is an obvious one to start with. It is clearly formed from the name of the supreme god of Babylon, Marduk, and may be intended to represent that god. If so, then Haman, whose nature is all evil, and who stands in relation to

Mordecai as the evil (one) subdued by the good (one), could be deemed to represent the chaos monster vanquished by the creator god Marduk. But the story is very remote from the myth and has really no more to do with it than would the story of any good man in conflict with a bad one.

Other names, however, besides that of Mordecai, have been thought to have connection with the names of gods: Haman and Vashti have been equated with the Elamite gods Human and Mashti, Mordecai and Esther with Marduk and Ishtar, both Babylonian gods. The Esther story might then be regarded as being built upon an ancient tradition of a conflict between the Elamite and Babylonian chief god and goddess. But again the story of Esther has nothing to do with such a conflict. All that we can safely say is that the author has chosen for some of his characters names with a resemblance to those of gods, whether intentionally or not cannot be said. The name Mordecai is found in Ezr. 2.2 (=Neh. 7.7) and, in a simpler form, Marduk, on an Aramaic letter of the fourth century B.C. (G. R. Driver, *Aramaic Documents*, 1957, letter VI), and is thus shown to have been an acceptable name among Jews in ordinary life. The other names, Esther, Haman and Vashti, occur only in Esther.

The author may have incorporated traditional material as well as legendary into his story, but the finished product is so clearly a unity that even if there had been written or oral material on which he drew it would be impossible to disentangle it. There may have been (a) a *Downfall of Vashti* story widely current among both Jews and non-Jews from which the author could have drawn details of practices and customs at the Persian court in addition to the main theme, and (b) a *Mordecai–Hadassah* (Esther) story, or even a *Mordecai–Haman* one which, if it did exist, would doubtless be popular among Jews. But this is mere speculation based on little more than the author's obviously wide knowledge of local customs.

4. CANONICITY OF THE BOOK OF ESTHER

The book was slow to gain acceptance as canonical, both Jewish and Christian authorities being somewhat shy of granting it the same recognition as other books in the Old Testament. There is no evidence of any copy of it among the books in the Qumran library. A Jewish rabbi named Samuel in the third century A.D. was of the opinion that Esther was not a sacred book, and it did not appear in lists of the canon made towards the end of the fourth century by Athanasius (*d.* 373) and Gregory of Nazianzus (*d.* 391). On the other hand, it seems to have been much read, and there were some who felt a need to improve on it by way of supplementing what the author had written. This supplementary material is to be found in the Apocrypha under the title 'The Additions to the Book of Esther'. They seem to have been added to the Greek form of the book and not the Hebrew, and to have been intended to minimize the obvious indifference to religion shown by the Hebrew book. Two of the additions are prayers attributed to Mordecai and Esther (13.8–18 and 14.1–15.16). Two others purport to give the exact words of two royal edicts (13.1–7 and 16.1–24), whilst a prologue and epilogue (11.2–12.6 and 10.4–13) set the story of Esther in the framework of a dream which Mordecai dreamt. (The chapter and verse numbers given above are traditional and come from the practice of numbering them in sequence *after* the canonical book, but in the Greek Bible the additions are printed at either end or within the text, i.e. 11.2–12.6 stands as prologue, 10.4–13 as epilogue, closed by 11.1, 13.1–7 follows 3.13, 13.8–18 and 14.1–15.6 follow 4.17 and finally 16.1–24 follows 8.12.) In its Hebrew form the book seems to have been expanded at a very early time by the addition of 9.20–10.3. 9.19 would suitably round off a book, especially if we complete the verse from certain manuscripts of the Greek with the words 'but those who live in cities keep also the fifteenth of Adar as a joyous and good day by sending portions to their neighbours'. This implies a difference in celebration in country and town. In 9.20ff., however, no such difference is discernible, and both days are established for celebration alike in town and country (9.21). The book was therefore probably expanded in this way at some time not known to bring into line with current practice.

5. PURIM

The culminating point of the book is the celebration of the fourteenth and fifteenth days of Adar (the former in the villages and
walled towns and the latter in towns and cities) as a festival of joy
and revelry. They were called 'days of Purim' (Est. 9.26, 31),
because the date on which Haman was to have carried out his
programme against the Jews was chosen by lot, *pûr*. The book of
Esther is the earliest reference to such a festival, the next known
reference being in 2 Mac. 15.36, which mentions Mordecai's day.
Subsequent references are found in the Mishnah and other rabbinic
literature. The word *pûr* is not a Hebrew word and its use in the
story may be because either it was the word likely to have been in
use in Persia at the time the story is cast or, which is more likely,
the festival was already in existence in Persia and its celebration
involved the casting of lots. The word *pûr* is thought to be of
Accadian origin, and if so must have passed into use in other
languages, perhaps as the observance of the festival was handed on.
It has been suggested that the festival may have begun as a
Babylonian New Year festival, but its origin is lost in obscurity.
The uncertainty that exists over the word *pûr* has led one critic at
least (Pfeiffer) to think that the author invented both the festival
and the name, the latter, in its plural form, Purim, being comparable
with Urim and Thummim.

The festival was celebrated with much joy and revelry, so much
so that 'a Babylonian authority of the fourth century, Raba, took
it that a man should drink till he cannot distinguish between
Cursed be Haman! and Blessed be Mordecai!' (G. F. Moore,
Judaism, vol. II, 1927, p. 53). The book of Esther was to be read by
all Jews at the time of the festival, either publicly or privately.

THE BOOK OF
ESTHER

THE BOOK OF

ESTHER

THE GREAT BANQUET 1.1–9

1. **Ahasuerus:** i.e. Xerxes (485–465 B.C.); cf. Ezr. 4.6, Dan. 9.1.
India to Ethiopia: i.e. the eastern and western limits. 'India' implies the river Indus as the natural frontier.
one hundred and twenty-seven provinces: in Dan. 6.1 the number is given as 120. Inscriptions show that the number varied from twenty-one to twenty-nine. Story-teller's licence is indulged here.

2. **Susa the capital:** see on Neh. 2.8 and Ezr. 4.9; 6.2. It was the winter residence —Neh. 1.1 mentions the ninth month, Chislev, and Est. 9.1 the twelfth month, Adar. The name Susa was given to the city as well as the fortress (capital), 3.15; 8.14f.; 9.6, 12, 15, 18.

3. **third year:** i.e. 482 B.C.
army chiefs: the second word is added to the Hebrew on the grounds that Xerxes would be unlikely to entertain the whole army. But if he could hold a feast lasting 180 days (verse 4), it would not be out of keeping to let him entertain the whole army.

4. **a hundred and eighty days:** roughly half the year.

5. **seven days:** this was at least the normal period for a wedding feast; cf. Gen. 29.21–28; Jg. 14.17.

6. **porphyry:** a red stone capable of taking a very high polish. LXX has emerald.
precious stones: this may refer to turquoise, which is native to Persia.

8. **according to the law:** this need not imply a known law about drinking; the Hebrew could as well be translated: 'drinking was according to this rule', the rule being stated in the next phrase—'no one was compelled'.

9. **Vashti:** but in fact Xerxes' wife was called Amestris. The name Vashti means something like 'best', 'desired', 'beauty'. There was no social custom to dictate that the women should celebrate by themselves, but continued feasting might well lead to drunken disorder and Vashti's refusal of the king's command, though necessary to the development of the story, may have been genuine enough, assuming some such feast did take place, if she anticipated lewdness of any kind.

VASHTI REFUSED TO ATTEND 1.10–12

10. Six of the seven names occur only here, and the other, **Harbona**, only here and 7.9. They are all Persian names: the meanings of these and other Persian names in Esther are uncertain in many cases. Some meaning will be given where possible.
Mehuman: perhaps to be associated with the root 'mn, and then meaning 'Faithful'.

Biztha: 'Eunuch' (?).

Harbona: 'Donkey-driver'.

Bigtha: 'Endowed with fortune' (?). This may be a short form of Bagadatha, 'Given by God' (Baga being perhaps another name for Mithra).

Abagtha: probably another form of Bigtha.

Zethar: 'Conqueror'.

Carkas: 'Vulture'.

Note: On these, and the seven names in verse 14, see J. Duchesne-Guillemin, 'Les Noms des Eunuques d'Assuerus', *Le Muséon*, LXVI (1953), pp. 105–08.

12. refused to come: an act of disobedience was essential for the progress of the story, and while it is easy enough to find a possible motive, as suggested above, it is not strictly necessary.

THE KING'S ANGER AND THE DEGRADATION OF VASHTI 1.13–22

13. knew the times: being astrologers and astronomers: but the word '*ēt* may perhaps be connected with a root '*ānat* (Arabic), 'to cause trouble', and be translated 'trouble', 'crime'; this would make these men versed in criminal matters.

14. Of the seven Persian names given here, only the last, **Memucan**, occurs again, in verses 16, 21.

Carshena: 'Overcome with sacred drink'.

Shethar: 'One who sets the kingdom free'; cf. Shethar-bozenai in Ezr. 5.3.

Admatha: 'Unrestrained'; cf. Greek Admetos.

Tarshish: either 'Thirsty' or 'Greedy'.

Meres: unknown, unless it is a short form of the following name.

Marsena: 'Subject of the (demon) Marshavan'.

Memucan: perhaps the name of a mountain used as a personal name.

saw the king's face: i.e. were in closest intimacy with him.

19. so that it may not be altered: cf. 8.8; Dan. 6.8, 12, 15. There is no other evidence for this and it may be a legend peculiar to Esther and Daniel. The punishment of Vashti for disobedience is natural in an Oriental monarchy and the political influence of the Magians is also in character, but the publication of the moral as a lesson to other wives is doubtless an embellishment limited to this story.

22. and speak according to the language of his people: but this is what he would naturally and properly do at home. LXX omits this phrase and thus removes the difficulty, but it is also possible, by slight emendation (*ûmᵉdabbēr kol nāšāw 'immô*), to read, 'and to control all his women folk around him' (*B.Z.A.W.*, 66 (1936), p. 176).

SEARCH FOR A QUEEN 2.1–4

1. remembered Vashti: simply recalling that he had no queen now and that steps should be taken to replace Vashti.

3. Hegai: also in verses 8, 15. Herodotus (IX, 33) mentions a courtier of Xerxes with this name. Meaning unknown.

ointments: the necessary face cream and other cosmetics which were used over a period of time in preparation for a visit to the king. The root meaning is 'rub', 'polish'.

ESTHER, A JEWESS AND WARD OF MORDECAI, IS AMONG THE CANDIDATES 2.5–11

5. Mordecai: presumably a name associated with the god Marduk and perhaps meaning 'man of Marduk'; apparently it was not felt inappropriate for a Jew to bear it—a Mordecai occurs in the list in Ezr. 2.2 and Neh. 7.7. There is therefore no need to look for any mythological significance in its use here.

Jair: elsewhere (a) a son of Manasseh (Num. 32.41, etc.), and (b) a judge in Gilead (Jg. 10.3). The name means, 'He (Yahweh) gives light'.

Shimei: a very common name; see Ezr. 10.33.

Kish: clearly meant to make the reader think of the father of Saul, in spite of the intervening time. Kish was an Arab tribal name (originally a deity).

6. Jeconiah: 'Yahweh stands firm', also called Jehoiachin, 'Yahweh will make firm'; was taken captive in 597. It was a trait of Jewish historians to foreshorten time on occasion, and it is not therefore surprising to find the writer of a historical novel doing so.

7. Hadassah, that is Esther: the names do not mean the same; Hadassah means 'Myrtle' and Esther is either another form of Ishtar, the name of the goddess, or it is a Persian word meaning 'Star'. The fact that two names are remembered for her may reflect two traditional ways of telling the story.

8. The inclusion of a Jewess is, of course, necessary to the story but improbable in fact.

9. favour: the Hebrew word is that usually translated 'steadfast love' (see Ezr. 3.11; Neh. 1.5), and it carries with it the ideas of loyalty and affection as well as favour.

seven: cf. the seven eunuchs in 1.10 and the seven Magians in 1.14.

10. not made known: explaining why she could be taken into the harem: Mordecai's nationality was apparently no secret.

THE TRADITIONAL PROCEDURE 2.12–14

13. whatever she desired: what this was we do not know; it might be a flower, or a perfume, or a charm.

14. Shaashgaz: occurs only here. Meaning not known.

ESTHER IS PUT IN PLACE OF VASHTI 2.15–18

15. Abihail: 'My father is might'; the name occurs also in 9.29 and elsewhere in Num. 3.35 and 1 Chr. 5.14. It occurs twice as a woman's name (1 Chr. 2.29; 2 Chr. 11.18).

16. Tebeth: this is the only occurrence of the name of this month in the O.T.

17. favour: see verse 9.

18. remission of taxes (*margin*, 'or a holiday'): since the Hebrew word simply means respite with no explicit references to taxes, the margin reading is to be preferred.

MORDECAI'S DEED ON THE KING'S BEHALF 2.19–23

19. When . . . the second time: the whole phrase is not in LXX, and its omission removes the difficulty that nowhere else is a second mustering of the virgins mentioned.

sitting at the king's gate: this may mean that he had some duty or other to perform at court, but in any case it enabled him to speak with Esther (verse 11). A comparable phrase is used in Dan. 2.49, 'Daniel remained at the king's court', where the Aramaic word means lit. 'gate'.

21. Bigthan: probably another form of the name Bigtha (1.10), but a different person here. The form Bigthana is given in 6.2.

Teresh: perhaps another form of the name Tarshish (1.14); 'Cupidity' ('Thirsty', 'Greedy').

23. gallows: lit. tree.

Book of the Chronicles: the court or royal chronicle.

HAMAN'S OPPORTUNITY 3.1–15

HAMAN'S PROMOTION AND MORDECAI'S REFUSAL OF HOMAGE 3.1–6

1. promoted Haman: as the villain of the piece Haman is introduced with economy of words: his name has been thought to be a form of Humman, an Elamite god; the name occurs only in Esther. The name of his father **Hammedatha** occurs only here, and might mean either 'Given in the same month', or 'Given by Humman', both having some reference to birth.

the Agagite: evidently intended by the author to remind his readers of Agag the Amalekite, whose name is used in Num. 24.7 as a symbol of might and who, according to 1 Sam. 15.8f., 32f., was a bitter enemy of Saul. Here the name is a symbol of a hated enemy of the Jews. The LXX translators were apparently uncertain about it; in some forms it is omitted and in some it is represented as Bougaios (the Bugaean).

2. did not bow down: to do so would be a virtual breaking of the first and second commandments.

4. The fact of Mordecai's nationality was now no secret, even if it had been so before, and the king's servants wanted to see if Haman would sanction this Jewish prejudice.

6. In excess of pride Haman vowed vengeance on the whole Jewish population with Mordecai.

LOTS CAST TO DECIDE ON A DAY OF REVENGE 3.7–11

7. What they seem to have done was to go through the calendar day by day and month by month under decision of the lot (*pûr*) until such time as a certain day of a certain month should be determined. The Hebrew text is not quite clear here, but the Greek ends the verse with 'the lot fell on the fourteenth day of the month Adar'. This makes it tolerably certain that the text should specify the day of the month, and the rest of the book makes two things clear: first, that the day chosen was actually the thirteenth day (verse 13), and second, that the Greek translators put fourteenth in their text here under the influence of 9.18, 19. The verse, thus emended, would then end, 'they cast *pûr*, that is, the lot, before Haman day after day, month after month, and the lot fell on the thirteenth day of the twelfth month, which is the month Adar'.

Pur: this is thought to be an Accadian word whose use was retained only in the name and tradition of this Purim festival.

9. Haman's desire to be rid of the Jews was strong enough to prompt him to make a substantial payment to the royal treasury from his own pocket, though doubtless he would expect to recover it from the booty.

10. signet ring: putting Haman in full authority.

11. The king offers the money back to Haman, probably not in magnanimous refusal but to be put to use in the furtherance of the project; both the money and the people are to be at Haman's disposal.

DECREE SANCTIONING ANNIHILATION OF THE JEWS ON THE THIRTEENTH OF ADAR
    3.12–15

12. thirteenth day of the first month: to decree such an act eleven months ahead is clearly fictional.

satraps: see on Ezr. 5.3; 6.7.

13. to destroy, to slay, and to annihilate: the piling up of verbs is rhetorical and conveys the idea of thoroughness.

15. Susa the capital . . . the city of Susa: thus distinguishing between the citadel where the royal palace was and the rest of the city.

perplexed: the Hebrew word could be translated by something stronger, e.g. 'was thrown into confusion'.

MORDECAI'S DISTRESS AND ESTHER'S RESPONSE TO HIS PASSIONATE APPEAL **4.1–17**

1. His nationality no longer a secret, Mordecai was able to give free vent to his feelings, but in such condition he was prevented from pursuing his usual occupation within the palace gates (2.19).

4. Although Esther had been charged by Mordecai (2.10, 20) not to reveal her nationality, she properly felt his distress keenly.

5. Hathach: like most of the names in the book, this is a Persian name and occurs only in this chapter; possibly meaning 'Companion'.

11. Herodotus knew of the Persian custom that anyone approaching the king unsummoned would be put to death unless the king gave immediate pardon (III, 118, 140).

13–14. Mordecai appeals to Esther's loyalty: she must either declare her nationality and face what may come when she appeals to the king, or she must face whatever punishment will come on her as a traitor to her own people.

14. from another quarter: a veiled reference to God.

who knows: an appeal to Esther to prove her mettle: to the devout Jew this could only mean the depth of her 'fear of God'. She responded by dedicating herself to the task.

THE DOWNFALL OF HAMAN 5.1–7.10

ESTHER ARRANGES A FEAST FOR THE KING AND HAMAN 5.1–8

This chapter is a fine example of story-teller's art; suspense is held while Esther procrastinates at the first day's dinner and invites her guests, the king and Haman, to a dinner the next day, at which she promises to reveal her wish. The story is the thing, and the king is a necessary side-character playing the part assigned to him.

2. golden sceptre: cf. 4.11.

3. half of my kingdom: cf. Mk 6.23.

8. tomorrow: this addition from the Greek improves the sense of the verse.

HAMAN IN HIS PRIDE IS PERSUADED TO ERECT A GALLOWS FOR MORDECAI 5.9–14

9. Mordecai is back at his position within the king's gate; this is a proper sequel to 4.17.

10. Zeresh: a Persian name, possibly meaning 'golden'; it occurs only as the name of Haman's wife.

14. gallows: see 2.23.

HAMAN IS MADE TO SUGGEST AND EXECUTE A SUITABLE WAY OF REWARDING MORDECAI
    FOR HIS EARLIER ACT ON THE KING'S BEHALF 6.1–11

1. could not sleep: lit. the sleep of the king fled; cf. Dan. 6.18, where a literal translation of the Hebrew is given in RSV. It may be noted that when Belshazzar could not sleep, 'no diversions were brought to him' because he was too worried about Daniel. Here the royal chronicle was read aloud to the king. This is a dramatic touch—admirably timed.

2. Cf. 2.21–23.

4. Again the story-teller reveals his art by bringing Haman on the scene just when he is wanted. Is it still midnight?

8. on whose head: i.e. the horse's head. A horse with a crown may be seen on Assyrian palace reliefs. (On the use of crowns, see G. Dalman, *Arbeit und Sitte in Palästina*, v (1937), p. 279.) This detail is not picked up again in the subsequent story.

9. let him: this change to singular from plural is supported by LXX and is necessary to sense. It involves only a change of pronunciation in Hebrew.

HAMAN IS PERPLEXED, BUT IS SUMMONED TO THE SECOND BANQUET 6.12–14

12. covered: but for mourning the head should be uncovered; if an Arabic cognate be followed, the verb could mean uncovered. The uncovered head was the exception and therefore the more fitted for mourning: it was forbidden to priests (Lev. 10.6; 21.10; cf. Ezek. 24.17).

13. This is the kernel of the book's message; the Jews will eventually come out on top.

14. Haman was so engrossed in nursing his injured pride, a most fitting punishment for him, that he seems to have forgotten the banquet until fetched for it.

HAMAN IS PUT IN A FALSE POSITION AND GETS HANGED ON THE GALLOWS HE HAD
   MADE **7.1–10**

2. second day: i.e. the second day's banquet; we are not meant to think that the banquet lasted more than one day.

4. In its present form this verse means that the loss of his Jewish subjects would be more grievous to the king than slavery would be to the Jews. The last phrase, however, could be translated 'for such a misfortune (to be sold as slaves) would not justify troubling the king'. The Jews were well used to slavery and could recover from it in time.

6. was in terror: thus giving himself away.

Esther speaks of 'this wicked Haman': it was a rabbinic fancy to discover that the numerical value of the Aramaic for 'the wicked Haman' was 666, the number of the beast (Rev. 13.18).

7. went into the palace garden: he had to be out of the way so that the scene might be set for Haman to compromise himself; it is therefore probably superfluous to argue that he needed time to think things out. The decree had been issued under his seal as if with his full knowledge.

8. couch . . . assault: very much like the story of Joseph (Gen. 39.7ff.). Thus by his innocent pleading for mercy Haman fell into the king's hands and gave him a ready excuse for summarily disposing of Haman. The king could scarcely have put him to death for a decree that had gone out in his own name.

they covered Haman's face: 'they' are doubtless the courtiers or court officers or eunuchs; it is often understood to be the sign of the death sentence, but there is no evidence that there was any such custom. It is possible that the verb could be taken intransitively and then given the meaning 'Haman's face was covered', that is, he covered it with his own hands out of shame, chagrin, and despair.

9–10. It is but another sign of the 'timeliness' of the narrative that the gallows was so readily to hand.

MORDECAI IS INSTALLED IN HAMAN'S PLACE AND ESTHER SECURES A COMPLETE REVERSAL
   OF HAMAN'S DECREE **8.1–17**

1. house of Haman: he being hung as a traitor his house was forfeit.

4. golden sceptre: see 4.11.

8. cannot be revoked: cf. 1.19. This, as worded, applies to the letter to be written by Mordecai and Esther concerning the Jews, but it could equally well apply to the edict already made by Haman in the king's name. The letter written by Mordecai and Esther aimed therefore at allowing the Jews to disarm their enemies and thus preventing the carrying out of the edict.

9. concerning the Jews: the Hebrew could also mean 'to the Jews', and this is surely right, as is implied by the end of the verse and because it permitted them to take action.

10. mounted couriers . . . swift horses: giving a sense of urgency that was really not there since the danger lay nearly nine months ahead.

11. armed force . . . with their children and women: the last phrase is to be regarded strictly on the principle of an eye for an eye, etc.; if the Persians were to attack Jewish women and children then the Jews could retaliate.

12. thirteenth: see 3.7.

15. Cf. 6.8.

17. declared themselves Jews: how much is meant? Probably proselytes in the more or less strict sense. With this we may compare the Judaizing of Samaria, Idumaea, and Galilee by Hyrcanus and Aristobulus (135–104 B.C.).

THE JEWS RETALIATE ON THE THIRTEENTH AND FOURTEENTH DAYS OF ADAR AND A
   DECREE MADE TO CELEBRATE THE OCCASION 9.1–32

2. such as sought their hurt: this was the only way in which the previous decree could be revoked.

fear of them had fallen: there had been nearly nine months for the Jews to prepare, and, what is more, the army held their position by favour of Mordecai. There had in fact been plenty of time to disarm, but the story demanded more than a mere semblance of retaliation.

7–9. The ten names occur only here in the O.T. They are all Persian names.

7. Parshandatha: 'Made for battle' (?).

Dalphon: 'Doorkeeper'.

Aspatha: 'Given by the (sacred) horse'.

8. Poratha: 'Given by good fortune'.

Adalia: meaning unknown.

Aridatha: 'Given by Hari', Hari being an epithet of the god Vishnu; but the name might also mean 'Created as a hero'.

9. Parmashta: meaning unknown.

Arisai: meaning unknown.

Aridai: either short for Aridatha, see above, or it may be another form of Haridayas, 'Delight of Hari'.

Vaizatha: 'Given by the best one', the 'best one' being Ormuzd=Ahura Mazdah.

12. The unconcern of the king at so great a loss is merely part of the story.

13. be hanged on the gallows: either the author has forgotten that they have been killed already or else the intention is to have the corpses hung up for greater dishonour (cf. Dt. 21.22).

15. fourteenth: the festival was kept on two days; the fourteenth in the country and the fifteenth in the cities, the difference being due to a different determination of the new moon. This second day's slaughter in Susa offers a basic reason for the two festival dates.

16. seventy-five thousand: an imaginary number.

laid no hands on the plunder: despite 8.11; this is probably added to create a good impression in favour of the Jews.

19. gladness . . . feasting . . . holidaymaking: cf. Neh. 8.10–12, where similar practices were followed for the festival which followed the law reading.

Some MSS. of LXX add 'but those who live in cities keep also the fifteenth of Adar as a joyous and good day by sending portions to their neighbours'. This may well be part of the original text and it rounds off the verse.

29. and Mordecai: in verses 20–28 Mordecai alone is the author of the letter, and what is now expected is that Esther as queen should confirm it. If we were to read 'gave full authority to Mordecai the Jew' (reading *l*ᵉ*mordoḵay* for *umordoḵay*) it would be easier.

second letter: i.e. 9.20ff., the first being 8.8, 9–14.

30. and truth: it is possible that this is intended to convey the same force as the Aramaic word for truth could do, i.e. physical well-being (see G. R. Driver, *Aramaic Documents of the Fifth Century B.C.*, 1957, p. 44), and we might translate, 'peace and prosperity'.

31. and Queen Esther: if the change suggested for verses 29 be accepted, this must be regarded as a consequential addition to this verse when 'and Mordecai' was read in verse 29. Moreover, Esther's part is to be mentioned in verse 32.

CONCLUDING SUMMARY 10.1–3

1. tribute: the Hebrew word normally means labour gangs, forced labourers, but in very late times it did come to mean tribute (as LXX translates). At all events, the verse seems to be very much out of context and it is difficult to decide which meaning the word should bear. Doubtless the author meant it to be something in favour of the Jews, and if it were tribute, i.e. incoming wealth, it might be regarded as fulfilling Isa. 60.5, 9.

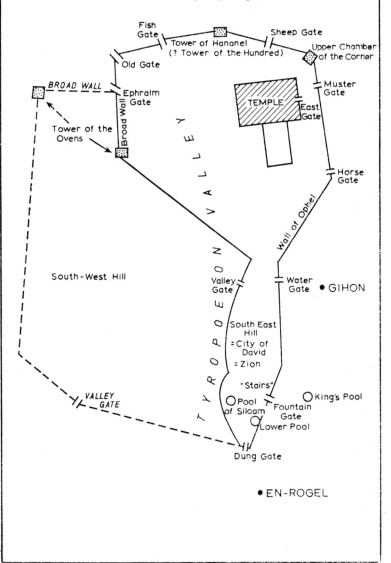

JERUSALEM
Diagram showing two possible lines of Nehemiah's Wall

Fish Gate

Tower of Hananel (? Tower of the Hundred)

Sheep Gate

Upper Chamber of the Corner

Old Gate

BROAD WALL

Ephraim Gate

Broad Wall

Muster Gate

TEMPLE

East Gate

Tower of the Ovens

V A L L E Y

Horse Gate

Wall of Ophel

South-West Hill

Valley Gate

Water Gate

● GIHON

T Y R O P O E O N

South East Hill
= City of David
= Zion

"Stairs"

VALLEY GATE

○ King's Pool

○ Pool of Siloam

Fountain Gate

○ Lower Pool

Dung Gate

● EN-ROGEL

INDEX

185